THE WINTER'S TALE

The RSC Shakespeare

Edited by Jonathan Bate and Eric Rasmussen

Chief Associate Editor: Héloïse Sénéchal

Associate Editors: Trey Jansen, Eleanor Lowe, Lucy Munro,
Dee Anna Phares, Jan Sewell

The Winter's Tale

Textual editing: Eric Rasmussen

Introduction and "Shakespeare's Career in the Theater": Jonathan Bate

Commentary: Charlotte Scott and Héloïse Sénéchal

Scene-by-Scene Analysis: Esme Miskimmin

In Performance: Clare Smout (RSC stagings) and Jan Sewell (overview)

The Director's Cut (interviews by Jonathan Bate and Kevin Wright):
Adrian Noble, Barbara Gaines, Dominic Cooke

The RSC Shakespeare

William Shakespeare

THE WINTER'S TALE

Edited by Jonathan Bate and Eric Rasmussen

Introduction by Jonathan Bate

The Modern Library
New York

CONTENTS

INTRODUCTION

OLD TALES

In about 1590 the dramatist George Peele wrote a play called *The Old Wives' Tale* in which an old woman is asked to tell "a merry winter's tale" in order to "drive away the time trimly." "Once upon a time," she begins, as all traditional storytellers do, "there was a king or a lord or a duke that had a fair daughter, the fairest that ever was, as white as snow and as red as blood: and once upon a time his daughter was stolen away." An old wives' or a winter's tale is like a fairy story: it is not supposed to be realistic and it is bound to have a happy ending. Along the way, there will be magic, dreams, coincidences, children lost and found. This is the style of play to which Shakespeare turned some twenty years after Peele, in the final phase of his career.

Shakespeare's late plays have come to be known as "romances." Although neither the dramatist himself nor the compilers of the First Folio used this generic classification, the term is helpful because it gestures toward the origin of such stories in ancient Greek prose romance, which was peopled by wanderers, separated lovers, oracles, shepherds, and heroes who undergo narrow escapes from disaster. The story of Apollonius of Tyre, the ultimate source for Shakespeare's co-written play *Pericles*, is a classic example of the genre. Robert Greene, another dramatist who was prominent in the early 1590s, wrote several prose romances in this tradition, among them *Pandosto: The Triumph of Time*, the story that is dramatized in *The Winter's Tale*. We do not know exactly what led Shakespeare, some time after writing the tragedies of *Lear* and *Macbeth*, to turn back to the style of Peele and Greene. Always attuned to changes in the wind, perhaps he sensed that a gentler mode of tragicomedy and pastoral romance, with a distinctly royalist agenda, suited the times: the King's Men seem to have had notable successes in these years with several dramas of this kind, including a revival of the old anonymous play of *Mucedorus*, which even featured an encounter with a bear.

The Winter's Tale does not, however, begin in the world of romance. The Sicilian opening of the story is full of court intrigue in the manner of *King Lear* and sexual jealousy reminiscent of *Othello*. There are accusations of conspiracy, a queen is tried for treason, and a king behaves like a tyrant. Only in the second half is there a redemptive movement from court to country: the structure is similar to that of *Cymbeline*, another Shakespearean tragicomedy written around the same time. In contrast to Sicilia, Bohemia is a place of benign chance, where the flight of a falcon leads a prince to his future bride and a thieving trickster inadvertently helps the plot toward its happy resolution. The arts of the court give way to the harmonies of nature. Though this is to oversimplify: Polixenes relies on "intelligence" and disguise, then threatens physical violence against Perdita. She is a princess assumed to be a shepherdess, who dresses up as a queen and speaks of the need to intermingle art and nature in the grafting of flowers: complex layers of illusion are at work.

AFFECTION, INFECTION, EXPRESSION

Critics have been much exercised by Leontes' explosion of anger when Hermione succeeds in persuading Polixenes to prolong his visit to Sicilia after he himself has failed to do so. Why does her courtesy lead instantly to a false accusation of adultery? Has Leontes' jealousy been festering for a long time? Is he angry because a woman has come between two close male friends? The theme was certainly a Shakespearean obsession which ran from the early *Two Gentlemen of Verona* through the sonnets to his last play, *The Two Noble Kinsmen*. Such questions are the prerogative of the reader more than the spectator in the playhouse. An audience watching a play can work out only a limited amount about the events that are imagined to have occurred before the action begins, and in the theatrical experience such events do not exist.

Theatrical attention is concentrated more on Leontes as he is than on how he got there. In a puzzling, tortuous self-analysis concerning the "infection" of his brains, he says that as mental states may be affected by things unreal, such as dreams, so they may also be affected by things that are real:

> . . . Can thy dam, may't be
> Affection?— Thy intention stabs the centre.
> Thou dost make possible things not so held,
> Communicat'st with dream — how can this be? —
> With what's unreal thou coactive art,
> And fellow'st nothing. Then 'tis very credent
> Thou mayst co-join with something, and thou dost,
> And that beyond commission, and I find it,
> And that to the infection of my brains
> And hard'ning of my brows.

Both syntax and semantics are crabbed. Leontes' fragmented sentences are symptoms of his mental disintegration. The referent of the key word "affection" is unstable: does it refer to the relationship between Hermione and Polixenes or to Leontes' own mental state? "Affection" could denote their sexual desire or his strong feeling in response to it, but the word could also signify delusion, sickness. The ambiguity is revelatory precisely because Leontes can no longer distinguish between what is going on in his own mind and the reality observed by everyone else on stage. Hermione speaks truer than she knows when, in the trial scene, she says, "My life stands in the level of your dreams."

The logical conclusion of Leontes' analysis ought to be that the thing that is exercising him, namely the supposed affair between his wife and his best friend, is nothing but a bad dream. But he obstinately draws the opposite conclusion. The irrationality of this move is itself a sign of the "infection" that is afflicting him. Honest Camillo sees this, but, for the very reason that he is "infected," Leontes himself cannot. His "distraction" makes him misinterpret every action, even as his very language becomes infected with dark, sexual double entendre: "stabs," "nothing," and "co-join" anticipate the subsequent grossness of "No barricado for a belly" and "she has been sluiced in's absence / And his pond fished by his next neighbor."

Whatever the origin of Leontes' suspicion, the dramatic interest is in the effect, the tendency of human beings who have fallen into holes to dig themselves ever deeper. No argument, not even the supposedly divine "truth" of the oracle, will convince Leontes of his error. Accordingly, what does persuade him to change his mind is an effect of emotion rather than reason: the shock, the raw grief, of his son's and wife's sudden death. The boy Mamillius is the one who has said that "A sad tale's best for winter" when his mother offers to tell him a story, and he it is who becomes victim of the winter-bound first half of the play. Leontes metaphorically freezes his wife out of his affections, with the unintended result that his son catches a literal chill and dies. Only after this can the action move to the regenerative world of romance. "Thou met'st with things dying, I with things newborn," remarks the Old Shepherd at the play's pivotal point when he scoops up the baby Perdita as Antigonus is torn to pieces by the bear.

The forms of Shakespeare's verse loosened and became more flexible as he matured as a writer. His early plays have a higher proportion of rhyme and a greater regularity in rhythm, the essential pattern being that of iambic pentameter (ten syllables, five stresses, the stress on every second syllable). In the early plays, lines are very frequently end-stopped: punctuation marks a pause at the line ending, meaning that the movement of the syntax (the grammatical construction) falls in with that of the meter (the rhythmical construction). In the later plays, there are far fewer rhyming couplets (sometimes rhyme features only as a marker to indicate that a scene is ending) and the rhythmic movement has far greater variety, freedom, and flow. Mature Shakespearean blank (unrhymed) verse is typically not end-stopped but "run on" (a feature known as "enjambment"): instead of pausing heavily at the line ending, the speaker hurries forward, the sense demanded by the grammar working in creative tension against the holding pattern of the meter. The heavier pauses migrate to the middle of the lines, where they are known as the "caesura" and where their placing varies. Much more often than in the early plays a single line of verse is shared between two speakers. And the pentameter itself becomes a more subtle instrument: the iambic beat is broken up, there is often an extra ("redundant") unstressed eleventh syllable at the end of the line (this is known as a "feminine ending"). There are more modulations between verse and prose. Occasionally the verse is so loose that neither the original typesetters of the plays when they were first printed nor the modern editors of scholarly texts can be entirely certain whether verse or prose is intended.

Iambic pentameter is the ideal medium for dramatic poetry in English because its rhythm and duration seem to fall in naturally with the speech patterns of the language. In its capacity to combine the ordinary variety of speech with the heightened precision of poetry, the supple, mature Shakespearean "loose pentameter" is perhaps the most expressive vocal instrument ever given to the actor. The verse can embody both the fragmentation of Leontes' reason and the lyrical abandon of Florizel's passion:

> . . . When you do dance, I wish you
> A wave o'th'sea, that you might ever do
> Nothing but that. Move still, still so,
> And own no other function . . .

Florizel's wish sweeps him over the line ending as if it were itself a wave. Across the next line break, the eternity of "ever do" is played against "Nothing but," a negative made positive. Then a heavy pause, momentarily suspending the flow of the words, followed by a dancelike pattern of repetition and reversal in "Move still, still so." The caesura darts from place to place, line by line. The verse is the dance.

A SCANDAL IN BOHEMIA—OR IN SICILY?

Robert Greene's popular romance *Pandosto* told the story of a King of Bohemia who mistakenly believed that his wife was pregnant by his old friend the King of Sicilia. Shakespeare's boldest alteration of this story when he dramatized it into *The Winter's Tale* was the resurrection of the wronged queen, but his most puzzling change to his source was the inversion of the kingdoms. The jealous fit falls upon Sicilia instead of Bohemia.

The winter weather in Prague is somewhat colder than that in Palermo. Would it not therefore have been better to follow the original by locating the chilly court of Leontes in snowy middle Europe and the summer shepherding in sunny Sicily, which was, besides, the reputed birthplace of Theocritus, father of the "pastoral" genre on which the play draws so heavily? Hermione is identified as the daughter of the Emperor of Russia. From both a geographical and a dynastic point of view, it would have been more plausible to marry her to the king of nearby Bohemia rather than that of a distant Mediterranean island.

Various explanations have been proffered for Shakespeare's curious reversal. Perhaps he wanted to make Perdita a daughter of Sicily in order to further her resemblance to Proserpina, her mythic prototype. Shakespeare would have read in Ovid's *Metamorphoses* of how this lovely princess was snatched away to the underworld when she was gathering flowers in a Sicilian field; her release for half the year was symbolic of the seasonal cycle from winter to spring. Perdita invokes Proserpina in her own flower speech, and she is the figure who symbolically transforms the atmosphere of the play from winter to summer. Or perhaps the alteration was because Sicilians were notoriously hot-blooded and prone to jealousy, whereas Bohemia was often the setting for romantic fables. Perhaps Shakespeare was being deliberately absurd in a conscious act of anti-realism: Sicily was an island, but the play gives no sense of this; Bohemia, by contrast, was landlocked: this makes Perdita's abandonment on its coast either a bad mistake (Ben Jonson's view of the matter) or a deliberate joke.

Although Shakespeare's late plays are "tales" or fables, they are not wholly divorced from hard questions of history and politics. *The Tempest* is very interested in statecraft and dynastic liaison, while *Cymbeline* is one of Shakespeare's two extended meditations on what political historians call the British Question (the relationship between England and the other parts of the island). *The Winter's Tale* opens, in the exchange between Camillo and Archidamus, with the language of courtiership, diplomacy, and royal compliment. The pastoral form, far from being escapist, was often the vehicle for such heavy matter.

Shakespeare wrote all his later plays in the knowledge that the King's Men were required to give more command performances at court than any other theater company. Court performances were often given in the presence of visiting royals or their ambassadors. In such circumstances, the diplomatic consequences of dramatic locations had to be a consideration. King James' wife was Danish. That must be why in *Macbeth* the traitor Macdonald is in league with a Norwegian force, whereas in the play's source it is a Danish one. It was part of Shakespeare's job not to give offense to the wrong people. However removed from historical reality the action may be, to invoke the kingdoms of Bohemia and Sicily, especially in front of court audiences that might include visiting diplomats, would inevitably create a penumbra of geopolitical associations.

In the time of Shakespeare's father, the difference between the two realms in terms of political association would have been minimal. As Holy Roman Emperor, Charles V ruled the greater part of Europe, including both Sicily and Bohemia. But Shakespeare himself lived after the division of the House of Habsburg into distinct Spanish and Austrian branches. In his time, the two kingdoms fell under separate spheres of influence. Sicilia—or more exactly the kingdom of the two Sicilies, one consisting of the island and the other of southern Italy—was at the heart of the Mediterranean empire of Philip II of Spain, while Bohemia (the western two-thirds of what is now the Czech Republic) became the core of the Holy Roman Empire. When Rudolf II became emperor in 1576, he moved the seat of his government from Vienna to Prague. In Shakespeare's time, the title King of Sicilia belonged to Spain, while the King of Bohemia was the senior secular elector of the Habsburg Empery.

The other crucial difference was religious: Sicily was Catholic, whereas for two hundred years the Bohemians had been divided from Rome—the Hussite rising of 1419–20 was perhaps the first enduring religious reformation in Europe. Anti-papal, anti-clerical, and highly moralistic, the Bohemians were effectively Protestants before Protestantism was invented.

Fictional and fanciful as *The Winter's Tale* may be, the fact is that when the play was written the King of Sicilia was Philip III of Spain and the King of Bohemia was the Emperor Rudolf II. There were strong links between the courts of James in London and Rudolf in Prague. Rudolf's court was famously hospitable to English intellectuals, ranging from John Dee the magician to a young woman who became one of the most famous poets in all Europe, Elizabeth Jane Weston. There were also striking resemblances between the two monarchs, especially their interest in magic and their desire for European peacemaking through interdenominational matchmaking. These two preoccupations were closely related: Rudolf's obsession with alchemy, natural magic, and Rosicrucianism was not some eccentric aberration of his melancholy personality, but rather—as was also the case with the magical interests of King James—a way to a deeper religious vision and unity beyond the confessional divisions that racked his empire. Magic and royal matchmaking were also, of course, distinctly late Shakespearean subjects. Paulina's awakening of Hermione's statue places an invocation of benign magical arts in the service of the restoration of harmony within and between the play's two ruling families.

Conversely, despite the Catholicism of James' queen and the king's various attempts to match his children to clients of Spain, the residual English hostility to all things Spanish, dating back to the Armada and beyond, had not gone away. In these circumstances, it seems eminently plausible that on deciding to dramatize a story about the kings of Sicilia and Bohemia, and knowing that the play would at some point go into the court repertoire, Shakespeare thought it would be politic to make the monarch with Spanish as opposed to Rudolfine associations the one who is irrational, cruel, and blasphemous. It is not that Leontes is in any sense a representation of Philip or Polixenes of Rudolf, but rather that extreme tact was required in the invocation of the names of European kingdoms.

Shakespeare's tact toward Bohemia, a synecdoche for the Austro-Germanic Habsburg territories, was indeed such that *The Winter's Tale* could be played at court without embarrassment during the 1612–13 festivities in celebration of the wedding of King James' daughter Elizabeth to the Habsburg princeling Frederick the Elector Palatine—who, as it happens, would later become King of Bohemia. Life imitates art: like Perdita, Elizabeth would become known as the "winter queen" in Bohemia.

Whether or not geopolitical sensitivity lay behind Shakespeare's transposition of Sicilia and Bohemia, *The Winter's Tale* can still be thought of as a play that works on a north–south axis. The weird temporal syncretism of the play enacts the early modern rebirth of classical civilization: Apollo thunders and Ovid's Pygmalion is reborn as Giulio Romano; the setting moves between the temple of the Delphic oracle on a balmy Greek island, a very English-seeming sheep-shearing feast, and a private chapel reached via a picture gallery and housing a Madonna-like statue. The essential geographical structure, meanwhile, is an opposition between a hot-blooded, court-dominated—and perhaps implicitly Catholic—south, and a more relaxed, temperate north in which ordinary people (shepherd and clown) have a voice, as they do in the Protestant world where the Bible is available in the vernacular.

LIVING ART

One of the best ways of discovering Shakespeare's core concerns in a play is to consider his major additions to his sources: it is a fair assumption that he is most himself when he departs from his originals. As one would expect from *Pandosto*, Leontes is easily the largest role in the play, twice as long as any other. But the next two most sizable parts—added together, they equal that of Leontes in length—are Camillo and Paulina. The figure of Leontes' honest counselor greatly expands the role of the king's cupbearer in *Pandosto*, while Paulina, Hermione's preserver and Leontes' conscience, has no equivalent in the source. The prominence of these roles suggests that the play is especially interested in the relationship between absolute power, with its potential to turn to tyranny, and the role of the wise counselor. How far can an adviser, or for that matter a playwright whose works are performed at court, go in speaking truths that their rulers might not want to hear? This was a perennial concern in the Elizabethan and Jacobean era.

The court of King James was different from that of Queen Elizabeth, not least because there was a royal family. Negotiations to find the right husband for the king's daughter were ongoing at the time of the play's composition and first court performance. Like the

Bohemian connection discussed above, this context is in the hinterland of the play's origin. It should not lead us to read the drama as a direct allegory of contemporary diplomacy. Leontes is in no sense a representation of King James. Besides, among the things that make the play a romance is the delightful representation of paternal informality and intimacy in the exchanges with Mamillius in the opening court scene. Real kings did not publicly mix the roles of patriarch and playmate in this way.

In Greene's *Pandosto*, when the Perdita figure arrives incognito at court near the climax of the story, the desiring eye of her father falls upon her, raising the specter of royal incest. One of Paulina's roles in *The Winter's Tale* is to divert Leontes from any thought of this kind: "Your eye hath too much youth in't," she remarks, reminding him that even in middle age his dead queen was more beautiful "Than what you look on now." Earlier in the same scene, Paulina has counseled the king against remarriage, eliciting the response:

> Thou speak'st truth.
> No more such wives: therefore, no wife. One worse,
> And better used, would make her sainted spirit
> Again possess her corpse, and on this stage —
> Where we offenders now — appear soul-vexed,
> And begin, 'Why to me?'

These lines brilliantly anticipate the moment when, thanks to the dramaturgical art of Paulina, the "sainted spirit" of Hermione really does appear to have a soul breathed back into it as she walks again on that same "stage."

In *Pandosto* the wronged queen does not return to life. The reanimation of what Leontes takes to be Hermione's statue is Shakespeare's invention. The wonder-filled final scene puts a seemingly life-giving art into the hands of Paulina. That art dramatizes the magical power of theater itself so that we in the audience, like the characters on stage, awaken our faith. The many-layered quality of the illusion—a boy actor pretending to be a female character; Hermione, who is herself pretending to be a statue—takes Shakespeare's art to an extreme level of self-consciousness. Fittingly, the scene is also an allusion to Ovid, the most self-conscious artist among Shakespeare's literary models.

In book ten of the *Metamorphoses*, the artist Pygmalion carves an ivory statue so realistic that it seems to be a real girl, so beautiful that he falls in love with it. He desperately wants to believe it is real and there are moments when the perfection of the art is such that the statue does seem to be struggling into life. With a little assistance from the goddess Venus, a kiss then animates the statue in a striking reversal of the usual Ovidian metamorphic pattern in which people are turned into things or animals. At a profound level, Pygmalion is a figure of Ovid himself: the artist who transforms mere words into living forms.

Shakespeare learned from Ovid's Pygmalion both an idea and a style. If you want something badly enough and you believe in it hard enough, you will eventually get it: though tragedy denies this possibility, comedy affirms it. This is the illusion that theater can foster. Ovid showed Shakespeare that the way to evoke this leap of faith is through pinpricks of sensation. The progression in the animation of Pygmalion's statue is both precise and sensuous: blood pulses through the veins, the lips respond, the ivory face flushes. Correspondingly, Leontes contrasts the warm life his queen once had with the coldness of the statue, but then he seems to see blood in the veins and warmth upon the lips. And when she descends and embraces him, she *is* warm.

At the beginning of the play Leontes complains that Hermione's body contact with Polixenes is "Too hot, too hot!"—he wants her to be frigidly chaste, even though she is pregnant. His jealous look is like that of the basilisk or the gorgon Medusa: he turns his wife to stone. In the final act, this metaphor becomes a metamorphosis as Paulina conjures up the illusion of Hermione's depetrification. The transformation is triumphantly realized on stage both linguistically and visually. "Does not the stone rebuke me / For being more stone than it?" asks Leontes, when confronted with the statue. The hardened image of his wife forces him to turn his gaze inward upon his own hard heart. The play ends with the melting of that heart and the rekindling of love, with its concordant release of Hermione back into softness, warmth, and life.

We know in our heads that we are not really watching a statue coming to life. Yet in a good production, at the moment of awakening we feel in our hearts that we are. The magic of the drama occurs in a strange but deeply satisfying space between the two poles of reality and illusion. Metamorphosis is a kind of translation that occurs in the passage from one state to another. Ovid's world, which is also evoked by Perdita's comparison of herself to Proserpina, goddess of spring, shuttles between human passions and natural phenomena. Shakespeare carried the magic of that world across into the medium of theater, where everything is illusion, but somehow—as he put it in the alternative title of another of his last plays, *Henry VIII*—"All Is True."

When Perdita, whose name means "lost one," is restored to her father, the oracle is fulfilled and there is some atonement for the death of Mamillius. Not, however, full restoration, for Mamillius himself will not return. The boy actor who played the part would almost certainly have doubled as Perdita in the second half of the play, visually transforming the dead son into a living daughter. Polixenes' son Florizel also stands in for Mamillius: he grows into what Leontes' son might have become. When he and Perdita are joined in marriage, the two kings and their kingdoms are united. Leontes has to accept that he will live on only through the female line. This is an appropriate punishment, given his earlier rejection of the female for having come between him and his "brother."

It will perhaps seem harsh to speak of punishment after the delights of the pastoral scene, the benign mischief of Autolycus, and the wonder of the moment when the supposed statue of Hermione is brought back to life. To do so is to resemble the Paulina who browbeats Leontes into maintaining his penance for sixteen years. When she finally softens and lets him into her art gallery, surely we, too, need to let go of our reason and our moral judgment. "It is required," as Paulina puts it, that we awake our faith. But can so much suffering evaporate in an instant of theatrical magic? Hermione's face is scarred with the marks of time, the wrinkles accumulated in her sixteen years' seclusion. And not even the joys of the impending union of the two houses can bring back the child whose "smutched" nose his father has so tenderly wiped in the first act.

ABOUT THE TEXT

Shakespeare endures through history. He illuminates later times as well as his own. He helps us to understand the human condition. But he cannot do this without a good text of the plays. Without editions there would be no Shakespeare. That is why every twenty years or so throughout the last three centuries there has been a major new edition of his complete works. One aspect of editing is the process of keeping the texts up to date—modernizing the spelling, punctuation, and typography (though not, of course, the actual words), providing explanatory notes in the light of changing educational practices (a generation ago, most of Shakespeare's classical and biblical allusions could be assumed to be generally understood, but now they can't).

Because Shakespeare did not personally oversee the publication of his plays, with some plays there are major editorial difficulties. Decisions have to be made as to the relative authority of the early printed editions, the pocket format "Quartos" published in Shakespeare's lifetime and the elaborately produced "First Folio" text of 1623, the original "Complete Works" prepared for the press after his death by Shakespeare's fellow actors, the people who knew the plays better than anyone else. *The Winter's Tale*, however, exists only in a Folio text that is reasonably well printed. The following notes highlight various aspects of the editorial process and indicate conventions used in the text of this edition:

Lists of Parts are supplied in the First Folio for only six plays: *The Winter's Tale* is one of them, so the list here is a lightly edited version of Folio's "The Names of the Actors." Capitals indicate that part of the name which is used for speech headings in the script (thus "LEONTES, King of Sicilia").

Locations are provided by the Folio for only two plays, of which *The Winter's Tale* is not one. Eighteenth-century editors, working in an age of elaborately realistic stage sets, were the first to provide detailed locations ("another part of the palace"). Given that Shakespeare wrote for a bare stage and often an imprecise sense of place, we have relegated locations to the explanatory notes at the foot of the page, where they are given at the beginning of each scene where the imaginary location is different from the one before. In the case of *The Winter's Tale*, the key aspect of location is the movement between Sicilia and Bohemia.

Act and Scene Divisions were provided in the Folio in a much more thoroughgoing way than in the Quartos. Sometimes, however, they were erroneous or omitted; corrections and additions supplied by editorial tradition are indicated by square brackets. Five-act division is based on a classical model, and act breaks provided the opportunity to replace the candles in the indoor Blackfriars playhouse which the King's Men used after 1608, but Shakespeare did not necessarily think in terms of a five-part structure of dramatic composition. The Folio convention is that a scene ends when the stage is empty. Nowadays, partly under the influence of film, we tend to consider a scene to be a dramatic unit that ends with either a change of imaginary location or a significant passage of time within the narrative. Shakespeare's fluidity of composition accords well with this convention, so in addition to act and scene numbers we provide a *running scene* count in the right margin at the beginning of each new scene, in the typeface used for editorial directions. Where there is a scene break caused by a momentary bare stage, but the location does not change and extra time does not pass, we use the convention *running scene continues*. There is inevitably a degree of editorial judgment in making such calls, but the system is very valuable in suggesting the pace of the plays.

Speakers' Names are often inconsistent in Folio. We have regularized speech headings, but retained an element of deliberate inconsistency in entry directions, in order to give the flavor of Folio.

Verse is indicated by lines that do not run to the right margin and by capitalization of each line. The Folio printers sometimes set verse as prose, and vice versa (either out of misunderstanding or for reasons of space). We have silently corrected in such cases, although in some instances there is ambiguity, in which case we have leaned toward the preservation of Folio layout. Folio sometimes uses contraction ("turnd" rather than "turned") to indicate whether or not the final "-ed" of a past participle is sounded, an area where there is variation for the sake of the five-beat iambic pentameter rhythm. We use the convention of a grave accent to indicate sounding (thus "turnèd" would be two syllables), but would urge actors not to overstress. In cases where one speaker ends with a verse half line and the next begins with the other half of the pentameter, editors since the late eighteenth century have indented the second line. We have abandoned this convention, since the Folio does not use it, and nor did actors' cues in the Shakespearean theater. An exception is made when the second speaker actively interrupts or completes the first speaker's sentence.

Spelling is modernized, but older forms are very occasionally maintained where necessary for rhythm or aural effect.

Punctuation in Shakespeare's time was as much rhetorical as grammatical. "Colon" was originally a term for a unit of thought in an argument. The semicolon was a new unit of punctuation (some of the Quartos lack them altogether). We have modernized punctuation throughout, but have given more weight to Folio punctuation than many editors, since, though not Shakespearean, it reflects the usage of his period. In particular, we have used the colon far more than many editors: it is exceptionally useful as a way of indicating how many Shakespearean speeches unfold clause by clause in a developing argument that gives the illusion of enacting the process of thinking in the moment. We have also kept in mind the origin of punctuation in classical times as a way of assisting the actor and orator: the comma suggests the briefest of pauses for breath, the colon a middling one, and a full stop or period a longer pause. Semicolons, by contrast, belong to an era of punctuation that was only just coming in during Shakespeare's time and that is coming to an end now: we have accordingly used them only where they occur in our copy texts (and not always then). Dashes are sometimes used for parenthetical interjections where the Folio has brackets. They are also used for interruptions and changes in train of thought. Where a change of addressee occurs within a speech, we have used a dash preceded by a full stop (or occasionally another form of punctuation). Often the identity of the respective addressees is obvious from the context. When it is not, this has been indicated in a marginal stage direction.

Entrances and Exits are fairly thorough in Folio, which has accordingly been followed as faithfully as possible. Where characters are omitted or corrections are necessary, this is indicated by square brackets (e.g. "[*and Attendants*]"). *Exit* is sometimes silently normalized to *Exeunt* and *Manet* anglicized to "remains." We trust Folio positioning of entrances and exits to a greater degree than most editors.

Editorial Stage Directions such as stage business, asides, indications of addressee and of characters' position on the gallery stage are used only sparingly in Folio. Other editions mingle directions of this kind with original Folio and Quarto directions, sometimes marking them by means of square brackets. We have sought to distinguish what could be described as *directorial* interventions of this kind from Folio-style directions (either original or supplied) by placing them in the right margin in a different typeface. There is a degree of subjectivity about which directions are of which kind, but the procedure is intended as a reminder to the reader and the actor that Shakespearean stage directions are often dependent upon editorial inference alone and are not set in stone. We also depart from editorial tradition in sometimes admitting uncertainty and thus printing permissive stage directions, such as an ***Aside?*** (often a line may be equally effective as an aside or a direct address—it is for each production or reading to make its own decision) or a ***may exit*** or a piece of business placed between arrows to indicate that it may occur at various different moments within a scene.

Line Numbers in the left margin are editorial, for reference and to key the explanatory and textual notes.

Explanatory Notes at the foot of each page explain allusions and gloss obsolete and difficult words, confusing phraseology, occasional major textual cruxes, and so on. Particular attention is given to non-standard usage, bawdy innuendo, and technical terms (e.g. legal and military language). Where more than one sense is given, commas indicate shades of related meaning, slashes alternative or double meanings.

Textual Notes at the end of the play indicate major departures from the Folio. They take the following form: the reading of our text is given in bold and its source given after an equals sign, with "F2" indicating a reading that derives from the Second Folio of 1632 and "Ed" one that derives from the subsequent editorial tradition. The rejected Folio ("F") reading is then given. Thus, for example: "**3.3.114 made** = Ed. F = mad" means that at Act 3 Scene 3 line 114, the Folio compositor has mistakenly printed "mad" and we have followed editorial tradition in correcting to "made."

MAJOR PARTS (*with percentages of lines/number of speeches/scenes on stage*): Leontes (20%/125/6), Paulina (10%/59/5), Camillo (9%/72/5), Autolycus (9%/67/3), Polixenes (8%/57/4), Florizel (6%/45/2), Hermione (6%/35/4), Clown (5%/64/4), Shepherd (4%/42/3), Perdita (4%/25/3), Antigonus (3%/19/3). An unusually large number of named parts have 20–30 lines, less than 1% of the text: Archidamus, Cleomenes, Dion, the boy Mamillius, Emilia, Dorcas, and Mopsa.

LINGUISTIC MEDIUM: 75% verse, 25% prose.

DATE: 1611. Performed at the Globe May 1611; dance of satyrs apparently borrows from a court entertainment of January 1611; performed at court November 1611 and again for royal wedding celebrations in early 1613. Some scholars argue for 1609–10 on assumption that the satyrs' dance is a later interpolation, but theaters were closed because of plague for many months of these earlier years.

SOURCES: A dramatization of Robert Greene's prose romance *Pandosto: The Triumph of Time* (1588, also known as *The History of Dorastus and Fawnia*). The survival and revival of the queen is a Shakespearean innovation, influenced by the story in Ovid's *Metamorphoses* (book ten) in which Pygmalion's statue comes to life.

TEXT: First Folio of 1623 is only early printed text. Typeset from a transcription by Ralph Crane, professional scribe to the King's Men, it is very well printed, with remarkably few textual problems.

THE WINTER'S TALE

LIST OF PARTS

LEONTES, King of Sicilia

HERMIONE, his queen

MAMILLIUS, their son, a child

PERDITA, their daughter

CAMILLO

ANTIGONUS

CLEOMENES

DION
} Lords at the Sicilian court

PAULINA, a lady, wife to Antigonus

EMILIA, a lady attending upon Hermione

POLIXENES, King of Bohemia

FLORIZEL, his son

ARCHIDAMUS, a lord of Bohemia

Old SHEPHERD, reputed father of Perdita

CLOWN, his son

AUTOLYCUS, a rogue, formerly in the service of Prince Florizel

Shepherds and Shepherdesses, including MOPSA and DORCAS

Twelve countrymen disguised as satyrs

A MARINER, a JAILER, other Lords, Gentlemen, Servants

TIME, as Chorus

Act 1 Scene 1

Enter Camillo and Archidamus

ARCHIDAMUS   If you shall chance, Camillo, to visit Bohemia, on the like occasion whereon my services are now on foot, you shall see, as I have said, great difference betwixt our Bohemia and your Sicilia.

5   CAMILLO   I think this coming summer the King of Sicilia means to pay Bohemia the visitation which he justly owes him.

ARCHIDAMUS   Wherein our entertainment shall shame us, we will be justified in our loves, for indeed—

10   CAMILLO   Beseech you—

ARCHIDAMUS   Verily, I speak it in the freedom of my knowledge: we cannot with such magnificence — in so rare — I know not what to say. We will give you sleepy drinks, that your senses, unintelligent of our insufficience, may, though they

15   cannot praise us, as little accuse us.

CAMILLO   You pay a great deal too dear for what's given freely.

ARCHIDAMUS   Believe me, I speak as my understanding instructs me and as mine honesty puts it to utterance.

CAMILLO   Sicilia cannot show himself over-kind to Bohemia.

20   They were trained together in their childhoods and there rooted betwixt them then such an affection which cannot choose but branch now. Since their more mature dignities and royal necessities made separation of their society, their encounters, though not personal, have been royally

25   attorneyed with interchange of gifts, letters, loving embassies, that they have seemed to be together, though absent, shook

---

1.1   *Location: Sicilia (now Sicily)*   1 Bohemia Bohemia, a central European kingdom, formerly part of the Austrian Empire; its capital was Prague   **2 on . . . occasion** in the same circumstances   **on foot** in employment   **6 Bohemia** the King of Bohemia   **8 Wherein . . . loves** in whatever manner our hospitality may shame us, we shall make up for it in our love for you   **11 Verily** truly   **in . . . knowledge** as my knowledge enables me to do   **12 rare** exceptional/excellent   **13 sleepy** sleep-inducing   **14 insufficience** inadequacy   **19 Sicilia** the King of Sicily   **20 trained** educated (plays on the sense of "directed or joined horticulturally")   **22 branch** flourish   **23 necessities** responsibilities   **25 attorneyed** represented   **embassies** messages

hands, as over a vast, and embraced, as it were, from the
ends of opposed winds. The heavens continue their loves.

30 ARCHIDAMUS   I think there is not in the world either malice or
matter to alter it. You have an unspeakable comfort of your
young prince Mamillius: it is a gentleman of the greatest
promise that ever came into my note.

CAMILLO   I very well agree with you in the hopes of him: it is a
gallant child; one that indeed physics the subject, makes old
35 hearts fresh. They that went on crutches ere he was born
desire yet their life to see him a man.

ARCHIDAMUS   Would they else be content to die?

CAMILLO   Yes; if there were no other excuse why they should
desire to live.

40 ARCHIDAMUS   If the king had no son, they would desire to live on
crutches till he had one.   *Exeunt*

Act 1 Scene 2   *running scene 1 continues*

*Enter Leontes, Hermione, Mamillius, Polixenes, Camillo [and
Attendants]*

POLIXENES   Nine changes of the wat'ry star hath been
The shepherd's note since we have left our throne
Without a burden. Time as long again
Would be filled up, my brother, with our thanks.
5   And yet we should, for perpetuity,
Go hence in debt: and therefore, like a cipher,
Yet standing in rich place, I multiply
With one 'We thank you' many thousands moe
That go before it.

10   LEONTES   Stay your thanks a while,
And pay them when you part.

27 **vast** boundless space   28 **ends . . . winds** opposite corners of the globe   **The** may the
30 **unspeakable** indescribable   **of** in the form of   32 **note** attention   34 **physics the subject**
gives health to the people   35 **ere** before   36 **desire . . . life** are determined to survive
37 **else** otherwise   **1.2**   1 **wat'ry star** the moon, which **changes** each month   2 **note**
observation   3 **burden** i.e. occupant   5 **perpetuity** ever   6 **cipher** zero that, worthless in
itself, may increase the value of a number it is added to   8 **moe** more   10 **Stay** restrain

POLIXENES   Sir, that's tomorrow.
I am questioned by my fears of what may chance
Or breed upon our absence, that may blow
No sneaping winds at home, to make us say
'This is put forth too truly'. Besides, I have stayed
To tire your royalty.

LEONTES   We are tougher, brother,
Than you can put us to't.

POLIXENES   No longer stay.

LEONTES   One sev'nnight longer.

POLIXENES   Very sooth, tomorrow.

LEONTES   We'll part the time between's then, and in that
I'll no gainsaying.

POLIXENES   Press me not, beseech you, so.
There is no tongue that moves, none, none i'th'world
So soon as yours could win me. So it should now,
Were there necessity in your request, although
'Twere needful I denied it. My affairs
Do even drag me homeward, which to hinder
Were in your love a whip to me, my stay
To you a charge and trouble. To save both,
Farewell, our brother.

LEONTES   Tongue-tied, our queen? Speak you.

HERMIONE   I had thought, sir, to have held my peace until
You had drawn oaths from him not to stay. You, sir,
Charge him too coldly. Tell him you are sure
All in Bohemia's well: this satisfaction
The bygone day proclaimed. Say this to him,
He's beat from his best ward.

LEONTES   Well said, Hermione.

---

13 questioned . . . truly' plagued by anxieties as to what might happen in my absence and concerned that no biting (**sneaping**) winds of hostility should make me conclude I was right to be afraid   19 put us to't prove by testing me   21 sev'nnight week   22 very sooth truly   23 between's between us   24 no gainsaying not be refused   29 needful necessary   31 Were . . . me would be a punishment to me (although well-intentioned)   32 charge burdensome responsibility   37 Charge entreat   38 this . . . day such reassuring news was announced yesterday   39 Say if you say   40 ward defensive position (fencing term)

HERMIONE   To tell, he longs to see his son, were strong.
But let him say so then, and let him go.
But let him swear so, and he shall not stay,
45   We'll thwack him hence with distaffs.—
Yet of your royal presence I'll adventure   *To Polixenes*
The borrow of a week. When at Bohemia
You take my lord, I'll give him my commission
To let him there a month behind the gest
50   Prefixed for's parting.— Yet, good deed, Leontes,
I love thee not a jar o'th'clock behind
What lady she her lord.— You'll stay?

POLIXENES   No, madam.

HERMIONE   Nay, but you will?

55   POLIXENES   I may not, verily.

HERMIONE   Verily?
You put me off with limber vows. But I,
Though you would seek t'unsphere the stars with oaths,
Should yet say 'Sir, no going.' Verily,
60   You shall not go; a lady's 'Verily' is
As potent as a lord's. Will you go yet?
Force me to keep you as a prisoner,
Not like a guest: so you shall pay your fees
When you depart, and save your thanks. How say you?
65   My prisoner? Or my guest? By your dread 'Verily',
One of them you shall be.

POLIXENES   Your guest, then, madam.
To be your prisoner should import offending,
Which is for me less easy to commit
70   Than you to punish.

---

42 tell say (to us)   **strong** i.e. as an argument   **43 But** only   **45 distaffs** cleft staffs around which wool or flax was wound for use in spinning   **46 adventure** risk   **48 take** receive **49 behind . . . parting** after the time (**gest**) appointed for his departure   **50 good deed** indeed **51 jar** tick   **behind . . . she** less than any noble woman (loves)   **57 limber vows** limp protestations   **58 t'unsphere the stars** to unhinge the cosmos (each star was thought to be contained within its own hollow sphere)   **63 pay . . . depart** Elizabethan prisoners were required to pay a fee on being released   **65 dread** greatly to be feared   **68 import offending** imply that I had offended

HERMIONE   Not your jailer, then,
But your kind hostess. Come, I'll question you
Of my lord's tricks and yours when you were boys.
You were pretty lordings then?

75 POLIXENES   We were, fair queen,
Two lads that thought there was no more behind
But such a day tomorrow as today,
And to be boy eternal.

HERMIONE   Was not my lord
80 The verier wag o'th'two?

POLIXENES   We were as twinned lambs that did frisk i'th'sun,
And bleat the one at th'other. What we changed
Was innocence for innocence. We knew not
The doctrine of ill-doing, nor dreamed
85 That any did. Had we pursued that life,
And our weak spirits ne'er been higher reared
With stronger blood, we should have answered heaven
Boldly 'Not guilty', the imposition cleared
Hereditary ours.

90 HERMIONE   By this we gather
You have tripped since.

POLIXENES   O, my most sacred lady,
Temptations have since then been born to's. For
In those unfledged days was my wife a girl;
95 Your precious self had then not crossed the eyes
Of my young play-fellow.

HERMIONE   Grace to boot!
Of this make no conclusion, lest you say
Your queen and I are devils. Yet go on.
100 Th'offences we have made you do we'll answer,

---

73 **Of** about   74 **pretty lordings** fine young gentlemen   76 **behind** to come   80 **verier wag** more mischievous fellow   82 **changed** exchanged   86 **weak . . . blood** childish dispositions/innocence never developed into adult passions   88 **the . . . ours** excepting the inherited (original) sin of all mankind/and have been spared inherited (original) sin   91 **tripped** sinned   93 **to's** to us   94 **unfledged** undeveloped, youthful   96 **play-fellow** i.e. Leontes   97 **Grace to boot!** Charming too!   98 **Of . . . conclusion** do not follow that statement (about temptation) to its logical conclusion   100 **answer** explain/respond to/repay

If you first sinned with us, and that with us
You did continue fault, and that you slipped not
With any but with us.

LEONTES   Is he won yet?

105 **HERMIONE**   He'll stay, my lord.

LEONTES   At my request he would not.—   *Aside?*
Hermione, my dearest, thou never spok'st
To better purpose.

HERMIONE   Never?

110 **LEONTES**   Never, but once.

HERMIONE   What? Have I twice said well? When was't before?
I prithee tell me. Cram's with praise, and make's
As fat as tame things. One good deed dying tongueless
Slaughters a thousand waiting upon that.

115 Our praises are our wages. You may ride's
With one soft kiss a thousand furlongs ere
With spur we heat an acre. But to th'goal:
My last good deed was to entreat his stay:
What was my first? It has an elder sister,

120 Or I mistake you — O, would her name were Grace! —
But once before I spoke to th'purpose: when?
Nay, let me have't: I long.

LEONTES   Why, that was when
Three crabbèd months had soured themselves to death,

125 Ere I could make thee open thy white hand
And clap thyself my love; then didst thou utter
'I am yours for ever.'

HERMIONE   'Tis grace indeed.—
Why, lo you now, I have spoke to th'purpose twice: *To Polixenes?*

---

101 sinned . . . us had sexual relations with us and continued to do so only with us and no others.   **112 Cram's** cram us (i.e. me)   **113 tame things** domestic pets (fat plays on her pregnancy)   **tongueless** unremarked upon   **114 Slaughters . . . that** means that all corresponding deeds go unrecognized as well   **115 ride's** ride us (with sexual connotations)   **116 furlong** a furlong is 220 yards (200 meters)   **ere . . . acre** before we will cover an acre as a result of (instead) being kicked with a spur   **119 sister** i.e. the first good deed Leontes mentioned   **120 would I** wish/if only   **Grace** i.e. virtue/honor/divine favor   **124 crabbèd** bitter, frustrating (crab apples were a notoriously sour fruit)   **126 clap** seal a bargain by striking hands reciprocally   **129 lo** look   **to th'purpose** effectively

130   The one forever earned a royal husband;
       Th'other for some while a friend.   *Takes Polixenes' hand*

LEONTES   Too hot, too hot!   *Aside*

       To mingle friendship far is mingling bloods.
       I have *tremor cordis* on me: my heart dances,
135   But not for joy, not joy. This entertainment
       May a free face put on, derive a liberty
       From heartiness, from bounty, fertile bosom,
       And well become the agent. 'T may, I grant.
       But to be paddling palms and pinching fingers,
140   As now they are, and making practised smiles,
       As in a looking-glass, and then to sigh, as 'twere
       The mort o'th'deer — O, that is entertainment
       My bosom likes not, nor my brows.— Mamillius,
       Art thou my boy?

145   MAMILLIUS   Ay, my good lord.

       LEONTES   I' fecks!

       Why, that's my bawcock. What? Hast smutched thy nose?—
       They say it is a copy out of mine.— Come, captain,   *Aside?*
       We must be neat; not neat, but cleanly, captain.
150   And yet the steer, the heifer and the calf
       Are all called neat.— Still virginalling   *Aside*
       Upon his palm?— How now, you wanton calf!
       Art thou my calf?

       MAMILLIUS   Yes, if you will, my lord.

---

131 friend companion (Leontes may pick up on the sense of "lover")   **133 mingling bloods** process believed to occur during sex, since semen was assumed to be chiefly composed of blood   **134** *tremor cordis* heart palpitations   **135 entertainment** hospitality (can have sexual connotations)   **136 free** innocent/open/generous   **137 heartiness** welcoming warmth   **bounty** generosity   **fertile bosom** profuse affection   **138 well . . . agent** still reflect well on the person behaving in such a way (Hermione)   **'T it**   **139 paddling . . . fingers** i.e. flirtatious gestures   **paddling** fingering   **140 practised** studied/flirtatious   **142 mort** horn sounded at the kill of a **deer**/death   **deer** puns on "dear"   **143 brows** forehead, from which cuckolds (men with unfaithful wives) were supposed to grow horns   **146 I' fecks!** In faith!   **147 bawcock** fine fellow (from French *beau coq*, meaning "fine cock, rooster")   **smutched** dirtied, smudged   **149 neat** clean, smart (puns on the sense of "horned cattle")   **150 steer** young male ox   **151 virginalling . . . palm** moving the fingers up and down, as if playing the virginals (a keyed instrument); with sexual innuendo   **152 wanton** wild/untrained/playful/lustful

155 LEONTES   Thou want'st a rough pash and the shoots that I have
To be full like me.— Yet they say we are   *Aside?*
Almost as like as eggs; women say so,
That will say anything. But were they false
As o'er-dyed blacks, as wind, as waters, false
160 As dice are to be wished by one that fixes
No bourn 'twixt his and mine, yet were it true
To say this boy were like me.— Come, sir page,   *To Mamillius*
Look on me with your welkin eye. Sweet villain!
Most dear'st, my collop! Can thy dam, may't be
165 Affection?— Thy intention stabs the centre.   *Aside?*
Thou dost make possible things not so held,
Communicat'st with dreams — how can this be? —
With what's unreal thou coactive art,
And fellow'st nothing. Then 'tis very credent
170 Thou mayst co-join with something, and thou dost,
And that beyond commission, and I find it,
And that to the infection of my brains
And hard'ning of my brows.
POLIXENES   What means Sicilia?
175 HERMIONE   He something seems unsettled.
POLIXENES   How, my lord?
LEONTES   What cheer? How is't with you, best brother?
HERMIONE   You look as if you held a brow of much distraction.
Are you moved, my lord?

---

155 **Thou want'st** you lack   **rough pash** shaggy head   **shoots** horns (signifying cuckoldry)
156 **full** complete, fully grown   159 **o'er-dyed blacks** fabric weakened by excessive
dyeing/fabric that has had black dye applied over a pre-existing color   **wind, as waters**
i.e. changeable, capricious   161 **bourn . . . mine** boundary between his and my possessions
(of which he intends to cheat me at **dice**)   163 **welkin** sky-blue   164 **collop** piece of flesh,
offspring   **Can thy dam** is your mother capable (of infidelity)   165 **Affection** strong
feeling/passion/animosity/delusion (sense apparently shifts between Hermione's supposed
erotic desire for Polixenes and Leontes' intense reaction)   **intention** intensity, forceful purpose
(which strikes to his heart, the **centre** of his being)   166 **not so held** deemed impossible
168 **thou coactive art** you collaborate   169 **fellow'st** are companion to   **credent** likely,
believable   170 **co-join** conjoin (sexual suggestion)   171 **commission** what is permitted
find discover, discern   173 **hard'ning . . . brows** i.e. as a cuckold, beginning to grow horns
174 **Sicilia** i.e. Leontes   175 **something seems** appears somewhat   179 **moved** distressed

180 LEONTES   No, in good earnest.—
          How sometimes nature will betray its folly,   *Aside?*
          Its tenderness, and make itself a pastime
          To harder bosoms!— Looking on the lines
          Of my boy's face, methoughts I did recoil
185   Twenty-three years, and saw myself unbreeched,
          In my green velvet coat; my dagger muzzled,
          Lest it should bite its master, and so prove,
          As ornaments oft do, too dangerous.
          How like, methought, I then was to this kernel,
190   This squash, this gentleman.— Mine honest friend,   *To Mamillius*
          Will you take eggs for money?

     MAMILLIUS   No, my lord, I'll fight.

     LEONTES   You will? Why, happy man be's dole! My brother,
          Are you so fond of your young prince as we
195   Do seem to be of ours?

     POLIXENES   If at home, sir,
          He's all my exercise, my mirth, my matter;
          Now my sworn friend and then mine enemy;
          My parasite, my soldier, statesman, all.
200   He makes a July's day short as December,
          And with his varying childness cures in me
          Thoughts that would thick my blood.

     LEONTES   So stands this squire
          Officed with me. We two will walk, my lord,
205   And leave you to your graver steps.— Hermione,
          How thou lovest us, show in our brother's welcome.
          Let what is dear in Sicily be cheap.
          Next to thyself and my young rover, he's
          Apparent to my heart.

---

182 make . . . bosoms provide entertainment to those with harder hearts   **185 unbreeched** i.e. a child, not yet in breeches (short trousers)   **186 muzzled** sheathed or with its tip protected **190 squash** unripe pea pod (familiar/contemptuous)   **191 take . . . money** i.e. be deceived into accepting something of inferior value (proverbial)   **193 happy . . . dole** may his destiny be good fortune/happiness   **197 exercise** usual occupation   **199 parasite** sponger, flattering courtier **201 childness** childlike ways   **202 Thoughts . . . blood** i.e. melancholy, thought to thicken the blood   **204 Officed** in such a role   **205 graver** slower, more sedate   **207 dear** expensive/ beloved   **cheap** inexpensive/common   **208 rover** wanderer   **209 Apparent** in line to

210   HERMIONE   If you would seek us,
        We are yours i'th'garden: shall's attend you there?
    LEONTES   To your own bents dispose you: you'll be found,
        Be you beneath the sky.— I am angling now,   *Aside*
        Though you perceive me not how I give line.
215   Go to, go to!
        How she holds up the neb, the bill to him!
        And arms her with the boldness of a wife
        To her allowing husband!

                [*Exeunt Polixenes, Hermione and Attendants*]
                Gone already?
        Inch-thick, knee-deep, o'er head and ears a forked one!—
220   Go, play, boy, play. Thy mother plays, and I
        Play too, but so disgraced a part, whose issue
        Will hiss me to my grave. Contempt and clamour
        Will be my knell. Go play, boy, play.— There have been,
        Or I am much deceived, cuckolds ere now.
225   And many a man there is, even at this present,
        Now while I speak this, holds his wife by th'arm,
        That little thinks she has been sluiced in's absence
        And his pond fished by his next neighbour, by
        Sir Smile, his neighbour. Nay, there's comfort in't
230   Whiles other men have gates and those gates opened,
        As mine, against their will. Should all despair
        That have revolted wives, the tenth of mankind
        Would hang themselves. Physic for't there's none:
        It is a bawdy planet, that will strike

---

211 shall's attend shall we wait for   **212 bents** inclinations   **found** discovered literally/
exposed morally   **215 Go to** expression of impatient dismissal   **216 neb, the bill** nose and
the mouth, i.e. she inclines her face as if to be kissed   **217 arms . . . husband** behaves as
though she were with her own husband   **219 forked** horned   **220 plays** ambiguous: amuses
herself/is busily engaged/practices deceit/has sexual intercourse; sense then shifts to "perform
a role"   **221 so . . . part** i.e. the cuckold, butt of jokes   **issue** outcome/end/action/offspring
(plays on the sense of "children")   **222 hiss** derisive response to Leontes' performance in role
of cuckold   **223 knell** funeral bells   **There have** perhaps elided "There've" for sake of meter
224 cuckolds men with unfaithful wives   **227 sluiced** flushed out with water, i.e. semen
228 pond plays on sense of "vagina"   **fished** plays on sense of "copulated with"   **230 gates**
i.e. vaginas   **232 revolted** unfaithful   **233 Physic** remedy   **234 bawdy** lewd   **strike** blast
with a malevolent influence

235 Where 'tis predominant; and 'tis powerful, think it,
From east, west, north and south. Be it concluded,
No barricado for a belly. Know't,
It will let in and out the enemy
With bag and baggage. Many thousand on's
240 Have the disease, and feel't not.— How now, boy?

MAMILLIUS   I am like you, they say.

LEONTES   Why that's some comfort. What, Camillo there?

CAMILLO   Ay, my good lord.   *Comes forward*

LEONTES   Go play, Mamillius, thou'rt an honest man.—
                                                  [*Exit Mamillius*]

245 Camillo, this great sir will yet stay longer.

CAMILLO   You had much ado to make his anchor hold:
When you cast out, it still came home.

LEONTES   Didst note it?

CAMILLO   He would not stay at your petitions, made
250 His business more material.

LEONTES   Didst perceive it?—
They're here with me already, whisp'ring, rounding   *Aside*
'Sicilia is a so-forth.' 'Tis far gone
When I shall gust it last.— How came't, Camillo,   *To Camillo*
255 That he did stay?

CAMILLO   At the good queen's entreaty.

LEONTES   At the queen's be't. 'Good' should be pertinent,
But so it is, it is not. Was this taken
By any understanding pate but thine?
260 For thy conceit is soaking, will draw in
More than the common blocks. Not noted, is't,
But of the finer natures? By some severals

235 **predominant** in the ascendant   237 **barricado . . . belly** i.e. defense against sexual
entry   239 **bag and baggage** plays on the sense of "penis and testicles"   **on's** of us
246 **ado** trouble, fuss   **his anchor hold** him (Polixenes) stay   247 **still came home** always
returned, i.e. failed to take hold   249 **petitions** requests, entreaties   250 **material** urgent
252 **They're . . . already** i.e. people are already talking about me   **rounding** talking secretly
253 **so-forth** so-and-so, i.e. cuckold   **'Tis . . . last** it must be far advanced, if I am the last to
realize it   254 **gust** taste   257 **pertinent** appropriate (as a description of her)   258 **so it is**
as matters stand   **taken** understood, perceived   259 **pate** head   260 **conceit is soaking**
understanding is receptive   261 **blocks** idiots   262 **But of** except by   **severals** individuals

Of head-piece extraordinary? Lower messes
Perchance are to this business purblind? Say.

265 CAMILLO   Business, my lord? I think most understand
Bohemia stays here longer.

LEONTES   Ha?

CAMILLO   Stays here longer.

LEONTES   Ay, but why?

270 CAMILLO   To satisfy your highness and the entreaties
Of our most gracious mistress.

LEONTES   Satisfy?
Th'entreaties of your mistress? Satisfy?
Let that suffice. I have trusted thee, Camillo,

275 With all the nearest things to my heart, as well
My chamber-councils, wherein, priest-like, thou
Hast cleansed my bosom, I from thee departed
Thy penitent reformed. But we have been
Deceived in thy integrity, deceived

280 In that which seems so.

CAMILLO   Be it forbid, my lord!

LEONTES   To bide upon't, thou art not honest: or,
If thou inclin'st that way, thou art a coward,
Which hoxes honesty behind, restraining

285 From course required: or else thou must be counted
A servant grafted in my serious trust
And therein negligent: or else a fool
That see'st a game played home, the rich stake drawn,
And tak'st it all for jest.

290 CAMILLO   My gracious lord,
I may be negligent, foolish and fearful.
In every one of these no man is free,

---

263 **head-piece** intellect   **Lower messes** inferior classes   264 **business** plays on "sexual
business"   **purblind** blind   272 **Satisfy** Leontes picks up on the sense of "gratify sexually"
275 **well** well as with   276 **chamber-councils** personal business   277 **cleansed my bosom**
heard my confession and given me absolution   278 **we** Leontes falls back on royal "we" to
assert authority   282 **bide** dwell   284 **hoxes** cripples   285 **counted** accounted, deemed
286 **grafted** planted   288 **game** plays on the sense of "sexual play/contest"   **home** to its
conclusion   **stake drawn** prize collected (plays on the sense of "penis ready for action")

But that his negligence, his folly, fear,
Among the infinite doings of the world,
295 Sometime puts forth. In your affairs, my lord,
If ever I were wilful-negligent,
It was my folly: if industriously
I played the fool, it was my negligence,
Not weighing well the end: if ever fearful
300 To do a thing, where I the issue doubted,
Whereof the execution did cry out
Against the non-performance, 'twas a fear
Which oft infects the wisest. These, my lord,
Are such allowed infirmities that honesty
305 Is never free of. But, beseech your grace,
Be plainer with me. Let me know my trespass
By its own visage; if I then deny it,
'Tis none of mine.

LEONTES   Ha' not you seen, Camillo —
310 But that's past doubt, you have, or your eye-glass
Is thicker than a cuckold's horn — or heard —
For to a vision so apparent rumour
Cannot be mute — or thought — for cogitation
Resides not in that man that does not think —
315 My wife is slippery? If thou wilt confess,
Or else be impudently negative,
To have nor eyes nor ears nor thought, then say
My wife's a hobby-horse, deserves a name
As rank as any flax-wench that puts to
320 Before her troth-plight: say't and justify't.

CAMILLO   I would not be a stander-by to hear

---

296 wilful-negligent deliberately neglectful   **299 weighing** considering, anticipating
300 issue outcome   **301 Whereof . . . non-performance** where, the deed being accomplished,
it became clear that it should indeed have been undertaken   **306 trespass** crime
307 visage face, appearance   **310 eye-glass** lens of the eye   **312 vision so apparent**
something so obvious   **313 cogitation** thought   **315 slippery** licentious/deceitful/unchaste
316 be . . . To shamelessly deny that you   **318 hobby-horse** whore   **319 rank** lustful   **flax-**
wench lowly woman (flax was spun on a—phallic—distaff, so this also signifies "whore/
lecherous woman")   **puts . . . troth-plight** has sex before her betrothal

My sovereign mistress clouded so, without
My present vengeance taken. 'Shrew my heart,
You never spoke what did become you less
325 Than this; which to reiterate were sin
As deep as that, though true.

LEONTES   Is whispering nothing?
Is leaning cheek to cheek? Is meeting noses?
Kissing with inside lip? Stopping the career
330 Of laughter with a sigh — a note infallible
Of breaking honesty? Horsing foot on foot?
Skulking in corners? Wishing clocks more swift?
Hours, minutes? Noon, midnight? And all eyes
Blind with the pin and web but theirs, theirs only,
335 That would unseen be wicked? Is this nothing?
Why then the world and all that's in't is nothing:
The covering sky is nothing, Bohemia is nothing,
My wife is nothing, nor nothing have these nothings,
If this be nothing.

340 CAMILLO   Good my lord, be cured
Of this diseased opinion, and betimes.
For 'tis most dangerous.

LEONTES   Say it be, 'tis true.

CAMILLO   No, no, my lord.

345 LEONTES   It is. You lie, you lie.
I say thou liest, Camillo, and I hate thee,
Pronounce thee a gross lout, a mindless slave,
Or else a hovering temporizer, that
Canst with thine eyes at once see good and evil,
350 Inclining to them both. Were my wife's liver

---

322 **clouded** i.e. defamed   323 **present** immediate   **'Shrew** curse (beshrew)   324 **become** befit, suit   325 **were . . . true** would be as sinful as the (adulterous) wrongs you describe, even if they were true   329 **career** full gallop   330 **note infallible** certain sign   331 **honesty** virtue, decency/chastity   **Horsing . . . foot** foot-treading, a favorite erotic signal of the period; plays on sexual sense of "mount," adopting sexual position   333 **Hours** wishing hours were   334 **pin and web** cataract   338 **nothing** of no significance; plays on "no thing" (i.e. vagina/no penis)   341 **betimes** quickly   348 **temporizer** procrastinator   350 **liver** thought to be the seat of sexual passion

> Infected as her life, she would not live
> The running of one glass.

CAMILLO   Who does infect her?

LEONTES   Why, he that wears her like her medal, hanging

355 About his neck, Bohemia: who, if I
     Had servants true about me that bare eyes
     To see alike mine honour as their profits,
     Their own particular thrifts, they would do that
     Which should undo more doing. Ay, and thou,

360 His cupbearer — whom I from meaner form
     Have benched and reared to worship, who mayst see
     Plainly as heaven sees earth and earth sees heaven,
     How I am galled — mightst bespice a cup
     To give mine enemy a lasting wink,

365 Which draught to me were cordial.

CAMILLO   Sir, my lord,
     I could do this, and that with no rash potion,
     But with a ling'ring dram that should not work
     Maliciously like poison. But I cannot

370 Believe this crack to be in my dread mistress,
     So sovereignly being honourable.
     I have loved thee—

LEONTES   Make that thy question, and go rot!
     Dost think I am so muddy, so unsettled,

375 To appoint myself in this vexation, sully
     The purity and whiteness of my sheets —
     Which to preserve is sleep, which being spotted
     Is goads, thorns, nettles, tails of wasps —

---

352 **glass** hourglass   354 **medal** miniature portrait of the beloved   356 **bare** bore, had
358 **particular thrifts** personal profit   359 **undo** prevent, ruin   **doing** action/sex
360 **cupbearer** servant who carried his master's cup and was responsible for serving wine
meaner form lower rank   361 **benched** given a position of authority   **worship** honor,
respectability   363 **galled** distressed, vexed   **bespice** season (with poison)   364 **lasting
wink** eternal sleep (death)   365 **cordial** health giving, heart restoring   367 **rash** immediately
effective   368 **dram** draught, tiny amount   369 **Maliciously** violently   370 **crack** moral
breach (with vaginal connotations)   **dread** noble, respected   373 **Make . . . rot!** If you are
going to dispute my accusations, then go and rot!   374 **muddy** dull-witted   375 **appoint . . .
vexation** put myself in this distress   377 **sleep** peace of mind   **spotted** stained

Give scandal to the blood o'th'prince my son —
380   Who I do think is mine and love as mine —
Without ripe moving to't? Would I do this?
Could man so blench?

CAMILLO   I must believe you, sir.
I do, and will fetch off Bohemia for't,
385   Provided that when he's removed, your highness
Will take again your queen as yours at first,
Even for your son's sake, and thereby for sealing
The injury of tongues in courts and kingdoms
Known and allied to yours.

LEONTES   Thou dost advise me
390   Even so as I mine own course have set down.
I'll give no blemish to her honour, none.

CAMILLO   My lord,
Go then; and with a countenance as clear
395   As friendship wears at feasts, keep with Bohemia
And with your queen. I am his cupbearer:
If from me he have wholesome beverage,
Account me not your servant.

LEONTES   This is all.
400   Do't and thou hast the one half of my heart;
Do't not, thou splitt'st thine own.

CAMILLO   I'll do't, my lord.

LEONTES   I will seem friendly, as thou hast advised me.   *Exit*

CAMILLO   O miserable lady! But, for me,
405   What case stand I in? I must be the poisoner
Of good Polixenes, and my ground to do't
Is the obedience to a master; one
Who, in rebellion with himself, will have

379 Give . . . blood raise questions about the legitimacy   381 ripe moving to't full, compelling reason for it   382 blench turn aside   384 fetch off kill (plays on the sense of "rescue")   387 for . . . tongues preventing damaging talk   390 Thou . . . down i.e. what you suggest is exactly what I had intended to do   394 countenance expression/appearance   395 keep keep company with   404 miserable doomed, unfortunate   405 case situation   406 ground reason, imperative   408 in . . . himself behaving uncharacteristically, defying his true nature

All that are his so too. To do this deed,

410　Promotion follows. If I could find example

Of thousands that had struck anointed kings

And flourished after, I'd not do't. But since

Nor brass nor stone nor parchment bears not one,

Let villainy itself forswear't. I must

415　Forsake the court. To do't, or no, is certain

To me a break-neck. Happy star, reign now!

Here comes Bohemia.

Enter Polixenes

POLIXENES　This is strange. Methinks　　　　　　*Aside*

My favour here begins to warp. Not speak?—

420　Good day, Camillo.

CAMILLO　Hail, most royal sir!

POLIXENES　What is the news i'th'court?

CAMILLO　None rare, my lord.

POLIXENES　The king hath on him such a countenance

425　As he had lost some province and a region

Loved as he loves himself. Even now I met him

With customary compliment, when he,

Wafting his eyes to th'contrary and falling

A lip of much contempt, speeds from me and

430　So leaves me to consider what is breeding

That changes thus his manners.

CAMILLO　I dare not know, my lord.

POLIXENES　How, dare not? Do not? Do you know, and dare not?

Be intelligent to me. 'Tis thereabouts.

435　For, to yourself, what you do know, you must,

And cannot say you dare not. Good Camillo,

Your changed complexions are to me a mirror

---

409 All . . . too all of his servants behave in such a way as well　**410 If** even if　**413 brass . . . parchment** monuments or materials on which history is recorded　**416 break-neck** i.e. death　**Happy** favorable　**419 warp** contract/go astray　**423 None rare** nothing exceptional　**425 As** as if　**427 customary compliment** usual courtesy　**428 Wafting . . . th'contrary** looking away　**falling** letting fall, pouting　**434 intelligent** informative, communicative　**'Tis thereabouts** it must be something of this sort, i.e. something you **dare not** say　**435 to . . . must** within your heart, if you know something, you cannot deny that you do　**437 complexions** appearance, expressions

Which shows me mine changed too, for I must be
A party in this alteration, finding
440   Myself thus altered with't.

CAMILLO   There is a sickness
Which puts some of us in distemper, but
I cannot name the disease, and it is caught
Of you that yet are well.

445 POLIXENES   How, caught of me?
Make me not sighted like the basilisk.
I have looked on thousands who have sped the better
By my regard, but killed none so. Camillo —
As you are certainly a gentleman, thereto
450   Clerk-like experienced, which no less adorns
Our gentry than our parents' noble names,
In whose success we are gentle — I beseech you,
If you know aught which does behove my knowledge
Thereof to be informed, imprison't not
455   In ignorant concealment.

CAMILLO   I may not answer.

POLIXENES   A sickness caught of me, and yet I well?
I must be answered. Dost thou hear, Camillo,
I conjure thee, by all the parts of man
460   Which honour does acknowledge, whereof the least
Is not this suit of mine, that thou declare
What incidency thou dost guess of harm
Is creeping toward me; how far off, how near,
Which way to be prevented, if to be.
465   If not, how best to bear it.

CAMILLO   Sir, I will tell you,
Since I am charged in honour and by him
That I think honourable: therefore mark my counsel,

---

442 **distemper** disordered constitution   444 **Of** from   446 **basilisk** mythical reptile that could kill with its sight and breath   447 **sped** fared/succeeded   448 **regard** look/favor, esteem   450 **Clerk-like** educated (and)   451 **gentry** gentlemanly role   452 **whose success** being descended from whom   **gentle** honorable   453 **aught** anything   **behove** benefit   459 **conjure** charge, solemnly appeal   **parts** qualities   460 **whereof . . . suit** not the least of which is (to answer) my request   462 **incidency** event   467 **charged** commanded   468 **mark** pay attention to

Which must be ev'n as swiftly followed as
470 I mean to utter it; or both yourself and me
Cry lost, and so goodnight!

POLIXENES   On, good Camillo.

CAMILLO   I am appointed him to murder you.

POLIXENES   By whom, Camillo?

475 CAMILLO   By the king.

POLIXENES   For what?

CAMILLO   He thinks, nay, with all confidence he swears,
As he had seen't or been an instrument
To vice you to't, that you have touched his queen
480 Forbiddenly.

POLIXENES   O, then my best blood turn
To an infected jelly and my name
Be yoked with his that did betray the best!
Turn then my freshest reputation to
485 A savour that may strike the dullest nostril
Where I arrive, and my approach be shunned,
Nay, hated too, worse than the great'st infection
That e'er was heard or read!

CAMILLO   Swear his thought over
490 By each particular star in heaven and
By all their influences; you may as well
Forbid the sea for to obey the moon
As or by oath remove or counsel shake
The fabric of his folly, whose foundation
495 Is piled upon his faith and will continue
The standing of his body.

POLIXENES   How should this grow?

CAMILLO   I know not. But I am sure 'tis safer to
Avoid what's grown than question how 'tis born.

---

469 ev'n even, just   **471 goodnight** i.e. the end   **473 him** by him/to be the one   **479 vice** force   **483 his . . . best** i.e. Judas, betrayer of Christ   **485 savour** smell   **strike** blast, have an evil influence over   **dullest** least receptive   **489 Swear . . . over** even if you swear what he says is untrue   **491 influences** an invisible substance was supposed to stream from stars and influence destiny   **492 for to** to   **493 or** either   **494 fabric** building, structure   **496 The . . . body** for the rest of his life   **497 grow** have developed

500 If therefore you dare trust my honesty,
That lies enclosèd in this trunk which you
Shall bear along impawned, away tonight!
Your followers I will whisper to the business,
And will by twos and threes at several posterns
505 Clear them o'th'city. For myself, I'll put
My fortunes to your service, which are here
By this discovery lost. Be not uncertain,
For by the honour of my parents, I
Have uttered truth, which if you seek to prove,
510 I dare not stand by; nor shall you be safer
Than one condemnèd by the king's own mouth,
Thereon his execution sworn.

POLIXENES   I do believe thee:
I saw his heart in's face. Give me thy hand.
515 Be pilot to me and thy places shall
Still neighbour mine. My ships are ready and
My people did expect my hence departure
Two days ago. This jealousy
Is for a precious creature: as she's rare,
520 Must it be great, and as his person's mighty,
Must it be violent, and as he does conceive
He is dishonoured by a man which ever
Professed to him, why, his revenges must
In that be made more bitter. Fear o'ershades me.
525 Good expedition be my friend, and comfort
The gracious queen, part of his theme, but nothing
Of his ill-ta'en suspicion. Come, Camillo.
I will respect thee as a father if
Thou bear'st my life off hence. Let us avoid.

---

501 **trunk** body   502 **impawned** as a pledge   503 **whisper** to inform secretly of
504 **posterns** back gates of the city   505 **Clear them** make their way out   506 **which . . . lost**
i.e. in revealing this information I have ruined my **fortunes**   509 **prove** test   510 **stand by**
reaffirm publicly   515 **pilot** guide   **thy . . . mine** your position/privileges shall always be
related to mine   **places** dignities, rank, honors   517 **hence departure** departure from here
523 **Professed** professed friendship   525 **Good expedition** prompt departure   526 **theme**
concern, motive   527 **ill-ta'en** misinformed, unjustified   529 **avoid** leave

530 CAMILLO   It is in mine authority to command
         The keys of all the posterns. Please your highness
         To take the urgent hour. Come, sir, away.   *Exeunt*

Act 2 Scene 1   *running scene 2*

Enter Hermione, Mamillius, Ladies

HERMIONE   Take the boy to you. He so troubles me,
         'Tis past enduring.
FIRST LADY   Come, my gracious lord,   *Takes Mamillius*
         Shall I be your playfellow?
5 MAMILLIUS   No, I'll none of you.
FIRST LADY   Why, my sweet lord?
MAMILLIUS   You'll kiss me hard and speak to me as if
         I were a baby still.— I love you better.   *To Second Lady*
SECOND LADY   And why so, my lord?
10 MAMILLIUS   Not for because
         Your brows are blacker — yet black brows, they say,
         Become some women best, so that there be not
         Too much hair there, but in a semicircle
         Or a half-moon made with a pen.
15 SECOND LADY   Who taught 'this?
MAMILLIUS   I learned it out of women's faces. Pray now
         What colour are your eyebrows?
FIRST LADY   Blue, my lord.
MAMILLIUS   Nay, that's a mock. I have seen a lady's nose
20   That has been blue, but not her eyebrows.
FIRST LADY   Hark ye.
         The queen your mother rounds apace. We shall
         Present our services to a fine new prince
         One of these days, and then you'd wanton with us,
25   If we would have you.

2.1   **5 none of** have nothing to do with   **10 for because** because   **12 so** provided   **15 'this**
you this   **22 rounds apace** grows larger rapidly (in pregnancy)   **24 wanton with us** (want
to) play with us

SECOND LADY   She is spread of late
Into a goodly bulk. Good time encounter her!

HERMIONE   What wisdom stirs amongst you? Come, sir, now
I am for you again. Pray you sit by us,
30   And tell's a tale.

MAMILLIUS   Merry or sad shall't be?

HERMIONE   As merry as you will.

MAMILLIUS   A sad tale's best for winter. I have one
Of sprites and goblins.

35   HERMIONE   Let's have that, good sir.
Come on, sit down. Come on, and do your best
To fright me with your sprites. You're powerful at it.

MAMILLIUS   There was a man—

HERMIONE   Nay, come, sit down, then on.

40   MAMILLIUS   Dwelt by a churchyard — I will tell it softly.   *Sits*
Yond crickets shall not hear it.

HERMIONE   Come on, then, and give't me in mine ear.   *They talk apart*

[*Enter Leontes, Antigonus, Lords and others*]

LEONTES   Was he met there? His train? Camillo with him?

A LORD   Behind the tuft of pines I met them. Never
45   Saw I men scour so on their way: I eyed them
Even to their ships.

LEONTES   How blest am I
In my just censure, in my true opinion!
Alack, for lesser knowledge! How accursed
50   In being so blest! There may be in the cup
A spider steeped, and one may drink, depart,
And yet partake no venom, for his knowledge
Is not infected: but if one present
Th'abhorred ingredient to his eye, make known
55   How he hath drunk, he cracks his gorge, his sides,

---

27 **Good . . . her!** May she have a happy labor!   29 **for** ready for   31 **sad** serious/mournful
34 **sprites** spirits   41 **Yond crickets** i.e. the other women over there   44 **tuft** thicket
45 **scour** move swiftly   46 **Even** all the way   48 **just censure** accurate/justifiable judgment
50 **In . . . infected** i.e. a **spider** (thought to be venomous) would not poison the drink it was
in unless the drinker knew of its presence   51 **steeped** soaked   55 **gorge** stomach/throat

With violent hefts. I have drunk, and seen the spider.
Camillo was his help in this, his pander.
There is a plot against my life, my crown.
All's true that is mistrusted. That false villain
60 Whom I employed was pre-employed by him.
He has discovered my design, and I
Remain a pinched thing; yea, a very trick
For them to play at will. How came the posterns
So easily open?

65 A LORD   By his great authority,
Which often hath no less prevailed than so
On your command.

LEONTES   I know't too well.—
Give me the boy. I am glad you did not nurse him.   *To Hermione*
70 Though he does bear some signs of me, yet you
Have too much blood in him.

HERMIONE   What is this? Sport?

LEONTES   Bear the boy hence. He shall not come   *To a Lord or Lady*
about her.
Away with him, and let her sport herself
75 With that she's big with,— for 'tis Polixenes   *To Hermione*
Has made thee swell thus.

                    [*The Lord or Lady exits with Mamillius*]

HERMIONE   But I'd say he had not;
And I'll be sworn you would believe my saying,
Howe'er you lean to th'nayward.

80 LEONTES   You, my lords,
Look on her, mark her well. Be but about
To say 'She is a goodly lady', and
The justice of your hearts will thereto add
''Tis pity she's not honest, honourable.'

---

56 **hefts** heaves   **I have drunk** perhaps elided "I've drunk" for sake of meter   57 **pander**
pimp, go-between   59 **mistrusted** suspected   **false** deceitful   62 **pinched** tormented   **trick**
trifle, toy   69 **nurse** breast-feed (babies of noble households were breast-fed by wet-nurses)
72 **Sport?** A joke?   74 **sport** entertain (plays on the sense of "have sex")   79 **Howe'er . . .
th'nayward** whatever you think to the contrary   83 **justice** rightful judgment   84 **honest**
truthful/chaste

85   Praise her but for this her without-door form,
Which on my faith deserves high speech, and straight
The shrug, the hum or ha, these petty brands
That calumny doth use — O, I am out —
That mercy does, for calumny will sear
90   Virtue itself: these shrugs, these hums and ha's,
When you have said 'She's goodly', come between
Ere you can say 'She's honest.' But be't known,
From him that has most cause to grieve it should be,
She's an adultress.

95   HERMIONE   Should a villain say so —
The most replenished villain in the world —
He were as much more villain. You, my lord,
Do but mistake.

LEONTES   You have mistook, my lady,
100   Polixenes for Leontes. O thou thing,
Which I'll not call a creature of thy place,
Lest barbarism, making me the precedent,
Should a like language use to all degrees
And mannerly distinguishment leave out
105   Betwixt the prince and beggar. I have said
She's an adult'ress. I have said with whom.
More, she's a traitor and Camillo is
A federary with her, and one that knows
What she should shame to know herself
110   But with her most vile principal, that she's
A bed-swerver, even as bad as those

---

85 **without-door** public, outward   86 **straight** immediately   87 **brands** stigmas/slanders
88 **calumny** slander   **out** wrong/angry/speechless   89 **That . . . itself** i.e. **mercy**, not slander,
uses shrugs to suggest that Hermione is unchaste; slander attacks actual **virtue** (which she
does not possess)   91 **come between** interrupt   96 **replenished** complete   97 **He . . .
villain** saying so would make him an even greater villain   99 **mistook** plays on the sense of
"wrongfully had sex with"   101 **I'll . . . place** i.e. I will not desecrate your high rank by calling
you what you really are (in fact Leontes does so: **creature** plays on the sense of "whore")
103 **a like** the same   **degrees** social classes   104 **mannerly distinguishment** the proper
distinction   108 **federary** confederate, accomplice   109 **know** plays on the sense of "have
sex"   111 **bed-swerver** unfaithful to the marital bed ("swerver" means offender, trespasser;
possible play on "swiver")

That vulgars give bold'st titles; ay, and privy
To this their late escape.

HERMIONE   No, by my life,
115   Privy to none of this. How will this grieve you,
When you shall come to clearer knowledge, that
You thus have published me. Gentle my lord,
You scarce can right me throughly then to say
You did mistake.

120   LEONTES   No. If I mistake
In those foundations which I build upon,
The centre is not big enough to bear
A school-boy's top. Away with her, to prison!
He who shall speak for her is afar off guilty
125   But that he speaks.

HERMIONE   There's some ill planet reigns:
I must be patient till the heavens look
With an aspect more favourable. Good my lords,
I am not prone to weeping — as our sex
130   Commonly are — the want of which vain dew
Perchance shall dry your pities: but I have
That honourable grief lodged here which burns
Worse than tears drown. Beseech you all, my lords,
With thoughts so qualified as your charities
135   Shall best instruct you, measure me; and so
The king's will be performed.

LEONTES   Shall I be heard?

HERMIONE   Who is't that goes with me? Beseech your highness
My women may be with me, for you see
140   My plight requires it. Do not weep, good fools.

---

112 **vulgars** common people   **bold'st titles** coarsest names   **privy To** secretly aware of
117 **published** publicly denounced   **Gentle my** my noble   118 **throughly** thoroughly
to say by saying   122 **centre** mainstay, support (i.e. if my supposition is incorrect, then the
whole structure of my mind/the world will collapse)   123 **top** spinning top, toy   124 **afar off**
indirectly/by implication   125 **But . . . speaks** merely by speaking up   126 **ill** malevolent
128 **aspect** astrological influence   130 **want** lack   131 **Perchance . . . pities** may perhaps
prevent you from feeling pity for me   132 **here** i.e. in my heart   134 **qualified** tempered,
moderated   **charities** senses of charity   135 **measure** judge   137 **heard** i.e. obeyed
140 **plight** situation, i.e. her pregnancy

There is no cause. When you shall know your mistress
Has deserved prison, then abound in tears
As I come out; this action I now go on
Is for my better grace.— Adieu, my lord.   *To Leontes*

145   I never wished to see you sorry, now
I trust I shall.— My women, come, you have leave.

LEONTES   Go, do our bidding. Hence!

[*Exit Hermione, guarded, with Ladies*]

A LORD   Beseech your highness, call the queen again.

ANTIGONUS   Be certain what you do, sir, lest your justice

150   Prove violence, in the which three great ones suffer:
Yourself, your queen, your son.

A LORD   For her, my lord,
I dare my life lay down and will do't, sir,
Please you t'accept it, that the queen is spotless

155   I'th'eyes of heaven and to you — I mean,
In this which you accuse her.

ANTIGONUS   If it prove
She's otherwise, I'll keep my stables where
I lodge my wife, I'll go in couples with her,

160   Than when I feel and see her no further trust her,
For every inch of woman in the world,
Ay, every dram of woman's flesh is false,
If she be.

LEONTES   Hold your peaces.

165   A LORD   Good my lord—

ANTIGONUS   It is for you we speak, not for ourselves.
You are abused and by some putter-on
That will be damned for't. Would I knew the villain,
I would land-damn him. Be she honour-flawed,

170   I have three daughters — the eldest is eleven

---

144 **better grace** higher virtue (in the eyes of God)   146 **leave** permission (to go)
158 **keep . . . wife** i.e. treat my wife as I would an animal/segregate my wife from all men (as
mares were from stallions in stables)   159 **in couples** leashed together (as hounds were for the
hunt)   160 **Than . . . her** not trust her except when I can see or feel her   162 **dram** tiny
portion   167 **putter-on** plotter, instigator   169 **land-damn** of unclear meaning; probably
"thrash pitilessly"

The second and the third, nine, and some five —
If this prove true, they'll pay for't. By mine honour,
I'll geld 'em all: fourteen they shall not see,
To bring false generations. They are co-heirs,
175   And I had rather glib myself than they
Should not produce fair issue.

LEONTES   Cease. No more.
You smell this business with a sense as cold
As is a dead man's nose. But I do see't and feel't
180   As you feel doing thus, and see withal
The instruments that feel.

ANTIGONUS   If it be so,
We need no grave to bury honesty:
There's not a grain of it the face to sweeten
185   Of the whole dungy earth.

LEONTES   What? Lack I credit?

FIRST LORD   I had rather you did lack than I, my lord,
Upon this ground. And more it would content me
To have her honour true than your suspicion,
190   Be blamed for't how you might.

LEONTES   Why, what need we
Commune with you of this, but rather follow
Our forceful instigation? Our prerogative
Calls not your counsels, but our natural goodness
195   Imparts this, which if you, or stupefied
Or seeming so in skill, cannot or will not
Relish a truth like us, inform yourselves
We need no more of your advice. The matter,

---

171 **some** about   173 **geld** spay, make infertile   174 **bring false generations** have illegitimate children   175 **glib** castrate   176 **fair issue** legitimate offspring   180 **doing thus** perhaps Leontes touches Antigonus or places Antigonus' hand on something   **withal** in addition   181 **instruments that feel** i.e. fingers   183 **honesty** chastity/fidelity/truth 184 **the . . . sweeten** to perfume the face   186 **credit** credibility, (others') belief   188 **Upon this ground** in this matter (plays on sense of "earth")   189 **suspicion** doubt   193 **instigation** incentive, direction   **Our . . . this** my royal privilege does not require your advice; I am informing you of this out of **natural goodness**   195 **or stupefied** either insensible   196 **in skill** falsely   197 **Relish** appreciate, understand

The loss, the gain, the ord'ring on't, is all
200 Properly ours.
ANTIGONUS   And I wish, my liege,
You had only in your silent judgement tried it,
Without more overture.
LEONTES   How could that be?
205 Either thou art most ignorant by age,
Or thou wert born a fool. Camillo's flight,
Added to their familiarity —
Which was as gross as ever touched conjecture,
That lacked sight only, nought for approbation
210 But only seeing, all other circumstances
Made up to th'deed — doth push on this proceeding.
Yet, for a greater confirmation —
For in an act of this importance 'twere
Most piteous to be wild — I have dispatched in post
215 To sacred Delphos, to Apollo's temple,
Cleomenes and Dion, whom you know
Of stuffed sufficiency. Now from the oracle
They will bring all, whose spiritual counsel had,
Shall stop or spur me. Have I done well?
220 A LORD   Well done, my lord.
LEONTES   Though I am satisfied and need no more
Than what I know, yet shall the oracle
Give rest to th'minds of others, such as he
Whose ignorant credulity will not
225 Come up to th'truth. So have we thought it good
From our free person she should be confined,

---

199 ord'ring on't management of it   200 Properly personally   201 liege lord, superior entitled to feudal allegiance and service   203 overture public disclosure   205 ignorant by age grown stupid with age   208 gross . . . only obvious as any suspicion that lacked only visible proof (gross plays on the senses of "coarse/vile")   209 nought for approbation nothing remained for proof   211 Made added   deed event/sexual act   proceeding course of action   214 wild rash   post haste   215 Delphos Delos, the island where Apollo the sun god was born and home to an oracle; possibly conflated with Delphi, the Greek town more famous for its oracle   217 stuffed sufficiency complete competency   218 had having been heard   223 he any man/Antigonus   225 Come up to face   226 From away from   free accessible/innocent/not imprisoned

Lest that the treachery of the two fled hence
Be left her to perform. Come, follow us.
We are to speak in public, for this business
230   Will raise us all.

ANTIGONUS   To laughter, as I take it,   *Aside*
If the good truth were known.   *Exeunt*

Act 2 Scene 2   *running scene 3*

Enter Paulina, a Gentleman [and Attendants]

PAULINA   The keeper of the prison, call to him.
Let him have knowledge who I am.   *Gentleman goes*
                                    Good lady,   *to the door*
No court in Europe is too good for thee.
What dost thou then in prison?

[Enter the Jailer]
                                    Now, good sir,
5   You know me, do you not?

JAILER   For a worthy lady,
And one who much I honour.

PAULINA   Pray you then,
Conduct me to the queen.

10   JAILER   I may not, madam.
To the contrary I have express commandment.

PAULINA   Here's ado, to lock up honesty and honour from
Th'access of gentle visitors! Is't lawful, pray you,
To see her women? Any of them? Emilia?

15   JAILER   So please you, madam,
To put apart these your attendants, I
Shall bring Emilia forth.

PAULINA   I pray now call her.—
Withdraw yourselves.

                    [Exeunt Gentleman and Attendants]

---

227 **treachery** i.e. suspected plot to kill Leontes   230 **raise** rouse, incite   **2.2**   **12 ado** a fuss
13 **gentle** noble/kind   **16 put apart** dismiss, leave

20 JAILER   And, madam,
I must be present at your conference.

PAULINA   Well, be't so, prithee.   [*Exit Jailer*]
Here's such ado to make no stain a stain
As passes colouring.

[*Enter Jailer with Emilia*]

25   Dear gentlewoman,
How fares our gracious lady?

EMILIA   As well as one so great and so forlorn
May hold together. On her frights and griefs —
Which never tender lady hath borne greater —
30   She is something before her time delivered.

PAULINA   A boy?

EMILIA   A daughter, and a goodly babe,
Lusty and like to live. The queen receives
Much comfort in't, says 'My poor prisoner,
35   I am innocent as you.'

PAULINA   I dare be sworn.
These dangerous unsafe lunes i'th'king, beshrew them!
He must be told on't, and he shall. The office
Becomes a woman best. I'll take't upon me.
40   If I prove honey-mouthed, let my tongue blister
And never to my red-looked anger be
The trumpet any more. Pray you, Emilia,
Commend my best obedience to the queen.
If she dares trust me with her little babe,
45   I'll show't the king and undertake to be
Her advocate to th'loud'st. We do not know
How he may soften at the sight o'th'child:

---

24 **passes colouring** surpasses dyeing/is beyond all attempts at justification
27 **forlorn** outcast   28 **On** on account of   30 **is . . . delivered** has given birth prematurely
33 **Lusty** robust   37 **lunes** fits of madness, attributed to changes of the moon   **beshrew**
curse   38 **on't** of it   **office** task   39 **Becomes** is suited to   40 **honey-mouthed** deceitful
41 **never . . . more** may my tongue never be allowed to declare my anger again   **red-looked**
dressed in red, like the military herald who preceded the trumpeter   43 **Commend . . .**
obedience send my devoted support   46 **Her . . . th'loud'st** her most vociferous representative

The silence often of pure innocence
Persuades when speaking fails.

50 EMILIA   Most worthy madam,
Your honour and your goodness is so evident
That your free undertaking cannot miss
A thriving issue. There is no lady living
So meet for this great errand. Please your ladyship
55 To visit the next room, I'll presently
Acquaint the queen of your most noble offer,
Who but today hammered of this design,
But durst not tempt a minister of honour,
Lest she should be denied.

60 PAULINA   Tell her, Emilia.
I'll use that tongue I have: if wit flow from't
As boldness from my bosom, let't not be doubted
I shall do good.

EMILIA   Now be you blest for it!
65 I'll to the queen.— Please you come something   *To Jailer*
nearer.

JAILER   Madam, if't please the queen to send the babe,
I know not what I shall incur to pass it,
Having no warrant.

PAULINA   You need not fear it, sir:
70 This child was prisoner to the womb and is
By law and process of great nature thence
Freed and enfranchised, not a party to
The anger of the king nor guilty of,
If any be, the trespass of the queen.

75 JAILER   I do believe it.

PAULINA   Do not you fear. Upon mine honour, I
Will stand betwixt you and danger.   *Exeunt*

---

52 free generous   **miss . . . issue** fail to achieve a positive outcome (**thriving issue** plays
on the sense of "healthy offspring")   **54 meet** suitable   **55 presently** immediately
57 hammered . . . design thought of this enterprise   **58 durst . . . honour** dared not ask a noble
person   **61 wit** good sense, wisdom   **67 I shall . . . it** punishment I risk to let it out of the prison

Act 2 Scene 3

Enter Leontes

	LEONTES	Nor night nor day no rest. It is but weakness
		To bear the matter thus, mere weakness. If
		The cause were not in being — part o'th'cause,
		She, th'adulteress, for the harlot king
5		Is quite beyond mine arm, out of the blank
		And level of my brain, plot-proof. But she
		I can hook to me — say that she were gone,
		Given to the fire, a moiety of my rest
		Might come to me again. Who's there?

[Enter a Servant]

10	SERVANT	My lord?
	LEONTES	How does the boy?
	SERVANT	He took good rest tonight.
		'Tis hoped his sickness is discharged.
	LEONTES	To see his nobleness!
15		Conceiving the dishonour of his mother,
		He straight declined, drooped, took it deeply,
		Fastened and fixed the shame on't in himself,
		Threw off his spirit, his appetite, his sleep,
		And downright languished. Leave me solely. Go,
20		See how he fares.— *[Exit Servant]*
		Fie, fie! No thought of him.
		The very thought of my revenges that way
		Recoil upon me — in himself too mighty,
		And in his parties, his alliance. Let him be
		Until a time may serve. For present vengeance,
25		Take it on her. Camillo and Polixenes
		Laugh at me, make their pastime at my sorrow.
		They should not laugh if I could reach them, nor
		Shall she within my power.

2.3   1 Nor neither   **3 in being** alive   **4 harlot** lascivious (Polixenes)   **5 blank** target
6 level aim, range   **7 hook** attach   **8 Given . . . fire** burned at the stake (punishment for
treason)   **moiety** part   **15 Conceiving** learning of   **19 solely** alone   **20 him** i.e. Polixenes
23 parties, his alliance supporters, his allies   **28 she** she who is

[*Enter Paulina, carrying the baby; Antigonus and Lords enter and try to hold her back*]

A LORD You must not enter.

30 PAULINA   Nay, rather, good my lords, be second to me.
Fear you his tyrannous passion more, alas,
Than the queen's life? A gracious innocent soul,
More free than he is jealous.

ANTIGONUS   That's enough.

35 SERVANT   Madam, he hath not slept tonight, commanded
None should come at him.

PAULINA   Not so hot, good sir,
I come to bring him sleep. 'Tis such as you,
That creep like shadows by him and do sigh
40 At each his needless heavings, such as you
Nourish the cause of his awaking. I
Do come with words as medicinal as true,
Honest as either, to purge him of that humour
That presses him from sleep.

45 LEONTES   What noise there, ho?

PAULINA   No noise, my lord, but needful conference
About some gossips for your highness.

LEONTES   How?
Away with that audacious lady! Antigonus,
50 I charged thee that she should not come about me.
I knew she would.

ANTIGONUS   I told her so, my lord,
On your displeasure's peril and on mine,
She should not visit you.

55 LEONTES   What? Canst not rule her?

PAULINA   From all dishonesty he can. In this,
Unless he take the course that you have done —

---

30 be second to support   **33 free** innocent   **37 hot** rash, hasty   **38 sleep** i.e. peace
40 needless heavings pointless sighs or groans   **41 awaking** sleeplessness   **43 either** both
humour mood/sickness   **46 needful conference** necessary conversation   **47 gossips**
godparents   **48 How?** What?   **53 On . . . peril** at the risk of your fury   **55 rule** control
56 From away from

Commit me for committing honour — trust it,
He shall not rule me.

60 ANTIGONUS   La you now, you hear.
When she will take the rein, I let her run.
But she'll not stumble.

PAULINA   Good my liege, I come.
And, I beseech you hear me, who professes
65 Myself your loyal servant, your physician,
Your most obedient counsellor, yet that dares
Less appear so in comforting your evils,
Than such as most seem yours. I say, I come
From your good queen.

70 LEONTES   Good queen?

PAULINA   Good queen, my lord, good queen. I say good queen,
And would by combat make her good, so were I
A man, the worst about you.

LEONTES   Force her hence.   *To Lords*

75 PAULINA   Let him that makes but trifles of his eyes
First hand me. On mine own accord I'll off.
But first I'll do my errand. The good queen,
For she is good, hath brought you forth a daughter —
Here 'tis — commends it to your blessing.   *Lays down the baby*

80 LEONTES   Out!
A mankind witch! Hence with her, out o'door.
A most intelligencing bawd!

PAULINA   Not so.
I am as ignorant in that as you
85 In so entitling me, and no less honest
Than you are mad, which is enough, I'll warrant,
As this world goes, to pass for honest.

---

58 **Commit** imprison   60 **La you now** there you are, then   67 **in . . . yours** when it comes
to condoning your wrongs than those who seem superficially to be most loyal   70 **queen**
may pun on "quean" (whore)   72 **by . . . good** prove her innocence by a duel   73 **the worst**
even the most lowly   75 **makes but trifles** thinks little of, i.e. she'll scratch them   76 **hand**
touch   **On . . . off** I'll go when I decide   80 **Out!** Away!   81 **mankind** masculine/furious
82 **intelligencing bawd** spying pimp   84 **ignorant** inexperienced, unknowing   85 **entitling**
calling   86 **warrant** assure (you)

LEONTES   Traitors!   *To Lords*
Will you not push her out?— Give her the bastard.   *To Antigonus*

90   Thou dotard, thou art woman-tired, unroosted
By thy dame Partlet here. Take up the bastard,
Take't up, I say: give't to thy crone.

PAULINA   Forever   *To Antigonus*
Unvenerable be thy hands, if thou

95   Tak'st up the princess by that forcèd baseness
Which he has put upon't!

LEONTES   He dreads his wife.

PAULINA   So I would you did. Then 'twere past all doubt
You'd call your children yours.

100   LEONTES   A nest of traitors!

ANTIGONUS   I am none, by this good light.

PAULINA   Nor I, nor any
But one that's here, and that's himself, for he
The sacred honour of himself, his queen's,

105   His hopeful son's, his babe's, betrays to slander,
Whose sting is sharper than the sword's; and will not —
For, as the case now stands, it is a curse
He cannot be compelled to't — once remove
The root of his opinion, which is rotten

110   As ever oak or stone was sound.

LEONTES   A callat
Of boundless tongue, who late hath beat her husband
And now baits me! This brat is none of mine.
It is the issue of Polixenes.

115   Hence with it, and together with the dam
Commit them to the fire!

PAULINA   It is yours.
And, might we lay th'old proverb to your charge,

---

90 **dotard** old fool   **woman-tired** henpecked   **unroosted** dislodged, usurped in domestic authority   91 **Partlet** traditional name for a hen   92 **crone** old woman/old ewe   94 **Unvenerable** unworthy of respect   95 **by . . . upon't** under that base name (of **bastard**) he has forced on it   97 **dreads** fears (Paulina's response seems to shift sense to "respects, reveres")   107 **as . . . opinion** i.e. as he is king, it is a shame he cannot be forced to uproot the basis of his belief   111 **callat** nag/whore   113 **baits** provokes (plays on **beats**)   115 **dam** mother (contemptuous, usually applied to animals)   118 **lay . . . charge** apply the old proverb to you

So like you, 'tis the worse. Behold, my lords,

120 Although the print be little, the whole matter

And copy of the father: eye, nose, lip,

The trick of's frown, his forehead, nay, the valley,

The pretty dimples of his chin and cheek, his smiles,

The very mould and frame of hand, nail, finger.

125 And thou, good goddess Nature, which hast made it

So like to him that got it, if thou hast

The ordering of the mind too, 'mongst all colours

No yellow in't, lest she suspect, as he does,

Her children not her husband's!

130 **LEONTES**   A gross hag.

And, lozel, thou art worthy to be hanged,   *To Antigonus*

That wilt not stay her tongue.

ANTIGONUS   Hang all the husbands

That cannot do that feat, you'll leave yourself

135 Hardly one subject.

LEONTES   Once more, take her hence.

PAULINA   A most unworthy and unnatural lord

Can do no more.

LEONTES   I'll ha' thee burnt.

140 **PAULINA**   I care not:

It is an heretic that makes the fire,

Not she which burns in't. I'll not call you tyrant.

But this most cruel usage of your queen —

Not able to produce more accusation

145 Than your own weak-hinged fancy — something savours

Of tyranny and will ignoble make you,

Yea, scandalous to the world.

LEONTES   On your allegiance,   *To Antigonus*

Out of the chamber with her! Were I a tyrant,

---

119 **'tis the worse** the child is the worse off for it   120 **print** copy   **matter** substance/image
122 **trick** manner, habit   **nay** even   **valley** perhaps the groove between the nose and the lip
or a cleft in the chin   126 **got** begot, conceived   127 **ordering . . . mind** temperament
128 **No yellow** let there be no yellow (traditionally the color of jealousy)   130 **hag** witch
131 **lozel** scoundrel   132 **stay her tongue** shut her up   141 **It . . . in't** i.e. it is *you*, the one
who orders the fire, who is a heretic as you are burning me unjustly   145 **weak-hinged fancy**
fragile, unsupported imaginings   **savours** smells

150   Where were her life? She durst not call me so,
If she did know me one. Away with her!

PAULINA   I pray you do not push me. I'll be gone.
Look to your babe, my lord, 'tis yours. Jove send her
A better guiding spirit! What needs these hands?
155   You that are thus so tender o'er his follies
Will never do him good, not one of you.
So, so. Farewell, we are gone.   *Exit*

LEONTES   Thou, traitor, hast set on thy wife to this.   *To Antigonus*
My child? Away with't! Even thou, that hast
160   A heart so tender o'er it, take it hence
And see it instantly consumed with fire.
Even thou and none but thou. Take it up straight.
Within this hour bring me word 'tis done,
And by good testimony, or I'll seize thy life,
165   With what thou else call'st thine. If thou refuse
And wilt encounter with my wrath, say so;
The bastard brains with these my proper hands
Shall I dash out. Go, take it to the fire,
For thou set'st on thy wife.

170 **ANTIGONUS**   I did not, sir.
These lords, my noble fellows, if they please,
Can clear me in't.

LORDS   We can. My royal liege,
He is not guilty of her coming hither.

175 **LEONTES**   You're liars all.

A LORD   Beseech your highness, give us better credit.
We have always truly served you, and beseech'
So to esteem of us, and on our knees we beg,
As recompense of our dear services
180   Past and to come, that you do change this purpose,

---

150 Where . . . life? i.e. I would have had her killed by now   **153 Jove** Roman king of the gods   **154 What . . . hands?** i.e. There is no need to manhandle me   **155 You** i.e. Leontes' attendants   **158 set on** put up   **162 straight** immediately   **164 testimony** authority/evidence   **167 proper** own   **176 credit** credibility/honor   **177 beseech** beseech you   **179 dear** heartfelt/valuable

Which being so horrible, so bloody, must
Lead on to some foul issue. We all kneel.

LEONTES   I am a feather for each wind that blows.
Shall I live on to see this bastard kneel
185 And call me father? Better burn it now
Than curse it then. But be it. Let it live.
It shall not neither.— You, sir, come you hither.   *To Antigonus*
You that have been so tenderly officious
With Lady Margery, your midwife there,
190 To save this bastard's life — for 'tis a bastard,
So sure as this beard's grey — what will you adventure
To save this brat's life?

ANTIGONUS   Anything, my lord,
That my ability may undergo
195 And nobleness impose. At least thus much:
I'll pawn the little blood which I have left
To save the innocent. Anything possible.

LEONTES   It shall be possible. Swear by this sword   *Holds out sword*
Thou wilt perform my bidding.

200 **ANTIGONUS**   I will, my lord.

LEONTES   Mark and perform it, see'st thou! For the fail
Of any point in't shall not only be
Death to thyself but to thy lewd-tongued wife,
Whom for this time we pardon. We enjoin thee,
205 As thou art liege-man to us, that thou carry
This female bastard hence and that thou bear it
To some remote and desert place quite out
Of our dominions; and that there thou leave it,
Without more mercy, to it own protection
210 And favour of the climate. As by strange fortune
It came to us, I do in justice charge thee,
On thy soul's peril and thy body's torture,

---

182 foul issue terrible outcome   **183 I . . . blows** I am exposed to every opinion   **189 Lady Margery** derogatory name for a woman; "Margery-prater" is a slang term for "hen"   **191 this beard's grey** probably refers to Antigonus' beard   **adventure** risk   **203 lewd-tongued** outspoken/lascivious   **204 enjoin** command   **205 liege-man** loyal servant   **207 desert** deserted   **209 it** its   **210 strange fortune** unnatural circumstances/foreign events, i.e. Polixenes

That thou commend it strangely to some place
Where chance may nurse or end it. Take it up.

215 ANTIGONUS   I swear to do this, though a present death
Had been more merciful. Come on, poor babe.   *Takes up baby*
Some powerful spirit instruct the kites and ravens
To be thy nurses! Wolves and bears, they say,
Casting their savageness aside, have done

220 Like offices of pity. Sir, be prosperous
In more than this deed does require; — and blessing
Against this cruelty fight on thy side,
Poor thing, condemned to loss!   *Exit [with the baby]*

LEONTES   No, I'll not rear

225 Another's issue.

Enter a Servant

SERVANT   Please your highness, posts
From those you sent to th'oracle are come
An hour since: Cleomenes and Dion,
Being well arrived from Delphos, are both landed,

230 Hasting to th'court.

FIRST LORD   So please you, sir, their speed
Hath been beyond account.

LEONTES   Twenty-three days
They have been absent: 'tis good speed, foretells

235 The great Apollo suddenly will have
The truth of this appear. Prepare you, lords.
Summon a session, that we may arraign
Our most disloyal lady, for, as she hath
Been publicly accused, so shall she have

240 A just and open trial. While she lives
My heart will be a burden to me. Leave me,
And think upon my bidding.   *Exeunt*

---

213 **commend . . . place** commit it to some foreign land   214 **nurse . . . it** nurture or kill it
215 **present** instant, immediate   217 **kites** birds of prey   **ravens** thought to be a bird of ill
omen   220 **Like** similar   221 **more** more ways   **require** deserves   222 **thy** addressed to the
baby   226 **posts** messengers   232 **beyond account** without precedent/beyond description
235 **suddenly** immediately   237 **session** legal hearing   **arraign** put on trial

Act 3 Scene 1

Enter Cleomenes and Dion

CLEOMENES   The climate's delicate, the air most sweet,
Fertile the isle, the temple much surpassing
The common praise it bears.

DION   I shall report,
5   For most it caught me, the celestial habits,
Methinks I so should term them, and the reverence
Of the grave wearers. O, the sacrifice!
How ceremonious, solemn and unearthly
It was i'th'off'ring!

10   CLEOMENES   But of all, the burst
And the ear-deaf'ning voice o'th'oracle,
Kin to Jove's thunder, so surprised my sense
That I was nothing.

DION   If th'event o'th'journey
15   Prove as successful to the queen — O, be't so! —
As it hath been to us rare, pleasant, speedy,
The time is worth the use on't.

CLEOMENES   Great Apollo
Turn all to th'best! These proclamations,
20   So forcing faults upon Hermione,
I little like.

DION   The violent carriage of it
Will clear or end the business: when the oracle,
Thus by Apollo's great divine sealed up,
25   Shall the contents discover, something rare
Even then will rush to knowledge. Go, fresh horses!
And gracious be the issue!   *Exeunt*

3.1   *Location: on the road*   1 delicate exquisite/fragrant   **5 caught** struck/charmed
habits clothing   **7 grave** reverend, wise   **12 Kin** similar   **surprised** assailed, overwhelmed
14 th'event the outcome   **16 rare** wonderful, exceptional   **17 worth . . . on't** well spent
22 violent . . . it rash way it has been executed   **24 great divine** chief priest   **25 discover**
reveal

Act 3 Scene 2

Enter Leontes, Lords, Officers

LEONTES   This sessions, to our great grief we pronounce,
Even pushes gainst our heart: the party tried
The daughter of a king, our wife, and one
Of us too much beloved. Let us be cleared
5   Of being tyrannous, since we so openly
Proceed in justice, which shall have due course,
Even to the guilt or the purgation.
Produce the prisoner.

OFFICER   It is his highness' pleasure that the queen
10   Appear in person here in court. Silence!

[Enter Hermione as to her trial, Paulina and Ladies attending]

LEONTES   Read the indictment.

OFFICER   Hermione, queen to the worthy Leontes,   *Reads*
King of Sicilia, thou art here accused and arraigned of high
treason, in committing adultery with Polixenes, King of
15   Bohemia, and conspiring with Camillo to take away the
life of our sovereign lord the king, thy royal husband: the
pretence whereof being by circumstances partly laid open,
thou, Hermione, contrary to the faith and allegiance of a
true subject, didst counsel and aid them, for their better
20   safety, to fly away by night.

HERMIONE   Since what I am to say must be but that
Which contradicts my accusation and
The testimony on my part no other
But what comes from myself, it shall scarce boot me
25   To say 'Not guilty': mine integrity
Being counted falsehood, shall, as I express it,
Be so received. But thus: if powers divine
Behold our human actions, as they do,
I doubt not then but innocence shall make

3.2   *Location: Sicilia*   4 Of by   7 Even . . . purgation until we have established guilt or
acquittal   17 pretence purpose   19 counsel advise/communicate with   24 boot profit
25 mine . . . received as I am thought to be a liar my claims shall be received accordingly

30   False accusation blush and tyranny
        Tremble at patience. You, my lord, best know,
        Whom least will seem to do so, my past life
        Hath been as continent, as chaste, as true,
        As I am now unhappy, which is more
35   Than history can pattern, though devised
        And played to take spectators. For behold me
        A fellow of the royal bed, which owe
        A moiety of the throne, a great king's daughter,
        The mother to a hopeful prince, here standing
40   To prate and talk for life and honour 'fore
        Who please to come and hear. For life, I prize it
        As I weigh grief, which I would spare: for honour,
        'Tis a derivative from me to mine,
        And only that I stand for. I appeal
45   To your own conscience, sir, before Polixenes
        Came to your court, how I was in your grace,
        How merited to be so. Since he came,
        With what encounter so uncurrent I
        Have strained t'appear thus: if one jot beyond
50   The bound of honour, or in act or will
        That way inclining, hardened be the hearts
        Of all that hear me, and my near'st of kin
        Cry fie upon my grave!

        LEONTES   I ne'er heard yet
55   That any of these bolder vices wanted
        Less impudence to gainsay what they did
        Than to perform it first.

---

31 patience endurance, suffering   **33 continent** restrained/faithful   **35 history** any
historical narrative or fictional tale   **pattern** show, provide a model for   **36 take spectators**
enthrall an audience   **37 which owe** who owns   **38 moiety** portion   **40 prate** prattle
41 For . . . spare I value life as I do grief, both of which I could do without   **42 for . . . for**
honor is handed down from me to my children and it is only for that reason that I make a
stand   **45 conscience** also "inward consciousness"   **46 grace** favor   **47 merited** deserved
48 With . . . thus by what unacceptable behavior have I transgressed that I appear on trial like
this   **encounter** behavior (plays on the sense of "sexual act")   **53 fie** shame   **54 I . . . first**
I've never heard that adulterers lacked the same audacity to deny (**gainsay**) their actions that
was required to perform them

HERMIONE   That's true enough.
Though 'tis a saying, sir, not due to me.

60   LEONTES   You will not own it.

HERMIONE   More than mistress of
Which comes to me in name of fault, I must not
At all acknowledge. For Polixenes,
With whom I am accused, I do confess

65   I loved him, as in honour he required,
With such a kind of love as might become
A lady like me, with a love even such,
So and no other, as yourself commanded:
Which, not to have done, I think had been in me

70   Both disobedience and ingratitude
To you and toward your friend, whose love had spoke,
Even since it could speak, from an infant, freely
That it was yours. Now, for conspiracy,
I know not how it tastes, though it be dished

75   For me to try how: all I know of it
Is that Camillo was an honest man.
And why he left your court, the gods themselves —
Wotting no more than I — are ignorant.

LEONTES   You knew of his departure, as you know

80   What you have underta'en to do in's absence.

HERMIONE   Sir,
You speak a language that I understand not:
My life stands in the level of your dreams,
Which I'll lay down.

85   LEONTES   Your actions are my dreams.
You had a bastard by Polixenes,
And I but dreamed it. As you were past all shame —
Those of your fact are so — so past all truth,
Which to deny concerns more than avails, for as

---

61 More . . . acknowledge I must not answer for more than those faults that I actually possess   **71 friend . . . yours** relative (Polixenes), who has professed his love freely for you since childhood   **73 for** as for   **74 dished** served up   **78 Wotting** knowing   **83 level . . . dreams** target, aim of your delusions   **84 Which** i.e. my life   **88 of your fact** who have committed your crime   **89 concerns . . . avails** is of more importance than practical advantage to you

90   Thy brat hath been cast out, like to itself,
      No father owning it — which is indeed
      More criminal in thee than it — so thou
      Shalt feel our justice, in whose easiest passage
      Look for no less than death.

95 HERMIONE   Sir, spare your threats.
      The bug which you would fright me with, I seek.
      To me can life be no commodity;
      The crown and comfort of my life, your favour,
      I do give lost, for I do feel it gone,
100   But know not how it went. My second joy,
      And first-fruits of my body, from his presence
      I am barred, like one infectious. My third comfort
      Starred most unluckily, is from my breast —
      The innocent milk in it most innocent mouth —
105   Haled out to murder. Myself on every post
      Proclaimed a strumpet, with immodest hatred
      The child-bed privilege denied, which 'longs
      To women of all fashion. Lastly, hurried
      Here to this place, i'th'open air, before
110   I have got strength of limit. Now, my liege,
      Tell me what blessings I have here alive,
      That I should fear to die? Therefore proceed:
      But yet hear this — mistake me not. No life,
      I prize it not a straw, but for mine honour,
115   Which I would free — if I shall be condemned
      Upon surmises, all proofs sleeping else
      But what your jealousies awake, I tell you

---

90 like to itself which, as a bastard, it should be   **93 in . . . death** i.e. the very mildest form of your punishment will be death, perhaps preceded by torture   **96 bug** imagined terror, fearful threat   **97 commodity** thing of value   **99 give** acknowledge, give up for   **103 Starred most unluckily** born under an unlucky star   **104 it** its   **105 Haled** dragged   **post** proclamations were nailed up publicly   **106 strumpet** harlot/whore   **immodest** outrageous   **107 child-bed privilege** rights extended to women after they had given birth, including bed-rest   **'longs** belongs   **108 fashion** ranks   **110 strength of limit** strength gained during the postnatal period of recuperation   **115 free** clear   **116 sleeping else** otherwise unforthcoming   **117 awake** create/muster

'Tis rigour and not law. Your honours all,
I do refer me to the oracle:

120   Apollo be my judge!

A LORD   This your request
Is altogether just: therefore bring forth,
And in Apollo's name, his oracle.   [Exeunt some Officers]

HERMIONE   The Emperor of Russia was my father.

125   O that he were alive, and here beholding
His daughter's trial! That he did but see
The flatness of my misery; yet with eyes
Of pity, not revenge!

[Enter Officers, with Cleomenes and Dion]

OFFICER   You here shall swear upon this sword of   Holds sword
justice,

130   That you, Cleomenes and Dion, have
Been both at Delphos, and from thence have brought
This sealed-up oracle, by the hand delivered
Of great Apollo's priest; and that since then,
You have not dared to break the holy seal

135   Nor read the secrets in't.

CLEOMENES and DION   All this we swear.

LEONTES   Break up the seals and read.

OFFICER   Hermione is chaste, Polixenes blameless,   Reads
Camillo a true subject, Leontes a jealous tyrant, his innocent

140   babe truly begotten, and the king shall live without an heir, if
that which is lost be not found.

LORDS   Now blessèd be the great Apollo!

HERMIONE   Praised!

LEONTES   Hast thou read truth?

145   OFFICER   Ay, my lord, even so as it is here set down.

LEONTES   There is no truth at all i'th'oracle:
The sessions shall proceed: this is mere falsehood.

[Enter a Servant]

SERVANT   My lord the king, the king!

---

118 rigour . . . law severity rather than justice (plays on the phrase "the rigor of the law")
127 flatness absoluteness   **140 truly begotten** conceived legitimately   **147 sessions** trial

LEONTES   What is the business?

150   SERVANT   O sir, I shall be hated to report it!
The prince your son, with mere conceit and fear
Of the queen's speed, is gone.

LEONTES   How? Gone?

SERVANT   Is dead.

155   LEONTES   Apollo's angry, and the heavens themselves
Do strike at my injustice.   *Hermione faints*
How now there!

PAULINA   This news is mortal to the queen. Look down
And see what death is doing.

LEONTES   Take her hence.

160   Her heart is but o'ercharged. She will recover.
I have too much believed mine own suspicion:
Beseech you, tenderly apply to her
Some remedies for life.—   [*Exeunt Ladies, carrying Hermione*]
Apollo, pardon
My great profaneness gainst thine oracle!

165   I'll reconcile me to Polixenes,
New woo my queen, recall the good Camillo,
Whom I proclaim a man of truth, of mercy.
For, being transported by my jealousies
To bloody thoughts and to revenge, I chose

170   Camillo for the minister to poison
My friend Polixenes, which had been done,
But that the good mind of Camillo tardied
My swift command, though I with death and with
Reward did threaten and encourage him,

175   Not doing it and being done. He, most humane
And filled with honour, to my kingly guest
Unclasped my practice, quit his fortunes here —
Which you knew great — and to the hazard
Of all incertainties himself commended,

---

151 **conceit** imagining   152 **speed** fate   157 **mortal** fatal   168 **transported** carried away, overcome   172 **tardied** held back from   175 **Not . . . done** depending on whether he did or did not do the deed   177 **Unclasped my practice** revealed my plot   179 **commended** entrusted

180 No richer than his honour. How he glisters
     Through my rust! And how his piety
     Does my deeds make the blacker!

PAULINA   Woe the while!
     O, cut my lace, lest my heart, cracking it,
185 Break too.

A LORD   What fit is this, good lady?

PAULINA   What studied torments, tyrant, hast for me?
     What wheels? Racks? Fires? What flaying? Boiling?
     In leads or oils? What old or newer torture
190 Must I receive, whose every word deserves
     To taste of thy most worst? Thy tyranny,
     Together working with thy jealousies —
     Fancies too weak for boys, too green and idle
     For girls of nine — O, think what they have done
195 And then run mad indeed, stark mad! For all
     Thy bygone fooleries were but spices of it.
     That thou betrayed'st Polixenes, 'twas nothing:
     That did but show thee, of a fool, inconstant
     And damnable ingrateful. Nor was't much,
200 Thou wouldst have poisoned good Camillo's honour,
     To have him kill a king. Poor trespasses.
     More monstrous standing by: whereof I reckon
     The casting forth to crows thy baby-daughter
     To be or none or little; though a devil
205 Would have shed water out of fire ere done't.
     Nor is't directly laid to thee, the death
     Of the young prince, whose honourable thoughts —
     Thoughts high for one so tender — cleft the heart
     That could conceive a gross and foolish sire

---

180 No richer than with nothing but   **glisters** shines   **184 lace** laces that fasten the corset,
cut to relieve faintness   **187 studied** planned   **188 wheels** to which victims were tied
and beaten   **Racks** torture instruments that stretched the limbs   **193 Fancies** imaginings
green immature   **idle** foolish   **196 bygone fooleries** previous mistakes   **spices** slight
tastes   **198 of** as   **inconstant** disloyal   **201 Poor trespasses** small crimes   **204 or** either
205 shed . . . done't wept from his fiery eyes, or while burning in hellfire before he would
commit such a sin   **208 tender** young   **cleft** broke   **209 conceive** understand   **sire** father

210 Blemished his gracious dam: this is not, no,
   Laid to thy answer. But the last — O, lords,
   When I have said, cry woe! The queen, the queen,
   The sweet'st, dear'st creature's dead, and vengeance for't
   Not dropped down yet.

215 A LORD The higher powers forbid!

   PAULINA I say she's dead. I'll swear't. If word nor oath
   Prevail not, go and see. If you can bring
   Tincture or lustre in her lip, her eye,
   Heat outwardly or breath within, I'll serve you

220 As I would do the gods. But, O thou tyrant,
   Do not repent these things, for they are heavier
   Than all thy woes can stir: therefore betake thee
   To nothing but despair. A thousand knees
   Ten thousand years together, naked, fasting,

225 Upon a barren mountain and still winter
   In storm perpetual, could not move the gods
   To look that way thou wert.

   LEONTES Go on, go on.
   Thou canst not speak too much. I have deserved

230 All tongues to talk their bitt'rest.

   A LORD Say no more.
   Howe'er the business goes, you have made fault   *To Paulina*
   I'th'boldness of your speech.

   PAULINA I am sorry for't;

235 All faults I make, when I shall come to know them,
   I do repent. Alas, I have showed too much
   The rashness of a woman. He is touched
   To th'noble heart. What's gone and what's past help
   Should be past grief. Do not receive affliction

240 At my petition; I beseech you, rather

---

211 Laid . . . answer something you are required to answer to **212 said** finished speaking
214 dropped down emerged **218 Tincture or lustre** color or brightness **221 heavier . . .
stir** more sorrowful/weightier than all your remorse/misery can shift **222 betake thee To**
prepare for/go to **225 still** permanent **227 look . . . wert** look in your direction, take pity on
you **232 Howe'er . . . speech** whatever the nature of events you have erred in being so
outspoken **240 petition** urging, request

Let me be punished, that have minded you
Of what you should forget. Now, good my liege,
Sir, royal sir, forgive a foolish woman.
The love I bore your queen — lo, fool again! —
245   I'll speak of her no more, nor of your children.
I'll not remember you of my own lord,
Who is lost too. Take your patience to you,
And I'll say nothing.

LEONTES   Thou didst speak but well
250   When most the truth, which I receive much better
Than to be pitied of thee. Prithee bring me
To the dead bodies of my queen and son.
One grave shall be for both: upon them shall
The causes of their death appear, unto
255   Our shame perpetual. Once a day I'll visit
The chapel where they lie, and tears shed there
Shall be my recreation. So long as nature
Will bear up with this exercise, so long
I daily vow to use it. Come and lead me
260   To these sorrows.   *Exeunt*

Act 3 Scene 3   *running scene 7*

Enter Antigonus [carrying the] babe, [and] a Mariner

ANTIGONUS   Thou art perfect then, our ship hath touched upon
The deserts of Bohemia?

MARINER   Ay, my lord, and fear
We have landed in ill time. The skies look grimly
5   And threaten present blusters. In my conscience,

241 **minded** reminded   246 **remember** remind   247 **patience** endurance, suffering
249 **Thou . . . truth** you spoke best when most truthfully   251 **of** by   253 **them** i.e. the
gravestones/burial monuments   257 **nature . . . exercise** I am physically able   259 **use**
undertake   **3.3** *Location: Bohemia (coast)*   1 **Thou . . . o'th'business** dialogue
between Antigonus and Mariner is set as verse, but may have been intended as prose
perfect certain   2 **deserts** deserted coastal areas   5 **present blusters** impending storms
conscience opinion

The heavens with that we have in hand are angry
And frown upon's.

ANTIGONUS   Their sacred wills be done! Go, get aboard.
Look to thy bark. I'll not be long before
10   I call upon thee.

MARINER   Make your best haste, and go not
Too far i'th'land: 'tis like to be loud weather.
Besides, this place is famous for the creatures
Of prey that keep upon't.

15   ANTIGONUS   Go thou away. I'll follow instantly.

MARINER   I am glad at heart
To be so rid o'th'business.   *Exit*

ANTIGONUS   Come, poor babe.
I have heard, but not believed, the spirits o'th'dead
20   May walk again. If such thing be, thy mother
Appeared to me last night, for ne'er was dream
So like a waking. To me comes a creature,
Sometimes her head on one side, some another.
I never saw a vessel of like sorrow,
25   So filled and so becoming. In pure white robes,
Like very sanctity, she did approach
My cabin where I lay, thrice bowed before me,
And, gasping to begin some speech, her eyes
Became two spouts; the fury spent, anon
30   Did this break from her: 'Good Antigonus,
Since fate, against thy better disposition,
Hath made thy person for the thrower-out
Of my poor babe, according to thine oath,
Places remote enough are in Bohemia.
35   There weep and leave it crying. And, for the babe
Is counted lost forever, Perdita,
I prithee call't. For this ungentle business

---

6 that . . . hand what we are undertaking   9 bark small ship   12 loud stormy   22 creature
being, figure   23 some another sometimes on the other side   24 vessel container, figure
25 filled . . . becoming full of sorrow and so beautiful   26 sanctity holiness   29 fury strong
passion   anon presently   35 for because   36 Perdita literally "the lost one"   37 ungentle
ignoble/cruel

Put on thee by my lord, thou ne'er shalt see
Thy wife Paulina more.' And so, with shrieks
40   She melted into air. Affrighted much,
I did in time collect myself and thought
This was so and no slumber. Dreams are toys,
Yet for this once, yea superstitiously,
I will be squared by this. I do believe
45   Hermione hath suffered death, and that
Apollo would, this being indeed the issue
Of King Polixenes, it should here be laid,
Either for life or death, upon the earth
Of its right father. Blossom, speed thee well.   *Lays down the baby*
50   There lie, and there thy character: there these,   *with a box and*
Which may, if fortune please, both breed thee, pretty,   *bundle*
And still rest thine. The storm begins. Poor wretch,   *Thunder*
That for thy mother's fault art thus exposed
To loss and what may follow! Weep I cannot,
55   But my heart bleeds. And most accursed am I
To be by oath enjoined to this. Farewell!
The day frowns more and more: thou'rt like to have
A lullaby too rough. I never saw
The heavens so dim by day. A savage clamour!
60   Well may I get aboard. This is the chase!
I am gone forever.

Exit, pursued by a bear

[*Enter a Shepherd*]

SHEPHERD   I would there were no age between ten and three-
and-twenty, or that youth would sleep out the rest, for there
is nothing in the between but getting wenches with child,

---

39 shrieks ghosts were traditionally supposed to shriek in high-pitched voices   **42 toys**
trifles   **44 squared** ruled   **49 speed** fare, survive   **50 character** written account of her
history and parentage   **these** gold and jewels later found with the baby   **51 breed . . . thine**
pay for your upbringing with sufficient left over   **53 fault** crime   **56 enjoined** committed,
obliged   **59 clamour** the noise of hunters and dogs or the roar of the bear   **60 chase** hunt
(of Antigonus)/hunted bear   *bear* a real polar bear cub was available at the time of the play's
first performance, but some scholars assume an actor in bear costume

65   wronging the ancientry, stealing, fighting — Hark you now!
Would any but these boiled-brains of nineteen and two-and-
twenty hunt this weather? They have scared away two of my
best sheep, which I fear the wolf will sooner find than the
master. If anywhere I have them, 'tis by the seaside,
70   browsing of ivy. Good luck, an't be thy will. What have we
here? Mercy on's, a bairn? A very pretty bairn!   *Sees the baby*
A boy or a child, I wonder? A pretty one, a very pretty one.
Sure, some scape. Though I am not bookish, yet I can read
waiting-gentlewoman in the scape. This has been some stair-
75   work, some trunk-work, some behind-door-work: they were
warmer that got this than the poor thing is here. I'll take it
up for pity — yet I'll tarry till my son come. He hallooed but
even now. Whoa, ho, hoa!

Enter Clown

CLOWN   Hilloa, loa!

80 SHEPHERD   What? Art so near? If thou'lt see a thing to talk on
when thou art dead and rotten, come hither. What ailest
thou, man?

CLOWN   I have seen two such sights, by sea and by land! But
I am not to say it is a sea, for it is now the sky: betwixt the
85   firmament and it you cannot thrust a bodkin's point.

SHEPHERD   Why, boy, how is it?

CLOWN   I would you did but see how it chafes, how it rages,
how it takes up the shore! But that's not to the point. O, the
most piteous cry of the poor souls! Sometimes to see 'em,
90   and not to see 'em. Now the ship boring the moon with her
main-mast, and anon swallowed with yeast and froth, as

---

65 ancientry elderly/ancestors   **66 boiled-brains** idiots   **67 this** in this   **70 browsing of**
feeding on   **an't be thy** if it be God's   **71 bairn** child   **72 child** baby girl   **73 scape** sexual
transgression   **bookish** well-read   **74 stair-work . . . behind-door-work** i.e. secret sexual
liaisons (**work** plays on the sense of "sexual activity" and **trunk** plays on the sense of "body")
76 warmer i.e. from sexual activity   **got** begot, conceived   **77 tarry** wait   **hallooed** called
out   **78 Clown** a rustic, comic character; the Shepherd's son   **80 on** about   **81 ailest**
troubles/prevents   **85 firmament** sky   **bodkin** pin/needle   **87 chafes** seethes   **88 takes up**
consumes/rebukes   **90 boring** piercing   **91 anon** then/shortly   **yeast** foam

you'd thrust a cork into a hogshead. And then for the land-
service, to see how the bear tore out his shoulder-bone. How
he cried to me for help and said his name was Antigonus, a
95   nobleman. But to make an end of the ship, to see how the sea
flap-dragoned it. But first, how the poor souls roared, and
the sea mocked them. And how the poor gentleman roared
and the bear mocked him, both roaring louder than the sea
or weather.

100   SHEPHERD   Name of mercy, when was this, boy?

CLOWN   Now, now. I have not winked since I saw these
sights. The men are not yet cold under water, nor the bear
half dined on the gentleman. He's at it now.

SHEPHERD   Would I had been by, to have helped the old man!

105   CLOWN   I would you had been by the ship side, to have
helped her; there your charity would have lacked footing.

SHEPHERD   Heavy matters, heavy matters! But look thee here,
boy. Now bless thyself. Thou met'st with things dying, I with
things newborn. Here's a sight for thee: look thee, a bearing-
110   cloth for a squire's child. Look thee here. Take up, take up,
boy. Open't. So, let's see — it was told me I should be rich by
the fairies — this is some changeling. Open't. What's within,
boy?

CLOWN   You're a made old man. If the sins of   *Opens the box*
115   your youth are forgiven you, you're well to live. Gold, all gold!

SHEPHERD   This is fairy gold, boy, and 'twill prove so. Up with't,
keep it close. Home, home, the next way. We are lucky, boy,
and to be so still requires nothing but secrecy. Let my sheep
go. Come, good boy, the next way home.

---

92 hogshead cask of alcohol   **land-service** combat on land/food served on land (i.e. events
on land)   **95 make . . . ship** finish the story of the ship/tell you how the ship met its end
96 flap-dragoned consumed (as in a game of flapdragon, where raisins are plucked from
burning brandy and swallowed)   **101 winked** shut my eyes   **104 by** nearby   **106 your . . .
footing** you would have been unable to stand (**footing** puns on the sense of "establishment of
a **charity**")   **107 Heavy** grave, sorrowful   **108 met'st** met   **109 bearing-cloth** christening
robe   **110 squire** i.e. one of a relatively high social position   **112 changeling** child taken
by the fairies, or the one substituted for it   **115 you're . . . live** you will live prosperously
116 fairy gold if not kept secret, riches brought by fairies were thought to bring bad luck
117 close secret   **next** nearest   **118 still** yet/always

120 CLOWN   Go you the next way with your findings. I'll go see if
the bear be gone from the gentleman and how much he hath
eaten. They are never curst but when they are hungry. If
there be any of him left, I'll bury it.

SHEPHERD   That's a good deed. If thou mayst discern by that
125 which is left of him what he is, fetch me to th'sight of him.

CLOWN   Marry, will I. And you shall help to put him
i'th'ground.

SHEPHERD   'Tis a lucky day, boy, and we'll do good deeds on't.

Exeunt

Act 4 Scene 1   *running scene 8*

Enter Time, the Chorus

TIME   I, that please some, try all, both joy and terror
Of good and bad, that makes and unfolds error,
Now take upon me, in the name of Time,
To use my wings. Impute it not a crime
5   To me or my swift passage, that I slide
O'er sixteen years and leave the growth untried
Of that wide gap, since it is in my power
To o'erthrow law and in one self-born hour
To plant and o'erwhelm custom. Let me pass
10   The same I am, ere ancient'st order was
Or what is now received. I witness to
The times that brought them in, so shall I do
To th'freshest things now reigning and make stale
The glistering of this present, as my tale
15   Now seems to it. Your patience this allowing,

122 curst vicious   125 what who   126 Marry by the Virgin Mary   4.1   *Location: the
theater*   1 try test (proverbial: "time tries all things")   both . . . Of bringer of both joy
and terror to the   2 unfolds reveals   4 wings Time was traditionally depicted as winged
6 growth untried development unexamined   8 self-born selfsame/self-created (by Time)
9 plant and o'erwhelm create and overrule   10 ere . . . received since the beginning of time,
before the oldest laws and customs were set down and before those of the present day
11 witness bear willing testimony   12 them i.e. law and custom   do be   13 stale . . .
present redundant and past what is now fresh and gleaming   15 seems to it seems old in
comparison to the present

I turn my glass and give my scene such growing
As you had slept between. Leontes leaving —
Th'effects of his fond jealousies so grieving
That he shuts up himself — imagine me,
20   Gentle spectators, that I now may be
In fair Bohemia, and remember well,
I mentioned a son o'th'king's, which Florizel
I now name to you, and with speed so pace
To speak of Perdita, now grown in grace
25   Equal with wond'ring. What of her ensues
I list not prophesy, but let Time's news
Be known when 'tis brought forth. A shepherd's daughter
And what to her adheres, which follows after,
Is th'argument of Time. Of this allow,
30   If ever you have spent time worse ere now.
If never, yet that Time himself doth say
He wishes earnestly you never may.   *Exit*

Act 4 Scene 2   *running scene 9*

Enter Polixenes and Camillo

POLIXENES   I pray thee, good Camillo, be no more importunate:
'tis a sickness denying thee anything, a death to grant this.

CAMILLO   It is fifteen years since I saw my country. Though I
have for the most part been aired abroad, I desire to lay my
5   bones there. Besides, the penitent king, my master, hath sent
for me, to whose feeling sorrows I might be some allay, or I
o'erween to think so, which is another spur to my departure.

16 glass hourglass   17 As as if   Leontes . . . himself leaving Leontes to the consequences
of his foolish jealousies, so distraught he shuts himself away   20 Gentle noble, wellborn/
excellent/polite, courteous   22 king's i.e. Polixenes'   23 pace proceed   25 Equal with
wond'ring as great as the admiration her grace inspires   26 list not prophesy wish not
to foretell   28 adheres pertains   29 argument subject matter   31 yet yet allow
4.2   *Location: Bohemia (court)*   1 importunate persistent, urging   2 'tis . . . denying it
makes me ill to deny   3 fifteen the discrepancy between Camillo's fifteen and Time's sixteen
years may be a scribal error or a slip on Shakespeare's part   4 been aired lived   6 feeling
heartfelt   allay comfort   7 o'erween presume

POLIXENES   As thou lovest me, Camillo, wipe not out the rest of
thy services by leaving me now: the need I have of thee thine
10   own goodness hath made: better not to have had thee than
thus to want thee. Thou, having made me businesses which
none without thee can sufficiently manage, must either stay
to execute them thyself or take away with thee the very
services thou hast done, which if I have not enough
15   considered, as too much I cannot, to be more thankful to
thee shall be my study, and my profit therein the heaping
friendships. Of that fatal country, Sicilia, prithee speak
no more, whose very naming punishes me with the
remembrance of that penitent, as thou call'st him, and
20   reconciled king, my brother, whose loss of his most precious
queen and children are even now to be afresh lamented. Say
to me, when sawest thou the Prince Florizel, my son? Kings
are no less unhappy, their issue not being gracious, than
they are in losing them when they have approved their
25   virtues.

CAMILLO   Sir, it is three days since I saw the prince. What his
happier affairs may be, are to me unknown. But I have
missingly noted, he is of late much retired from court and is
less frequent to his princely exercises than formerly he hath
30   appeared.

POLIXENES   I have considered so much, Camillo, and with some
care — so far that I have eyes under my service which look
upon his removedness, from whom I have this intelligence,
that he is seldom from the house of a most homely shepherd:
35   a man, they say, that from very nothing, and beyond
the imagination of his neighbours, is grown into an
unspeakable estate.

---

11 want be without   **made me businesses** handled affairs for me   **15 considered** rewarded
16 heaping friendships growth of Camillo's kindnesses/increase of mutual friendship
17 fatal deadly   **20 reconciled** remorseful, confessed   **23 unhappy** miserable/unfortunate
gracious virtuous   **24 approved** proved   **28 missingly noted** noticed in his absence
retired absent   **29 exercises** activities, pastimes   **32 eyes . . . service** employees to watch
him   33 removedness absence/where he goes   **37 unspeakable estate** indescribable wealth

CAMILLO   I have heard, sir, of such a man, who hath a
daughter of most rare note. The report of her is extended
40   more than can be thought to begin from such a cottage.

POLIXENES   That's likewise part of my intelligence: but, I fear,
the angle that plucks our son thither. Thou shalt accompany
us to the place where we will, not appearing what we are,
have some question with the shepherd, from whose
45   simplicity I think it not uneasy to get the cause of my son's
resort thither. Prithee be my present partner in this business,
and lay aside the thoughts of Sicilia.

CAMILLO   I willingly obey your command.

POLIXENES   My best Camillo, we must disguise ourselves.

Exeunt

Act 4 Scene 3   *running scene 10*

Enter Autolycus singing

AUTOLYCUS   When daffodils begin to peer,
        With hey, the doxy over the dale,
        Why then comes in the sweet o'the year,
        For the red blood reigns in the winter's pale.

5   The white sheet bleaching on the hedge,
        With hey, the sweet birds, O, how they sing!
        Doth set my pugging tooth an edge.
        For a quart of ale is a dish for a king.

        The lark, that tirra-lirra chants,
10   With hey, the thrush and the jay,

---

39 **rare note** exceptional report   40 **begin** originate   42 **angle** fishhook   44 **question**
conversation   45 **uneasy** difficult   46 **present** immediate   **4.3 *Location: Bohemia
(rural) Autolycus*** literally, "the wolf himself" or "the lone wolf"; in classical mythology, he
was a crafty thief   1 **peer** peep out/appear   2 **doxy** whore/low woman   3 **sweet o'** sweetest
part of   4 **pale** paleness/domain   5 **sheet . . . hedge** spring-cleaning involved washing linen,
which was hung out to dry on hedges   7 **set . . . edge** unclear; the general sense seems to be
"whet my appetite for thieving" ("to pug" means "to tug or pull," hence possibly "to steal");
alternative possibility is sexual ("pug" meant mistress/whore and "tooth" was associated with
desire, as in "toothsome")

Are summer songs for me and my aunts,
While we lie tumbling in the hay.
I have served Prince Florizel and in my time wore three-pile,
but now I am out of service.

15   But shall I go mourn for that, my dear?
The pale moon shines by night,
And when I wander here and there,
I then do most go right.

If tinkers may have leave to live,
20   And bear the sow-skin budget,
Then my account I well may give,
And in the stocks avouch it.
My traffic is sheets. When the kite builds, look to lesser linen.
My father named me Autolycus, who being, as I am, littered
25   under Mercury, was likewise a snapper-up of unconsidered
trifles. With die and drab I purchased this caparison, and my
revenue is the silly cheat. Gallows and knock are too
powerful on the highway. Beating and hanging are terrors to
me. For the life to come, I sleep out the thought of it. A prize,
30   a prize!   *He sees the Clown*
Enter Clown   *approaching*
CLOWN   Let me see, every 'leven wether tods, every tod yields
pound and odd shilling. Fifteen hundred shorn, what comes
the wool to?

---

11 **aunts** whores, wenches   12 **tumbling** having sex   13 **three-pile** costly thick velvet
14 **out of service** unemployed   19 **tinkers** menders of metal pots and kettles (also applied to
beggars and thieves)   **leave to live** permission to live freely   20 **sow-skin budget** pigskin
toolbag   22 **in . . . avouch it** affirm that I am a tinker (rather than a vagabond) and thus
escape punishment   **stocks** instrument of punishment in which the arms or legs were
confined   23 **traffic** trade, goods   **kite . . . linen** the kite (a bird of prey) supposedly stole
pieces of cloth to build its nest; Autolycus steals **sheets** that have been left out to dry
24 **littered under** fathered by/born under the influence of (the connotations of animal
birth recall Autolycus' wolfishness)   25 **Mercury** Roman god of thieves/the planet
unconsidered disregarded, unattended   26 **die** i.e. gambling   **drab** whoring/pimping
caparison clothing, outfit   27 **silly cheat** petty deception/foolish victim of my trickery
Gallows and knock hanging and beating (punishments of a highwayman)   29 **For . . .
come** as for the future/the afterlife   31 **'leven wether tods** eleven sheep will produce 12 kg
(a **tod**) of wool   32 **odd** one

AUTOLYCUS   If the springe hold, the cock's mine.   *Aside*

35   CLOWN   I cannot do't without counters. Let me see, what am
I to buy for our sheep-shearing feast? Three pound of sugar,
five pound of currants, rice — what will this sister of mine
do with rice? But my father hath made her mistress of the
feast, and she lays it on. She hath made me four-and-twenty
40   nosegays for the shearers — three-man-song-men all, and
very good ones — but they are most of them means and
basses; but one puritan amongst them, and he sings psalms
to hornpipes. I must have saffron to colour the warden pies.
Mace, dates? — none, that's out of my note. Nutmegs,
45   seven; a race or two of ginger, but that I may beg. Four
pound of prunes, and as many of raisins o'th'sun.

AUTOLYCUS   O, that ever I was born!   *Grovels on*

CLOWN   I'th'name of me.   *the ground*

AUTOLYCUS   O, help me, help me! Pluck but off these rags, and
50   then, death, death!

CLOWN   Alack, poor soul, thou hast need of more rags to lay
on thee, rather than have these off.

AUTOLYCUS   O, sir, the loathsomeness of them offends me more
than the stripes I have received, which are mighty ones and
55   millions.

CLOWN   Alas, poor man, a million of beating may come to a
great matter.

AUTOLYCUS   I am robbed, sir, and beaten. My money and apparel
ta'en from me, and these detestable things put upon me.

60   CLOWN   What, by a horseman, or a footman?

---

34 **springe** trap   **cock** woodcock, a proverbially stupid bird   35 **counters** round metal
disks used for calculating   36 **sheep-shearing feast** festival held between May and July; the
shearing of the sheep was accompanied by general celebrations   39 **lays it on** sets about it
thoroughly   **made me** made   40 **nosegays** posies of flowers   **three-man-song-men** men
who sing three-part songs   41 **means** boy altos or adult countertenors   42 **puritan** pious
Protestant, opposed to excessive festivity   43 **hornpipes** wind instruments/lively vigorous
dance/piece of music for such a dance; the **puritan** is so religious he will only sing psalms to
them   **warden pies** made from a variety of pear   44 **Mace** spice made from nutmeg   **out
of my note** not on my list   45 **race** root   46 **o'th'sun** sun-dried   48 **I'th'name of me** a mild,
and unusual, oath   54 **stripes** lashes of a whip   57 **great matter** serious consequences/
infected wounds   60 **horseman . . . footman** highwayman or robber on foot (who would wear
inferior **garments**)

AUTOLYCUS   A footman, sweet sir, a footman.

CLOWN   Indeed, he should be a footman by the garments he
has left with thee. If this be a horseman's coat, it hath seen
very hot service. Lend me thy hand, I'll help thee. Come, lend
65   me thy hand.   *Helps him to his feet*

AUTOLYCUS   O, good sir, tenderly, O!

CLOWN   Alas, poor soul!

AUTOLYCUS   O, good sir, softly, good sir! I fear, sir, my shoulder-
blade is out.

70   CLOWN   How now? Canst stand?

AUTOLYCUS   Softly, dear sir. Good sir, softly. You ha'   *Picks his pocket.*
done me a charitable office.

CLOWN   Dost lack any money? I have a little money for thee.

AUTOLYCUS   No, good sweet sir. No, I beseech you, sir. I have a
75   kinsman not past three quarters of a mile hence, unto whom
I was going. I shall there have money, or anything I want.
Offer me no money, I pray you. That kills my heart.

CLOWN   What manner of fellow was he that robbed you?

AUTOLYCUS   A fellow, sir, that I have known to go about with
80   troll-my-dames. I knew him once a servant of the prince. I
cannot tell, good sir, for which of his virtues it was, but he
was certainly whipped out of the court.

CLOWN   His vices, you would say. There's no virtue whipped
out of the court. They cherish it to make it stay there; and yet
85   it will no more but abide.

AUTOLYCUS   Vices, I would say, sir. I know this man well. He hath
been since an ape-bearer, then a process-server, a bailiff,
then he compassed a motion of the prodigal son, and
married a tinker's wife within a mile where my land and
90   living lies, and, having flown over many knavish professions,
he settled only in rogue. Some call him Autolycus.

---

64 hot service active use, i.e. excessive wear   **69 out** dislocated   **80 troll-my-dames** loose
women/whores   **85 abide** stay briefly   **87 ape-bearer** showman with a performing monkey
process-server officer who serves a summons   **88 compassed a motion** traveled around
with a puppet show   **prodigal son** in the New Testament parable, the younger son who
squanders his inheritance but is forgiven by his father (Luke 15)   **90 living** property   **flown
over** dabbled with

CLOWN   Out upon him! Prig, for my life, prig. He haunts
wakes, fairs and bear-baitings.

AUTOLYCUS   Very true, sir. He, sir, he. That's the rogue that put
95   me into this apparel.

CLOWN   Not a more cowardly rogue in all Bohemia; if you
had but looked big and spit at him, he'd have run.

AUTOLYCUS   I must confess to you, sir, I am no fighter. I am false
of heart that way, and that he knew, I warrant him.

100   CLOWN   How do you now?

AUTOLYCUS   Sweet sir, much better than I was. I can stand and
walk. I will even take my leave of you, and pace softly
towards my kinsman's.

CLOWN   Shall I bring thee on the way?

105   AUTOLYCUS   No, good-faced sir. No, sweet sir.

CLOWN   Then fare thee well. I must go buy spices for our
sheep-shearing.   *Exit*

AUTOLYCUS   Prosper you, sweet sir! Your purse is not hot enough
to purchase your spice. I'll be with you at your sheep-
110   shearing too. If I make not this cheat bring out another and
the shearers prove sheep, let me be unrolled and my name
put in the book of virtue!

[*Sings*] *song*   Jog on, jog on, the footpath way,
               And merrily hent the stile-a:
115   A merry heart goes all the day,
               Your sad tires in a mile-a.   *Exit*

Act 4 Scene 4   *running scene 11*

Enter Florizel [*wearing shepherd's clothing, and*] *Perdita*

FLORIZEL   These your unusual weeds to each part of you
Does give a life: no shepherdess, but Flora

---

92 Prig thief/tinker   **93 wakes** country festivals   **98 false of heart** fearful   **102 softly** gently
105 good-faced honest, kind   **108 hot** full (plays on the sense of "spicy")   **110 cheat**
deception   **bring out** lead to   **111 sheep** i.e. to be stupid   **unrolled** removed from the list of
thieves and vagabonds   **114 hent** grasp   **4.4   1 unusual weeds** special (festival) clothes
2 Flora Roman goddess of flowers

Peering in April's front. This your sheep-shearing
Is as a meeting of the petty gods,
5 And you the queen on't.

PERDITA   Sir, my gracious lord,
To chide at your extremes it not becomes me —
O, pardon, that I name them! Your high self,
The gracious mark o'th'land, you have obscured
10 With a swain's wearing, and me, poor lowly maid,
Most goddess-like pranked up. But that our feasts
In every mess have folly and the feeders
Digest it with a custom, I should blush
To see you so attired, swoon, I think,
15 To show myself a glass.

FLORIZEL   I bless the time
When my good falcon made her flight across
Thy father's ground.

PERDITA   Now Jove afford you cause!
20 To me the difference forges dread. Your greatness
Hath not been used to fear. Even now I tremble
To think your father, by some accident,
Should pass this way as you did. O, the Fates!
How would he look, to see his work so noble
25 Vilely bound up? What would he say? Or how
Should I, in these my borrowed flaunts, behold
The sternness of his presence?

FLORIZEL   Apprehend
Nothing but jollity. The gods themselves,
30 Humbling their deities to love, have taken

---

3 Peering . . . front appearing at the beginning of April   4 petty minor   7 chide . . .
extremes rebuke your exaggerations   9 mark o'th'land object of public attention   obscured
concealed, disguised   10 swain's wearing rustic clothing   11 pranked up dressed up,
adorned   12 mess group of diners/collection of dishes   folly lewd or foolish behavior
13 Digest . . . custom tolerate it because it is a tradition   15 show . . . glass look at myself
in a mirror   20 difference i.e. in rank   22 accident chance event   25 Vilely bound up
humbly/degradingly dressed (literally, bound like a book)   26 flaunts fancy clothes
27 sternness majesty   28 Apprehend be apprehensive about, imagine

The shapes of beasts upon them: Jupiter
Became a bull, and bellowed: the green Neptune
A ram, and bleated: and the fire-robed god,
Golden Apollo, a poor humble swain,
35   As I seem now. Their transformations
Were never for a piece of beauty rarer,
Nor in a way so chaste, since my desires
Run not before mine honour, nor my lusts
Burn hotter than my faith.

40   PERDITA   O, but, sir,
Your resolution cannot hold, when 'tis
Opposed, as it must be, by th'power of the king.
One of these two must be necessities,
Which then will speak, that you must change this purpose,
45   Or I my life.

FLORIZEL   Thou dearest Perdita,
With these forced thoughts, I prithee darken not
The mirth o'th'feast. Or I'll be thine, my fair,
Or not my father's. For I cannot be
50   Mine own, nor anything to any, if
I be not thine. To this I am most constant,
Though destiny say no. Be merry, gentle.
Strangle such thoughts as these with anything
That you behold the while. Your guests are coming:
55   Lift up your countenance, as it were the day
Of celebration of that nuptial which
We two have sworn shall come.

PERDITA   O lady Fortune,
Stand you auspicious!

---

31 Jupiter . . . bull in classical mythology the Roman supreme god Jupiter transformed himself
into a bull and abducted Europa   32 Neptune . . . ram the Roman sea god Neptune took on
the shape of a ram to carry off Theopane   34 Apollo . . . swain the classical sun god Apollo
disguised himself as a shepherd to seduce a mortal nymph   37 in a way for an undertaking/in
a manner   38 Run not before do not overtake   45 I my life possibly Perdita anticipates being
threatened with death   47 forced unnatural/uneasy   48 Or either   52 Though even if
53 with . . . while i.e. by occupying yourself with anything else in the meantime   55 as as if
59 Stand you be/remain (Fortune was traditionally fickle)

60 FLORIZEL   See, your guests approach.
    Address yourself to entertain them sprightly,
    And let's be red with mirth.

[*Enter Shepherd, Clown, Mopsa, Dorcas and others, with Polixenes and Camillo disguised*]

SHEPHERD   Fie, daughter! When my old wife lived, upon
    This day she was both pantler, butler, cook,
65 Both dame and servant, welcomed all, served all,
    Would sing her song and dance her turn: now here,
    At upper end o'th'table, now i'th'middle,
    On his shoulder, and his, her face o'fire
    With labour and the thing she took to quench it,
70 She would to each one sip. You are retired,
    As if you were a feasted one and not
    The hostess of the meeting. Pray you bid
    These unknown friends to's welcome, for it is
    A way to make us better friends, more known.
75 Come, quench your blushes and present yourself
    That which you are, mistress o'th'feast. Come on,
    And bid us welcome to your sheep-shearing,
    As your good flock shall prosper.

PERDITA   Sir, welcome.   *To Polixenes*
80 It is my father's will I should take on me
    The hostess-ship o'th'day.— You're welcome, sir.—   *To Camillo*
    Give me those flowers there, Dorcas.— Reverend sirs,
    For you there's rosemary and rue. These keep   *Gives flowers*
    Seeming and savour all the winter long.
85 Grace and remembrance be to you both,
    And welcome to our shearing!

POLIXENES   Shepherdess,
    A fair one are you — well you fit our ages
    With flowers of winter.

---

61 **Address** prepare   **sprightly** in a lively, cheerful manner   64 **pantler** pantry maid
65 **dame** hostess   68 **On his** at one person's   70 **to ... sip** toast each person   **retired**
withdrawn   83 **rosemary** herb symbolizing **remembrance**   **rue** herb symbolizing repentance
and **grace**   84 **Seeming and savour** appearance and smell   88 **fit** suit, match

90 PERDITA   Sir, the year growing ancient,
            Not yet on summer's death, nor on the birth
            Of trembling winter, the fairest flowers o'th'season
            Are our carnations and streaked gillyvors,
            Which some call nature's bastards. Of that kind
95   Our rustic garden's barren, and I care not
            To get slips of them.

    POLIXENES   Wherefore, gentle maiden,
            Do you neglect them?

    PERDITA   For I have heard it said
100   There is an art which in their piedness shares
            With great creating nature.

    POLIXENES   Say there be.
            Yet nature is made better by no mean
            But nature makes that mean, so over that art,
105   Which you say adds to nature, is an art
            That nature makes. You see, sweet maid, we marry
            A gentler scion to the wildest stock,
            And make conceive a bark of baser kind
            By bud of nobler race. This is an art
110   Which does mend nature, change it rather, but
            The art itself is nature.

    PERDITA   So it is.

    POLIXENES   Then make your garden rich in gillyvors,
            And do not call them bastards.

115 PERDITA   I'll not put
            The dibble in earth to set one slip of them.
            No more than were I painted I would wish
            This youth should say 'twere well and only therefore

---

90 the year . . . winter i.e. in autumn   **93 gillyvors** gillyflowers, a type of dual-colored
carnation   **94 nature's bastards** gillyflowers are a result of cross-pollination   **96 slips**
cuttings (plays on sense of "sexual lapse")   **97 Wherefore** why   **98 neglect** reject   **99 For**
because   **100 an . . . nature** i.e. artificial cross-breeding, in its effect of creating streaked
color, only imitates nature's skill   **piedness** being multicolored   **103 mean** method
104 over . . . makes i.e. man and his materials are created by nature, therefore anything he
does is essentially natural too   **107 gentler scion** nobler shoot   **stock** stem/ancestry
109 race root/ancestry, i.e. through cross-breeding, a superior plant is generated from a baser
one   **110 mend** improve   **116 dibble** tool for making holes in which to plant seedlings   **set**
plant   **117 painted** wearing makeup

Desire to breed by me. Here's flowers for you: *Gives flowers*
120   Hot lavender, mints, savory, marjoram,
The marigold, that goes to bed wi'th'sun
And with him rises weeping. These are flowers
Of middle summer, and I think they are given
To men of middle age. You're very welcome.
125   CAMILLO   I should leave grazing, were I of your flock,
And only live by gazing.
PERDITA   Out, alas!
You'd be so lean that blasts of January
Would blow you through and through.—
130   Now, my fair'st friend,   *To Florizel*
I would I had some flowers o'th'spring that might
Become your time of day,— and yours, and   *To Shepherdesses*
yours,
That wear upon your virgin branches yet
Your maidenheads growing.— O Proserpina,
135   For the flowers now that, frighted, thou let'st fall
From Dis's wagon! Daffodils,
That come before the swallow dares, and take
The winds of March with beauty: violets, dim,
But sweeter than the lids of Juno's eyes
140   Or Cytherea's breath: pale primroses
That die unmarried, ere they can behold
Bright Phoebus in his strength — a malady
Most incident to maids: bold oxlips and
The crown imperial: lilies of all kinds,
145   The flower-de-luce being one. O, these I lack,

---

120 Hot herbs were divided into "hot" or "cold" varieties based on their supposed qualities
savory a type of herb   **121 goes . . . weeping** the **marigold** closes at sunset and opens, filled
with dew, at sunrise   **127 Out, alas!** exclamation of dismay   **134 maidenheads** virginities
Proserpina in Ovid's *Metamorphoses*, Proserpina, the daughter of Ceres, is abducted by **Dis**
(Pluto) as she gathers flowers, and is taken in his chariot (**wagon**) to the underworld where he
rules   **137 dares** i.e. return from its migration   **take** bewitch   **138 dim** modest/drooping
139 Juno queen of the Roman gods   **140 Cytherea** Venus   **142 Phoebus** the sun god
malady . . . maids i.e. greensickness, a type of anemia that caused pallor and weakness;
it affected adolescent girls   **144 crown imperial** a lily first imported into England from
Constantinople in the late sixteenth century   **145 flower-de-luce** fleur-de-lis, heraldic lily
(actually a type of iris)

To make you garlands of, and my sweet friend,
To strew him o'er and o'er!

FLORIZEL   What, like a corpse?

PERDITA   No, like a bank for love to lie and play on.

150   Not like a corpse. Or if, not to be buried,
But quick and in mine arms. Come, take your flowers.
Methinks I play as I have seen them do
In Whitsun pastorals. Sure this robe of mine
Does change my disposition.

155   **FLORIZEL**   What you do
Still betters what is done. When you speak, sweet,
I'd have you do it ever: when you sing,
I'd have you buy and sell so, so give alms,
Pray so, and, for the ord'ring your affairs,

160   To sing them too. When you do dance, I wish you
A wave o'th'sea, that you might ever do
Nothing but that. Move still, still so,
And own no other function. Each your doing,
So singular in each particular,

165   Crowns what you are doing in the present deeds,
That all your acts are queens.

PERDITA   O Doricles,
Your praises are too large. But that your youth,
And the true blood which peeps fairly through't,

170   Do plainly give you out an unstained shepherd,
With wisdom I might fear, my Doricles,
You wooed me the false way.

FLORIZEL   I think you have
As little skill to fear as I have purpose

175   To put you to't. But come, our dance, I pray.

---

150 if if so   **151 quick** alive   **153 Whitsun pastorals** morris dances and plays celebrating
Whitsun, seven Sundays after Easter   **156 Still** always   **158 alms** charity to the poor or sick
159 ord'ring arranging of   **162 still** plays on the sense of "motionless"   **163 own . . . function**
perform no other activity   **your doing** thing you do   **164 singular** exceptional (plays on the
sense of "individual, **particular**")   **particular** individual aspect   **165 what . . . deeds** your
present actions   **167 Doricles** the name Florizel has assumed   **169 true** honorable/faithful
170 give you out proclaim you to be   **172 the false way** with dishonorable intentions
174 skill cause

Your hand, my Perdita. So turtles pair,
That never mean to part.

PERDITA   I'll swear for 'em.   *They stand aside*

POLIXENES   This is the prettiest low-born lass that ever   *To Camillo*
180   Ran on the greensward. Nothing she does or seems
But smacks of something greater than herself,
Too noble for this place.

CAMILLO   He tells her something
That makes her blood look out. Good sooth, she is
185   The queen of curds and cream.

CLOWN   Come on, strike up!

DORCAS   Mopsa must be your mistress. Marry, garlic,
To mend her kissing with!

MOPSA   Now, in good time!

190   CLOWN   Not a word, a word. We stand upon our manners.
Come, strike up!   *Music*

Here a dance of Shepherds and Shepherdesses

POLIXENES   Pray, good shepherd, what fair swain is this
Which dances with your daughter?

SHEPHERD   They call him Doricles, and boasts himself
195   To have a worthy feeding; but I have it
Upon his own report and I believe it.
He looks like sooth. He says he loves my daughter.
I think so too, for never gazed the moon
Upon the water as he'll stand and read,
200   As 'twere, my daughter's eyes. And to be plain,
I think there is not half a kiss to choose
Who loves another best.

POLIXENES   She dances featly.

SHEPHERD   So she does anything, though I report it,
205   That should be silent. If young Doricles

---

176 turtles turtledoves, thought to mate for life   **180 greensward** grass   **184 blood look
out** blush   **sooth** truth   **185 curds and cream** derived from milk and thus associated with
shepherds   **187 mistress** dance partner   **188 mend . . . with** i.e. improve her breath (so bad
that even **garlic** would help)   **189 in good time** expression of indignation   **190 stand upon**
insist on   **194 boasts** say he boasts   **195 worthy feeding** rich pasture, grazing land
197 like sooth truthful   **203 featly** skillfully

Do light upon her, she shall bring him that
Which he not dreams of.

Enter Servant

SERVANT   O, master, if you did but hear the pedlar at the door,
you would never dance again after a tabor and pipe. No, the
210   bagpipe could not move you. He sings several tunes faster
than you'll tell money. He utters them as he had eaten
ballads and all men's ears grew to his tunes.

CLOWN   He could never come better. He shall come in. I love
a ballad but even too well, if it be doleful matter merrily set
215   down, or a very pleasant thing indeed and sung lamentably.

SERVANT   He hath songs for man or woman, of all sizes. No
milliner can so fit his customers with gloves. He has the
prettiest love-songs for maids, so without bawdry, which is
strange, with such delicate burdens of dildos and fadings,
220   'jump her and thump her'. And where some stretch-
mouthed rascal would, as it were, mean mischief and break
a foul gap into the matter, he makes the maid to answer
'Whoop, do me no harm, good man', puts him off, slights
him, with 'Whoop, do me no harm, good man'.

225   POLIXENES   This is a brave fellow.

CLOWN   Believe me, thou talkest of an admirable conceited
fellow. Has he any unbraided wares?

SERVANT   He hath ribbons of all the colours i'th'rainbow;
points more than all the lawyers in Bohemia can learnedly
230   handle, though they come to him by th'gross: inkles,

---

206 light upon choose her (for marriage)   *Servant* i.e. the Old Shepherd's servant (whose
presence indicates that though humble, the household is not impoverished)   209 tabor
small drum used for morris dancing   211 tell count out   212 ballads narrative songs sung
and sold by itinerant peddlers   grew listened attentively/were drawn to   213 better at a
better time   217 milliner vendor of fashionable hats and gloves   218 bawdry lewdness
219 burdens refrains   dildos and fadings nonsense words used in refrains (plays on the
senses of "false penis" and "moment after orgasm")   220 "jump . . . her" also with sexual
connotations   stretched-mouthed wide-mouthed/obscene   221 break . . . matter interrupt
the song with an obscenity (gap plays on the sense of "vagina")   223 Whoop exclamation
of outcry or excitement   225 brave excellent/impudent   226 admirable conceited
extraordinarily witty, ingenious   227 unbraided untarnished, not shop-soiled ("braid" plays
on the sense of "ribbon")   229 points laces used to attach doublet and hose (plays on the
sense of "arguments")   230 by th'gross wholesale   inkles linen tape

caddisses, cambrics, lawns. Why, he sings 'em over as they were gods or goddesses. You would think a smock were a she-angel, he so chants to the sleeve-hand and the work about the square on't.

235 CLOWN Prithee bring him in, and let him approach singing.

PERDITA Forewarn him that he use no scurrilous words in's tunes.

Servant goes to door

CLOWN You have of these pedlars, that have more in them than you'd think, sister.

240 PERDITA Ay, good brother, or go about to think.

Enter Autolycus, singing   *He wears a false beard and carries a pack*

AUTOLYCUS Lawn as white as driven snow,   *Song*
    Cypress black as e'er was crow,
    Gloves as sweet as damask roses,
    Masks for faces and for noses,
245   Bugle bracelet, necklace amber,
    Perfume for a lady's chamber,
    Golden quoifs and stomachers,
    For my lads to give their dears,
    Pins and poking-sticks of steel,
250   What maids lack from head to heel.
    Come buy of me, come. Come buy, come buy.
    Buy lads, or else your lasses cry. Come buy!

CLOWN If I were not in love with Mopsa, thou shouldst take no money of me, but being enthralled as I am, it will also be
255   the bondage of certain ribbons and gloves.

MOPSA I was promised them against the feast, but they come not too late now.

---

231 **caddisses** yarn tape used for garters   **cambrics** fine linen from Cambray in Flanders   **lawns** fine linen   **'em over** about them   232 **smock** woman's undergarment   233 **sleeve-hand** cuff   **work about** embroidery on   234 **square** square piece of material on the chest area   238 **You have** there are some   240 **go about** wish   242 **Cypress** lightweight crepe fabric   243 **sweet** scented   244 **Masks** worn by women to protect the complexion from the sun   245 **Bugle** glittering   247 **quoifs** close-fitting caps   **stomachers** decorated fronts for women's dresses   249 **poking-sticks** rod for stiffening the folds of a ruff (with possible phallic play)   254 **enthralled** enslaved (by love)   255 **bondage** (buying and) binding up   256 **against** in preparation for

DORCAS   He hath promised you more than that, or there be liars.

260   MOPSA   He hath paid you all he promised you. Maybe he has paid you more, which will shame you to give him again.

CLOWN   Is there no manners left among maids? Will they wear their plackets where they should bear their faces? Is there not milking-time, when you are going to bed, or kiln-hole, to whistle of these secrets, but you must be tittle-tattling before all our guests? 'Tis well they are whisp'ring. Clamour your tongues, and not a word more.

MOPSA   I have done. Come, you promised me a tawdry-lace and a pair of sweet gloves.

270   CLOWN   Have I not told thee how I was cozened by the way and lost all my money?

AUTOLYCUS   And indeed, sir, there are cozeners abroad: therefore it behoves men to be wary.

CLOWN   Fear not thou, man, thou shalt lose nothing here.

275   AUTOLYCUS   I hope so, sir, for I have about me many parcels of charge.

CLOWN   What hast here? Ballads?

MOPSA   Pray now, buy some. I love a ballad in print alife, for then we are sure they are true.

280   AUTOLYCUS   Here's one to a very doleful tune, how a usurer's wife was brought to bed of twenty money-bags at a burden and how she longed to eat adders' heads and toads carbonadoed.

MOPSA   Is it true, think you?

285   AUTOLYCUS   Very true, and but a month old.

DORCAS   Bless me from marrying a usurer!

---

258 more than that presumably marriage   **260 paid you** had sex with you/given you   **261 paid . . . again** refers to pregnancy and the **shame** of an illegitimate child   **263 plackets . . . faces** i.e. reveal their most private affairs in public   **plackets** slits in skirts or petticoats (hence "vagina")   **264 kiln-hole** fire hole at an oven (somewhere to gossip)   **267 Clamour** silence   **268 tawdry-lace** Saint Audrey's lace, a decorative neckerchief   **270 cozened** tricked   **272 abroad** roaming about   **273 behoves** befits   **276 charge** value   **278 alife** on my life   **280 usurer** moneylender   **281 brought . . . of** delivered   **at a burden** in one birth   **283 carbonadoed** scored and grilled

AUTOLYCUS   Here's the midwife's name to't, one Mistress Tale-
porter, and five or six honest wives that were present. Why
should I carry lies abroad?

290   MOPSA   Pray you now, buy it.

CLOWN   Come on, lay it by, and let's first see more ballads.
We'll buy the other things anon.

AUTOLYCUS   Here's another ballad of a fish that appeared upon
the coast on Wednesday the fourscore of April, forty
295   thousand fathom above water, and sung this ballad against
the hard hearts of maids. It was thought she was a woman
and was turned into a cold fish for she would not exchange
flesh with one that loved her. The ballad is very pitiful and as
true.

300   DORCAS   Is it true too, think you?

AUTOLYCUS   Five justices' hands at it, and witnesses more than
my pack will hold.

CLOWN   Lay it by too; another.

AUTOLYCUS   This is a merry ballad, but a very pretty one.

305   MOPSA   Let's have some merry ones.

AUTOLYCUS   Why, this is a passing merry one and goes to the
tune of 'Two maids wooing a man'. There's scarce a maid
westward but she sings it. 'Tis in request, I can tell you.

MOPSA   We can both sing it. If thou'lt bear a part, thou shalt
310   hear. 'Tis in three parts.

DORCAS   We had the tune on't a month ago.

AUTOLYCUS   I can bear my part. You must know 'tis my
occupation. Have at it with you.

[*They sing the*] song

AUTOLYCUS   Get you hence, for I must go

315   Where it fits not you to know.

DORCAS   Whither?

---

287 **Tale-porter** i.e. "tale-bearer" or bringer of "tail" (vagina), hence pimp   291 **lay it by** set it
aside   294 **fourscore** eightieth (four times twenty)   **forty thousand fathom** 240,000 feet
(about 74,000 meters)   297 **exchange flesh** have sex   301 **justices'** magistrates'   **hands**
signatures   302 **pack** bag, pack of goods   306 **passing** extremely   308 **request** demand
309 **bear a part** sing a part/play a role/handle genitals   311 **on't** of it   313 **Have . . . you** let's
begin

	MOPSA	O, whither?
	DORCAS	Whither?
	MOPSA	It becomes thy oath full well,
320		Thou to me thy secrets tell.
	DORCAS	Me too, let me go thither.
	MOPSA	Or thou goest to th'grange or mill.
	DORCAS	If to either, thou dost ill.
	AUTOLYCUS	Neither.
325	DORCAS	What, neither?
	AUTOLYCUS	Neither.
	DORCAS	Thou hast sworn my love to be.
	MOPSA	Thou hast sworn it more to me.
		Then whither goest? Say, whither?

330 CLOWN   We'll have this song out anon by ourselves. My
father and the gentlemen are in sad talk, and we'll not
trouble them. Come, bring away thy pack after me.
Wenches, I'll buy for you both. Pedlar, let's have the first
choice. Follow me, girls.   [*Exit with Dorcas and Mopsa*]

335 AUTOLYCUS   And you shall pay well for 'em.

Song Will you buy any tape,   *Follows them, singing*
          Or lace for your cape,
          My dainty duck, my dear-a?
          Any silk, any thread,
340   Any toys for your head,
          Of the new'st and finest, finest wear-a?
          Come to the pedlar.
          Money's a meddler.
          That doth utter all men's ware-a.   *Exit*

[*Enter Servant*]

345 SERVANT   Master, there is three carters, three shepherds,
three neat-herds, three swine-herds, that have made
themselves all men of hair. They call themselves Saltiers, and

---

322 Or either   grange farmhouse   323 ill wrong   330 have . . . anon finish this song later
331 sad serious   340 toys ornaments, trinkets   344 utter offer for sale   ware-a wares,
goods   345 carters cart drivers   346 neat-herds cowherds   made . . . hair dressed in hairy
disguises, presumably animal skins, to resemble satyrs   347 Saltiers malapropism for "satyrs"
(mythical creatures, part man, part goat)

they have a dance which the wenches say is a gallimaufry of gambols, because they are not in't. But they themselves are
350 o'th'mind, if it be not too rough for some that know little but bowling, it will please plentifully.

SHEPHERD   Away! We'll none on't; here has been too much homely foolery already. I know, sir, we weary you.

POLIXENES   You weary those that refresh us. Pray let's see these
355 four threes of herdsmen.

SERVANT   One three of them, by their own report, sir, hath danced before the king, and not the worst of the three but jumps twelve foot and a half by th'square.

SHEPHERD   Leave your prating. Since these good men are
360 pleased, let them come in. But quickly now.

SERVANT   Why, they stay at door, sir.   *Goes to the door*

Here a dance of twelve Satyrs

POLIXENES   O, father, you'll know more of that   *To Shepherd*
      hereafter.—

Is it not too far gone? 'Tis time to part them.   *To Camillo*
He's simple and tells much.—

                    How now, fair shepherd!   *To Florizel*
365 Your heart is full of something that does take
Your mind from feasting. Sooth, when I was young
And handed love as you do, I was wont
To load my she with knacks. I would have ransacked
The pedlar's silken treasury and have poured it
370 To her acceptance. You have let him go
And nothing marted with him. If your lass
Interpretation should abuse and call this
Your lack of love or bounty, you were straited

---

348 gallimaufry of gambols chaotic mixture of leaps   **351 bowling** i.e. a gentle, sedate activity   **353 homely** simple   **355 threes** trios   **358 by th'square** with great precision   **359 prating** chattering   **361 stay** are waiting   **362 father** respectful term of address for an old man   **you'll . . . hereafter** presumably refers to a conversation the men were having during the dance   **364 He's simple** the Shepherd is ignorant/humble   **367 handed** handled   **wont** accustomed   **368 she with knacks** lady with trifles, presents   **371 marted** bargained/bought   **372 Interpretation should abuse** should misinterpret   **373 bounty** generosity   **straited** at a loss

For a reply, at least if you make a care

375 Of happy holding her.

FLORIZEL   Old sir, I know

She prizes not such trifles as these are.

The gifts she looks from me are packed and locked

Up in my heart, which I have given already,

380 But not delivered. O, hear me breathe my life

Before this ancient sir, whom, it should seem,

Hath sometime loved.— I take thy hand, this hand,   *To Perdita*

As soft as dove's down and as white as it,

Or Ethiopian's tooth, or the fanned snow that's bolted

385 By th'northern blasts twice o'er.   *Takes her hand*

POLIXENES   What follows this?

How prettily th'young swain seems to wash

The hand was fair before! I have put you out.

But to your protestation: let me hear

390 What you profess.

FLORIZEL   Do, and be witness to't.

POLIXENES   And this my neighbour too?

FLORIZEL   And he, and more

Than he, and men, the earth, the heavens, and all;

395 That were I crowned the most imperial monarch,

Thereof most worthy, were I the fairest youth

That ever made eye swerve, had force and knowledge

More than was ever man's, I would not prize them

Without her love; for her employ them all,

400 Commend them and condemn them to her service

Or to their own perdition.

POLIXENES   Fairly offered.

CAMILLO   This shows a sound affection.

---

374 make . . . her care about keeping her happy   **378 looks** looks for   **380 delivered**
i.e. legally, through formal betrothal   **breathe my life** i.e. pledge my love   **382 sometime**
formerly, at some time   **384 bolted** sifted, refined   **385 blasts** winds   **387 wash** clean/
whitewash   **388 was** that was   **put you out** disconcerted you (by interrupting); also used
for actor forgetting his lines   **389 to** return to   **protestation** declaration   **396 Thereof** of all
monarchs   **400 Commend . . . perdition** either commit them to her service, or consign them
to ruin

SHEPHERD   But, my daughter,
405   Say you the like to him?

PERDITA   I cannot speak
So well, nothing so well. No, nor mean better.
By th'pattern of mine own thoughts I cut out
The purity of his.

410 SHEPHERD   Take hands, a bargain!
And, friends unknown, you shall bear witness to't.
I give my daughter to him, and will make
Her portion equal his.

FLORIZEL   O, that must be
415   I'th'virtue of your daughter: one being dead,
I shall have more than you can dream of yet,
Enough then for your wonder. But come on,
Contract us 'fore these witnesses.

SHEPHERD   Come, your hand.
420   And, daughter, yours.

POLIXENES   Soft, swain, awhile, beseech you.
Have you a father?

FLORIZEL   I have, but what of him?

POLIXENES   Knows he of this?

425 FLORIZEL   He neither does nor shall.

POLIXENES   Methinks a father
Is at the nuptial of his son a guest
That best becomes the table. Pray you once more,
Is not your father grown incapable
430   Of reasonable affairs? Is he not stupid
With age and alt'ring rheums? Can he speak? Hear?
Know man from man? Dispute his own estate?

---

408 By . . . his through understanding the purity of my own thoughts I recognize that of his (a
dressmaking metaphor)   413 portion dowry   415 one being dead i.e. when Polixenes dies
and Florizel inherits the throne   418 Contract . . . witnesses the formal betrothal; a pledge of
marriage uttered before witnesses was legally binding   421 Soft wait a moment   swain
country gallant or lover/young man/rustic   428 becomes befits   429 incapable Of unable
to understand (through senility)   431 alt'ring rheums weakening catarrh or similar ailments
of old age   432 Dispute deal with

Lies he not bed-rid? And again does nothing
But what he did being childish?

435 FLORIZEL   No, good sir.
He has his health and ampler strength indeed
Than most have of his age.

POLIXENES   By my white beard,
You offer him, if this be so, a wrong
440 Something unfilial. Reason my son
Should choose himself a wife, but as good reason
The father, all whose joy is nothing else
But fair posterity, should hold some counsel
In such a business.

445 FLORIZEL   I yield all this.
But for some other reasons, my grave sir,
Which 'tis not fit you know, I not acquaint
My father of this business.

POLIXENES   Let him know't.

450 FLORIZEL   He shall not.

POLIXENES   Prithee let him.

FLORIZEL   No, he must not.

SHEPHERD   Let him, my son. He shall not need to grieve
At knowing of thy choice.

455 FLORIZEL   Come, come, he must not.
Mark our contract.

POLIXENES   Mark your divorce, young sir,   *Takes off disguise*
Whom son I dare not call. Thou art too base
To be acknowledged. Thou a sceptre's heir,
460 That thus affects a sheep-hook!— Thou, old   *To Shepherd*
    traitor,
I am sorry that by hanging thee I can
But shorten thy life one week.— And thou, fresh   *To Perdita*
    piece

---

433 does . . . childish i.e. suffers dementia and returns to a state of childish dependency
440 unfilial not like a son, unnatural   **Reason** it is reasonable that   **443 posterity** family,
descendants   **hold some counsel** be involved, consulted   **445 yield** grant   **456 Mark** witness
460 affects aspires to/seeks to obtain/loves/assumes the character of/puts on a pretense of
sheep-hook shepherd's crook, and by implication a shepherd girl (derogatory)

Of excellent witchcraft, who of force must know
The royal fool thou cop'st with—

465 SHEPHERD   O, my heart!

POLIXENES   I'll have thy beauty scratched with briers and made
More homely than thy state.— For thee, fond boy,   *To Florizel*
If I may ever know thou dost but sigh
That thou no more shalt see this knack, as never
470 I mean thou shalt, we'll bar thee from succession,
Not hold thee of our blood, no, not our kin,
Far than Deucalion off. Mark thou my words.
Follow us to the court.— Thou churl, for this time,   *To Shepherd*
Though full of our displeasure, yet we free thee
475 From the dead blow of it.— And you,   *To Perdita*
    enchantment,—
Worthy enough a herdsman — yea, him too,
That makes himself, but for our honour therein,
Unworthy thee — if ever henceforth thou
These rural latches to his entrance open,
480 Or hoop his body more with thy embraces,
I will devise a death as cruel for thee
As thou art tender to't.   *Exit*

PERDITA   Even here undone!
I was not much afeard, for once or twice
485 I was about to speak and tell him plainly,
The selfsame sun that shines upon his court
Hides not his visage from our cottage but
Looks on alike.— Will't please you, sir, be gone?   *To Florizel*
I told you what would come of this. Beseech you

---

463 excellent skilled   of force by necessity   464 cop'st with deal with/embrace   467 homely
ugly/humble   fond foolish/doting   469 knack toy/piece of trickery   470 succession i.e. to
the throne   471 Not . . . blood disown you   472 Far . . . off less linked in kinship than to
Deucalion, in classical mythology the common ancestor of humankind and thus the most
distant relation possible   473 churl rustic/villain, i.e. the Shepherd   475 dead . . . it
i.e. execution   enchantment enchantress, witch, i.e. Perdita   476 him i.e. Florizel
477 That . . . thee i.e. were it not for his royal blood, his behavior has made him even unworthy
of a lowly person like you   479 rural latches metaphorical gates that lead from Perdita's rustic
world into Florizel's   482 tender acutely receptive   483 undone ruined   487 visage face
488 alike both alike

490 Of your own state take care. This dream of mine —
     Being now awake, I'll queen it no inch further,
     But milk my ewes and weep.

CAMILLO   Why, how now, father!
     Speak ere thou diest.

495 SHEPHERD   I cannot speak, nor think
     Nor dare to know that which I know.— O, sir,   *To Florizel*
     You have undone a man of fourscore three,
     That thought to fill his grave in quiet, yea,
     To die upon the bed my father died,
500 To lie close by his honest bones; but now
     Some hangman must put on my shroud and lay me
     Where no priest shovels in dust.— O cursèd wretch,   *To Perdita*
     That knew'st this was the prince, and wouldst adventure
     To mingle faith with him! Undone, undone!
505 If I might die within this hour, I have lived
     To die when I desire.   *Exit*

FLORIZEL   Why look you so upon me?
     I am but sorry, not afeard. Delayed,
     But nothing altered. What I was, I am.
510 More straining on for plucking back, not following
     My leash unwillingly.

CAMILLO   Gracious my lord,
     You know your father's temper. At this time
     He will allow no speech — which I do guess
515 You do not purpose to him — and as hardly
     Will he endure your sight as yet, I fear.
     Then, till the fury of his highness settle,
     Come not before him.

FLORIZEL   I not purpose it.
520 I think, Camillo?

---

497 **fourscore three** eighty-three   498 **fill . . . quiet** die peacefully   502 **no . . . dust** criminals
were denied a Christian burial   503 **adventure** dare   504 **mingle faith** exchange vows
(perhaps with play on the belief in the mingling of blood during sex)   510 **straining . . . back**
determined for being deterred   **following . . . unwillingly** being dragged against my will
515 **purpose** intend   **hardly** with great difficulty/unwillingly   520 **I think, Camillo?** Camillo
either takes off his disguise or is recognized by Florizel, even with it on

CAMILLO   Even he, my lord.   *May remove his disguise*

PERDITA   How often have I told you 'twould be thus!
How often said, my dignity would last
But till 'twere known!

525 FLORIZEL   It cannot fail but by
The violation of my faith, and then
Let nature crush the sides o'th'earth together
And mar the seeds within! Lift up thy looks.
From my succession wipe me, father. I

530 Am heir to my affection.

CAMILLO   Be advised.

FLORIZEL   I am, and by my fancy. If my reason
Will thereto be obedient, I have reason.
If not, my senses, better pleased with madness,

535 Do bid it welcome.

CAMILLO   This is desperate, sir.

FLORIZEL   So call it, but it does fulfil my vow.
I needs must think it honesty. Camillo,
Not for Bohemia, nor the pomp that may

540 Be thereat gleaned, for all the sun sees or
The close earth wombs or the profound seas hides
In unknown fathoms, will I break my oath
To this my fair beloved: therefore, I pray you
As you have ever been my father's honoured friend,

545 When he shall miss me — as, in faith, I mean not
To see him any more — cast your good counsels
Upon his passion. Let myself and fortune
Tug for the time to come. This you may know,
And so deliver, I am put to sea

550 With her whom here I cannot hold on shore.
And most opportune to her need, I have

---

523 dignity worth   **524 But** only   **526 violation . . . faith** breaking of my oaths   **528 seeds**
i.e. of life   **Lift . . . looks** look at me/be cheerful   **529 wipe** erase   **531 Be advised** be
cautious, think carefully   **532 fancy** feelings, love   **536 desperate** extreme/rash/dangerous
538 honesty right, honorable   **539 pomp** splendor, ostentation   **541 close** secret/enclosed
wombs holds within   **profound** deep   **547 passion** rage   **548 Tug** contend with one
another   **549 deliver** report

A vessel rides fast by, but not prepared
For this design. What course I mean to hold
Shall nothing benefit your knowledge, nor
555 Concern me the reporting.

CAMILLO   O, my lord,
I would your spirit were easier for advice,
Or stronger for your need.

FLORIZEL   Hark, Perdita.—   *Takes her aside*
560 I'll hear you by and by.   *To Camillo*

CAMILLO   He's irremovable,   *Aside*
Resolved for flight. Now were I happy, if
His going I could frame to serve my turn,
Save him from danger, do him love and honour,
565 Purchase the sight again of dear Sicilia
And that unhappy king, my master, whom
I so much thirst to see.

FLORIZEL   Now, good Camillo,
I am so fraught with curious business that
570 I leave out ceremony.

CAMILLO   Sir, I think
You have heard of my poor services, i'th'love
That I have borne your father?

FLORIZEL   Very nobly
575 Have you deserved. It is my father's music
To speak your deeds, not little of his care
To have them recompensed as thought on.

CAMILLO   Well, my lord,
If you may please to think I love the king
580 And through him what's nearest to him, which is
Your gracious self, embrace but my direction,

---

552 **rides fast by** anchored nearby   553 **What . . . hold** where I intend to go   554 **Shall . . .
reporting** will not benefit you to hear or me to tell you   557 **for advice** to advise
561 **irremovable** determined   563 **frame . . . turn** use for my purposes   565 **Purchase** obtain
569 **fraught** burdened   **curious** difficult   570 **ceremony** courtesy (toward you)   572 **poor**
meager   576 **not . . . on** and important to him to reward your service as fully as he values it
581 **embrace . . . direction** accept my advice, adopt my plan

If your more ponderous and settled project
May suffer alteration. On mine honour,
I'll point you where you shall have such receiving
585 As shall become your highness, where you may
Enjoy your mistress, from the whom I see,
There's no disjunction to be made, but by —
As heavens forfend! — your ruin. Marry her,
And, with my best endeavours in your absence,
590 Your discontenting father strive to qualify
And bring him up to liking.

FLORIZEL   How, Camillo,
May this, almost a miracle, be done?
That I may call thee something more than man
595 And after that trust to thee.

CAMILLO   Have you thought on
A place whereto you'll go?

FLORIZEL   Not any yet,
But as th'unthought-on accident is guilty
600 To what we wildly do, so we profess
Ourselves to be the slaves of chance and flies
Of every wind that blows.

CAMILLO   Then list to me.
This follows, if you will not change your purpose
605 But undergo this flight: make for Sicilia,
And there present yourself and your fair princess,
For so I see she must be, 'fore Leontes;
She shall be habited as it becomes
The partner of your bed. Methinks I see
610 Leontes opening his free arms and weeping
His welcomes forth, asks thee there 'Son, forgiveness',

---

582 **ponderous** weighty   **settled** fixed, determined   583 **suffer alteration** permit
some adjustments   584 **receiving** a reception   586 **Enjoy** make love to/love freely
587 **disjunction** separation   588 **forfend** forbid   590 **discontenting** discontented   **qualify**
pacify   591 **liking** giving his approval   595 **after . . . to** ever after trust   596 **on** of
599 **th'unthought . . . do** this unexpected event is responsible for our rash behavior now
601 **flies . . . blows** blown about like flies in the wind   603 **list** listen   608 **habited** dressed

As 'twere i'th'father's person, kisses the hands
Of your fresh princess; o'er and o'er divides him
'Twixt his unkindness and his kindness. Th'one
615   He chides to hell and bids the other grow
Faster than thought or time.

FLORIZEL   Worthy Camillo,
What colour for my visitation shall I
Hold up before him?

620 CAMILLO   Sent by the king your father
To greet him and to give him comforts. Sir,
The manner of your bearing towards him, with
What you as from your father shall deliver —
Things known betwixt us three — I'll write you down,
625   The which shall point you forth at every sitting
What you must say, that he shall not perceive
But that you have your father's bosom there
And speak his very heart.

FLORIZEL   I am bound to you.
630   There is some sap in this.

CAMILLO   A course more promising
Than a wild dedication of yourselves
To unpathed waters, undreamed shores, most certain
To miseries enough, no hope to help you,
635   But as you shake off one to take another.
Nothing so certain as your anchors, who
Do their best office if they can but stay you
Where you'll be loath to be. Besides, you know
Prosperity's the very bond of love,
640   Whose fresh complexion and whose heart together
Affliction alters.

---

612 As . . . person as though he were your father   **613 divides . . . kindness** veers between chastising himself for his past unkindness/unnatural behavior and endeavoring to be kind/fatherly now   **618 colour** pretext   **622 bearing** behavior   **623 as** as if   **625 point . . . sitting** direct you at every discussion (with regard to)   **627 bosom** most personal thoughts   **630 sap** life   **633 unpathed** uncharted   **635 one** one misery   **636 nothing . . . as** your only certainty   **637 stay** hold, keep   **639 Prosperity's . . . love** good fortune secures love   **641 Affliction alters** (love) is changed by adversity

PERDITA   One of these is true:
I think affliction may subdue the cheek,
But not take in the mind.

645 CAMILLO   Yea? Say you so?
There shall not at your father's house these seven years
Be born another such.

FLORIZEL   My good Camillo,
She's as forward of her breeding as
650 She is i'th'rear our birth.

CAMILLO   I cannot say 'tis pity
She lacks instructions, for she seems a mistress
To most that teach.

PERDITA   Your pardon, sir. For this
655 I'll blush you thanks.

FLORIZEL   My prettiest Perdita!
But, O, the thorns we stand upon!— Camillo,
Preserver of my father, now of me,
The medicine of our house, how shall we do?
660 We are not furnished like Bohemia's son,
Nor shall appear in Sicilia.

CAMILLO   My lord,
Fear none of this. I think you know my fortunes
Do all lie there. It shall be so my care
665 To have you royally appointed as if
The scene you play were mine. For instance, sir,
That you may know you shall not want, one   *They talk apart*
    word.

Enter Autolycus

AUTOLYCUS   Ha, ha! What a fool honesty is! And trust, his sworn
brother, a very simple gentleman. I have sold all my
670 trumpery: not a counterfeit stone, not a ribbon, glass,

---

643 **subdue the cheek** make the complexion pale   644 **take in** affect/conquer   646 **seven years** i.e. for a long time   647 **such** such as Perdita   649 **as . . . birth** as superior to her lowly upbringing as she is inferior to us in rank   652 **instructions** education   660 **furnished** dressed/equipped   661 **appear** appear so   663 **fortunes** wealth   665 **appointed** provided for   666 **mine** written/performed by me   **instance** proof   667 **want** go without   670 **trumpery** worthless finery   **stone** gem   **glass** mirror

pomander, brooch, table-book, ballad, knife, tape, glove, shoe-tie, bracelet, horn-ring, to keep my pack from fasting. They throng who should buy first, as if my trinkets had been hallowed and brought a benediction to the buyer, by which
675 means I saw whose purse was best in picture, and what I saw, to my good use I remembered. My clown, who wants but something to be a reasonable man, grew so in love with the wenches' song, that he would not stir his pettitoes till he had both tune and words, which so drew the rest of the herd to me
680 that all their other senses stuck in ears. You might have pinched a placket, it was senseless; 'twas nothing to geld a codpiece of a purse. I would have filed keys off that hung in chains. No hearing, no feeling, but my sir's song, and admiring the nothing of it. So that in this time of lethargy I
685 picked and cut most of their festival purses, and had not the old man come in with a whoo-bub against his daughter and the king's son and scared my choughs from the chaff, I had not left a purse alive in the whole army.   *Camillo, Florizel and*

CAMILLO   Nay, but my letters, by this means being there   *Perdita*
690 So soon as you arrive, shall clear that doubt.   *come forward*
FLORIZEL   And those that you'll procure from King Leontes—
CAMILLO   Shall satisfy your father.
PERDITA   Happy be you!
     All that you speak shows fair.
695 **CAMILLO**   Who have we here?   *Sees Autolycus*
     We'll make an instrument of this, omit
     Nothing may give us aid.

---

671 pomander ball of sweet-smelling substances carried about for ornament or to prevent infection   **table-book** notebook   **672 horn-ring** ring made from horn, thought to possess magical qualities   **fasting** i.e. being empty   **674 hallowed** sacred   **benediction** blessing
675 best in picture looked best (to steal)   **676 use** purpose/opportunity/profit   **wants** lacks   **677 something** some thing   **grew** plays on the phallic sense of "became erect"
678 pettitoes feet (literally, pig's trotters)   **680 stuck in ears** were devoted to hearing
681 placket literally, slit in a petticoat, hence "vagina"   **geld . . . purse** cut a purse free from the codpiece it is attached to/castrate (**geld**) a scrotum   **683 my sir's** i.e. the Clown's
684 nothing meaninglessness/silliness (puns on musical "noting," which was pronounced similarly)   **686 whoo-bub** hullabaloo   **687 choughs** small chattering birds of crow family, especially jackdaws (plays on "chuffs," meaning "rustics")   **chaff** wares, pickings/husks of grain after threshing/refuse   **692 satisfy** appease   **697 Nothing** nothing that

AUTOLYCUS   If they have overheard me now, why, hanging.   *Aside*

CAMILLO   How now, good fellow? Why shakest thou so? Fear
700   not, man. Here's no harm intended to thee.

AUTOLYCUS   I am a poor fellow, sir.

CAMILLO   Why, be so still. Here's nobody will steal that from
thee. Yet for the outside of thy poverty we must make an
exchange: therefore discase thee instantly — thou must
705   think there's a necessity in't — and change garments with
this gentleman. Though the pennyworth on his side be the
worst, yet hold thee, there's some boot.   *Gives money*

AUTOLYCUS   I am a poor fellow, sir.— I know ye well   *Aside*
enough.

710   CAMILLO   Nay, prithee, dispatch: the gentleman is half flayed
already.

AUTOLYCUS   Are you in earnest, sir? I smell the trick on't.   *Aside*

FLORIZEL   Dispatch, I prithee.

AUTOLYCUS   Indeed, I have had earnest, but I cannot with
715   conscience take it.

CAMILLO   Unbuckle, unbuckle.   *Florizel and Autolycus*
Fortunate mistress — let my prophecy   *exchange clothes*
Come home to ye! — you must retire yourself
Into some covert; take your sweetheart's hat
720   And pluck it o'er your brows, muffle your face,
Dismantle you, and, as you can, disliken
The truth of your own seeming, that you may —
For I do fear eyes over — to shipboard
Get undescried.

725   PERDITA   I see the play so lies
That I must bear a part.

CAMILLO   No remedy.
Have you done there?

---

703 **outside . . . poverty** i.e. poor clothing   704 **discase** undress   705 **think** believe,
understand   706 **pennyworth** bargain   707 **some boot** something more   710 **dispatch**
hurry   **flayed** stripped   712 **in earnest** sincere (sense then shifts to "advance payment")
trick knack/habit/trickery   **on't** of it, i.e. duping people   718 **Come . . . ye** be fulfilled
719 **covert** hiding place   720 **pluck** pull   721 **Dismantle you** take off your outer clothes
disliken disguise   722 **seeming** appearance   723 **eyes over** spies   724 **undescried**
undetected   725 **lies** plays on the sense of "dissimulates"   727 **remedy** alternative

FLORIZEL   Should I now meet my father,
730   He would not call me son.
CAMILLO   Nay, you shall have no hat.   *Gives hat to Perdita*
Come, lady, come. Farewell, my friend.
AUTOLYCUS   Adieu, sir.
FLORIZEL   O Perdita, what have we twain forgot!
735   Pray you a word.
CAMILLO   What I do next, shall be to tell the king   *Aside*
Of this escape and whither they are bound.
Wherein my hope is I shall so prevail
To force him after, in whose company
740   I shall review Sicilia, for whose sight
I have a woman's longing.
FLORIZEL   Fortune speed us!
Thus we set on, Camillo, to th'seaside.
CAMILLO   The swifter speed the better.
                              Exeunt [Florizel, Perdita and Camillo]
745   AUTOLYCUS   I understand the business, I hear it. To have an open
ear, a quick eye, and a nimble hand, is necessary for a
cutpurse; a good nose is requisite also, to smell out work for
th'other senses. I see this is the time that the unjust man
doth thrive. What an exchange had this been without boot?
750   What a boot is here with this exchange? Sure, the gods do
this year connive at us, and we may do anything extempore.
The prince himself is about a piece of iniquity, stealing away
from his father with his clog at his heels. If I thought it were
a piece of honesty to acquaint the king withal, I would not
755   do't. I hold it the more knavery to conceal it; and therein am
I constant to my profession.
Enter Clown and Shepherd   *Carrying fardel and box*
Aside, aside. Here is more matter for a hot brain.   *He stands aside*

---

734 **twain** two   739 **after** in pursuit   740 **review** see again   741 **woman's** i.e. overwhelming
742 **speed** favor/hasten   747 **cutpurse** one who steals by cutting purses which were worn
hanging from the waist   749 **exchange** conversation/exchange of garments/financial
transaction   **without boot** even without payment   750 **boot** benefit/profit/shoe   751 **connive**
at conspire with   **extempore** on a whim, spontaneously   752 **piece of iniquity** wrongful act
753 **clog** burden (block of wood tied to man or animal to prevent escape)/mistress   754 **withal**
with this   756 **constant** faithful   *fardel* bundle   757 **hot** enthusiastic, active

Every lane's end, every shop, church, session, hanging, yields a careful man work.

760   CLOWN   See, see. What a man you are now! There is no other way but to tell the king she's a changeling and none of your flesh and blood.

SHEPHERD   Nay, but hear me.

CLOWN   Nay, but hear me.

765   SHEPHERD   Go to, then.

CLOWN   She being none of your flesh and blood, your flesh and blood has not offended the king, and so your flesh and blood is not to be punished by him. Show those things you found about her, those secret things, all but what she 770   has with her. This being done, let the law go whistle, I warrant you.

SHEPHERD   I will tell the king all, every word, yea, and his son's pranks too; who, I may say, is no honest man, neither to his father nor to me, to go about to make me the king's 775   brother-in-law.

CLOWN   Indeed, brother-in-law was the farthest off you could have been to him and then your blood had been the dearer by I know how much an ounce.

AUTOLYCUS   Very wisely, puppies!   *Aside*

780   SHEPHERD   Well, let us to the king. There is that in this fardel will make him scratch his beard.

AUTOLYCUS   I know not what impediment this complaint   *Aside* may be to the flight of my master.

CLOWN   Pray heartily he be at palace.

785   AUTOLYCUS   Though I am not naturally honest, I am so   *Aside* sometimes by chance: let me pocket up my pedlar's excrement.— How now, rustics! Whither are you   *Takes off his* bound?   *false beard*

SHEPHERD   To th'palace, an it like your worship.

---

758 session court session   **759 careful** attentive, cunning   **761 changeling** fairy child (usually substituted for a stolen mortal baby)   **765 Go to** go ahead   **778 I . . . ounce** i.e. nothing at all   **779 puppies** i.e. silly ones   **780 fardel** bundle   **782 complaint** lament, grounds for grievance   **783 master** i.e. Florizel   **786 pocket up** put away   **787 excrement** i.e. mustache/beard   **789 an it like** if it please

790   AUTOLYCUS   Your affairs there? What? With whom? The condition of that fardel, the place of your dwelling, your names, your ages, of what having, breeding, and any thing that is fitting to be known, discover.

CLOWN   We are but plain fellows, sir.

795   AUTOLYCUS   A lie; you are rough and hairy. Let me have no lying; it becomes none but tradesmen, and they often give us soldiers the lie, but we pay them for it with stamped coin, not stabbing steel: therefore they do not give us the lie.

CLOWN   Your worship had like to have given us one, if you 800   had not taken yourself with the manner.

SHEPHERD   Are you a courtier, an't like you, sir?

AUTOLYCUS   Whether it like me or no, I am a courtier. See'st thou not the air of the court in these enfoldings? Hath not my gait in it the measure of the court? Receives not thy nose 805   court-odour from me? Reflect I not on thy baseness court-contempt? Think'st thou, for that I insinuate or toaze from thee thy business, I am therefore no courtier? I am courtier cap-a-pie; and one that will either push on or pluck back thy business there: whereupon I command thee to open thy 810   affair.

SHEPHERD   My business, sir, is to the king.

AUTOLYCUS   What advocate hast thou to him?

SHEPHERD   I know not, an't like you.

CLOWN   Advocate's the court-word for a pheasant.   *Aside to* 815   Say you have none.   *the Shepherd*

SHEPHERD   None, sir. I have no pheasant, cock nor hen.

---

791 **condition** nature   792 **having** means, wealth   793 **discover** reveal   794 **plain** simple (Autolycus plays on sense of "smooth")   796 **give . . . lie** deceive us/accuse us of lying (a valid cause for a duel)   797 **pay . . . lie** i.e. even if cheated or insulted, since soldiers **pay** with legitimate currency rather than by stabbing, tradesmen cannot claim to have given anything (free goods/**the lie**), and a duel is thus avoided   799 **one** the lie/a duel   800 **taken . . . manner** behaved properly/caught yourself in time   803 **enfoldings** clothing   804 **gait** posture, bearing   **measure** graceful movement   805 **baseness** lowly status, which the court would find contemptuous   806 **for that** because   **insinuate** draw out subtly   **toaze** tease out 808 **cap-a-pie** from head to toe   809 **open thy affair** disclose your business   812 **advocate** representative   814 **pheasant** the only courts known to the Clown are those of local justices; he assumes Autolycus refers to bribing the judge with a gift

AUTOLYCUS   How blessed are we that are not simple men!   *Aside*
Yet nature might have made me as these are, therefore I will
not disdain.

820   CLOWN   This cannot be but a great courtier.   *To Shepherd*

SHEPHERD   His garments are rich, but he wears them not
handsomely.

CLOWN   He seems to be the more noble in being fantastical.
A great man, I'll warrant; I know by the picking on's teeth.

825   AUTOLYCUS   The fardel there? What's i'th'fardel? Wherefore that
box?

SHEPHERD   Sir, there lies such secrets in this fardel and box,
which none must know but the king, and which he shall
know within this hour, if I may come to th'speech of him.

830   AUTOLYCUS   Age, thou hast lost thy labour.

SHEPHERD   Why, sir?

AUTOLYCUS   The king is not at the palace. He is gone aboard a
new ship to purge melancholy and air himself, for, if thou
be'st capable of things serious, thou must know the king is
835   full of grief.

SHEPHERD   So 'tis said, sir, about his son, that should have
married a shepherd's daughter.

AUTOLYCUS   If that shepherd be not in hand-fast, let him fly; the
curses he shall have, the tortures he shall feel, will break the
840   back of man, the heart of monster.

CLOWN   Think you so, sir?

AUTOLYCUS   Not he alone shall suffer what wit can make heavy
and vengeance bitter, but those that are germane to him,
though removed fifty times, shall all come under the
845   hangman, which though it be great pity, yet it is necessary.
An old sheep-whistling rogue a ram-tender, to offer to have
his daughter come into grace! Some say he shall be stoned,

---

820 but anyone but   823 fantastical imaginative/eccentric   824 picking on's teeth
the way he picks his teeth (ornate toothpicks were a mark of fashion)   830 Age old man
834 be'st . . . serious are able to understand important things   838 hand-fast arrested
fly flee, escape   842 wit . . . heavy ingenuity can make brutal   843 germane related
846 sheep-whistling rogue rascal who whistles to his sheep   ram-tender one who looks
after rams   offer attempt   847 grace favor at court

but that death is too soft for him, say I. Draw our throne
into a sheep-cote? All deaths are too few, the sharpest too
850 easy.

CLOWN   Has the old man e'er a son, sir, do you hear, an't like
you, sir?

AUTOLYCUS   He has a son, who shall be flayed alive, then
'nointed over with honey, set on the head of a wasp's nest,
855 then stand till he be three quarters and a dram dead, then
recovered again with aqua-vitae or some other hot infusion,
then, raw as he is, and in the hottest day prognostication
proclaims, shall he be set against a brick wall, the sun
looking with a southward eye upon him, where he is to
860 behold him with flies blown to death. But what talk we of
these traitorly rascals, whose miseries are to be smiled at,
their offences being so capital? Tell me, for you seem to
be honest plain men, what you have to the king. Being
something gently considered, I'll bring you where he is
865 aboard, tender your persons to his presence, whisper him in
your behalfs; and if it be in man besides the king to effect
your suits, here is man shall do it.

CLOWN   He seems to be of great authority. Close   *To Shepherd*
with him, give him gold; and though authority be a stubborn
870 bear, yet he is oft led by the nose with gold. Show the inside of
your purse to the outside of his hand, and no more ado.
Remember 'stoned' and 'flayed alive'.

SHEPHERD   An't please you, sir, to undertake the business for
us, here is that gold I have. I'll make it as much   *Offers gold*
875 more and leave this young man in pawn till I bring it you.

AUTOLYCUS   After I have done what I promised?

SHEPHERD   Ay, sir.

---

849 **sheep-cote** building sheltering sheep   854 **'nointed** anointed, covered   855 **dram**
tiny bit   856 **aqua-vitae** liquor   857 **prognostication proclaims** the calendar forecasts
860 **blown** swollen with flies' eggs (laid in wounds)   862 **capital** worthy of the death penalty
863 **to** to say to   **Being . . . considered** as I am deemed noble/esteemed at court   865 **tender**
offer, present   **him** in to him on   866 **man** any man   868 **Close** make a deal   874 **that**
what   875 **in pawn** as security

AUTOLYCUS   Well, give me the moiety.— Are you a   *Takes gold/To*
party in this business?   *Clown*

880   CLOWN   In some sort, sir. But though my case be a pitiful
one, I hope I shall not be flayed out of it.

AUTOLYCUS   O, that's the case of the shepherd's son. Hang him,
he'll be made an example.

CLOWN   Comfort, good comfort! We must to the   *To Shepherd*
885   king and show our strange sights. He must know 'tis none of
your daughter nor my sister. We are gone else. Sir, I will give
you as much as this old man does when the business is
performed, and remain, as he says, your pawn till it be
brought you.

890   AUTOLYCUS   I will trust you. Walk before toward the seaside. Go
on the right hand, I will but look upon the hedge and follow
you.

CLOWN   We are blest in this man, as I may say, even blest.

SHEPHERD   Let's before as he bids us. He was provided to do
895   us good.

[*Exeunt Shepherd and Clown*]

AUTOLYCUS   If I had a mind to be honest, I see fortune would
not suffer me. She drops booties in my mouth. I am courted
now with a double occasion: gold and a means to do the
prince my master good; which who knows how that may
900   turn back to my advancement? I will bring these two
moles, these blind ones, aboard him. If he think it fit to
shore them again and that the complaint they have to the
king concerns him nothing, let him call me rogue for being
so far officious, for I am proof against that title and what
905   shame else belongs to't. To him will I present them. There
may be matter in it.   *Exit*

---

878 **moiety** half   880 **case** circumstances/skin   886 **gone else** dead otherwise   890 **before**
ahead of me   891 **look . . . hedge** i.e. urinate   897 **suffer** allow   **booties** booty, benefits
courted wooed   898 **occasion** opportunity   901 **him** i.e. Florizel's ship   902 **shore them**
put them ashore   904 **officious** interfering   **proof against** impervious to   906 **matter**
serious business/reward

Act 5 Scene 1

Enter Leontes, Cleomenes, Dion, Paulina [and] Servants

CLEOMENES   Sir, you have done enough, and have performed
  A saint-like sorrow. No fault could you make,
  Which you have not redeemed; indeed, paid down
  More penitence than done trespass. At the last,
5 Do as the heavens have done, forget your evil.
  With them forgive yourself.

LEONTES Whilst I remember
  Her and her virtues, I cannot forget
  My blemishes in them, and so still think of
10 The wrong I did myself, which was so much
  That heirless it hath made my kingdom and
  Destroyed the sweet'st companion that e'er man
  Bred his hopes out of. True?

PAULINA Too true, my lord.
15 If, one by one, you wedded all the world,
  Or from the all that are took something good
  To make a perfect woman, she you killed
  Would be unparalleled.

LEONTES I think so. Killed?
20 She I killed? I did so: but thou strik'st me
  Sorely, to say I did. It is as bitter
  Upon thy tongue as in my thought. Now, good now,
  Say so but seldom.

CLEOMENES   Not at all, good lady.
25 You might have spoken a thousand things that would
  Have done the time more benefit and graced
  Your kindness better.

PAULINA You are one of those
  Would have him wed again.

5.1   *Location: Sicilia*   2 sorrow i.e. penitence   **3 paid . . . trespass** endured and
repented more than the sin warranted   **9 in them** with regard to them   **16 the . . . are** all
existing women   **22 good now** expression of entreaty   **26 done . . . benefit** been more
helpful

30   DION   If you would not so,
                You pity not the state, nor the remembrance
                Of his most sovereign name, consider little
                What dangers by his highness' fail of issue
                May drop upon his kingdom and devour
35   Incertain lookers on. What were more holy
                Than to rejoice the former queen is well?
                What holier than, for royalty's repair,
                For present comfort and for future good,
                To bless the bed of majesty again
40   With a sweet fellow to't?
          PAULINA   There is none worthy,
                Respecting her that's gone. Besides, the gods
                Will have fulfilled their secret purposes.
                For has not the divine Apollo said?
45   Is't not the tenor of his oracle,
                That King Leontes shall not have an heir
                Till his lost child be found? Which that it shall
                Is all as monstrous to our human reason
                As my Antigonus to break his grave
50   And come again to me, who, on my life,
                Did perish with the infant. 'Tis your counsel
                My lord should to the heavens be contrary,
                Oppose against their wills.— Care not for issue.   *To Leontes*
                The crown will find an heir. Great Alexander
55   Left his to th'worthiest, so his successor
                Was like to be the best.
          LEONTES   Good Paulina,
                Who hast the memory of Hermione,
                I know, in honour — O, that ever I
60   Had squared me to thy counsel! Then, even now,

---

32 sovereign name royal lineage, i.e. through an heir   **33 fail of issue** childlessness
35 Incertain lookers on subjects or spectators who are unsure and anxious about the future
36 well i.e. in heaven   **42 Respecting** compared to   **45 tenor** substance   **48 monstrous**
incredible, unnatural   **50 on my life** I am certain   **51 counsel** advice   **54 Great . . .**
th'worthiest Alexander the Great reportedly urged his followers simply to choose the worthiest
man as his successor   **60 squared me** conformed

I might have looked upon my queen's full eyes,
Have taken treasure from her lips—

PAULINA   And left them
More rich for what they yielded.

65 LEONTES   Thou speak'st truth.
No more such wives: therefore, no wife. One worse,
And better used, would make her sainted spirit
Again possess her corpse, and on this stage —
Where we offenders now — appear soul-vexed,
70 And begin, 'Why to me?'

PAULINA   Had she such power,
She had just such cause.

LEONTES   She had, and would incense me
To murder her I married.

75 PAULINA   I should so.
Were I the ghost that walked, I'd bid you mark
Her eye, and tell me for what dull part in't
You chose her. Then I'd shriek, that even your ears
Should rift to hear me and the words that followed
80 Should be 'Remember mine.'

LEONTES   Stars, stars,
And all eyes else dead coals! Fear thou no wife;
I'll have no wife, Paulina.

PAULINA   Will you swear
85 Never to marry but by my free leave?

LEONTES   Never, Paulina, so be blest my spirit!

PAULINA   Then, good my lords, bear witness to his oath.

CLEOMENES   You tempt him over-much.

PAULINA   Unless another,
90 As like Hermione as is her picture,
Affront his eye.

---

61 full perfect   **66 One . . . used** i.e. if I married an inferior woman and treated her better
(than Hermione)   **67 her** i.e. Hermione's   **68 and** i.e. and do so/and appear   **69 now**
i.e. now stand (or perhaps a printer's error for "mourn")   **soul-vexed** tormented (dying with
a troubled soul was thought to make the dead rise as ghosts)   **70 Why** i.e. why offer this insult
72 had would have   **75 should so** would also incite you to do so   **76 mark** note, observe
79 rift split   **80 mine** i.e. my eyes   **82 eyes else** other eyes   **85 leave** permission   **88 tempt**
test   **91 Affront** come before

CLEOMENES   Good madam—

PAULINA   I have done.

Yet, if my lord will marry — if you will, sir,
No remedy, but you will — give me the office
To choose you a queen. She shall not be so young
As was your former, but she shall be such
As, walked your first queen's ghost, it should take joy
To see her in your arms.

LEONTES   My true Paulina,

We shall not marry till thou bid'st us.

PAULINA   That

Shall be when your first queen's again in breath.
Never till then.

Enter a Servant

SERVANT   One that gives out himself Prince Florizel,
Son of Polixenes, with his princess, she
The fairest I have yet beheld, desires access
To your high presence.

LEONTES   What with him? He comes not

Like to his father's greatness. His approach,
So out of circumstance and sudden, tells us
'Tis not a visitation framed, but forced
By need and accident. What train?

SERVANT   But few,

And those but mean.

LEONTES   His princess, say you, with him?

SERVANT   Ay, the most peerless piece of earth, I think,
That e'er the sun shone bright on.

PAULINA   O, Hermione,

As every present time doth boast itself

---

95 **office** task, responsibility   98 **walked . . . ghost** were the ghost of Hermione to walk
104 *Servant* so called in Folio, but clearly a gentleman courtier (he has once written
poetry in praise of Hermione)   105 **gives out himself** claims to be   109 **What** i.e. what
attendants, company   111 **out of circumstance** without ceremony   112 **framed** planned
113 **accident** chance event   **train** retinue (has he with him)   115 **mean** humble
117 **peerless . . . earth** perfect mortal   120 **As . . . now** as every present moment claims to be
superior to what's past, so must you (Hermione) yield for the living

Above a better gone, so must thy grave
Give way to what's seen now! Sir, you yourself   *To Servant*
Have said and writ so, but your writing now
Is colder than that theme: 'She had not been,
125   Nor was not to be equalled.' Thus your verse
Flowed with her beauty once; 'tis shrewdly ebbed,
To say you have seen a better.

SERVANT   Pardon, madam.
The one I have almost forgot — your pardon —
130   The other, when she has obtained your eye,
Will have your tongue too. This is a creature,
Would she begin a sect, might quench the zeal
Of all professors else, make proselytes
Of who she but bid follow.

135   PAULINA   How? Not women?

SERVANT   Women will love her that she is a woman
More worth than any man: men that she is
The rarest of all women.

LEONTES   Go, Cleomenes.
140   Yourself, assisted with your honoured friends,
Bring them to our embracement.— Still, 'tis strange   *To Paulina*
He thus should steal upon us.   [*Exeunt Cleomenes and others*]

PAULINA   Had our prince,
Jewel of children, seen this hour, he had paired
145   Well with this lord, there was not full a month
Between their births.

LEONTES   Prithee no more; cease. Thou know'st
He dies to me again when talked of. Sure,
When I shall see this gentleman, thy speeches
150   Will bring me to consider that which may
Unfurnish me of reason. They are come.

Enter Cleomenes and others, [with] Florizel and Perdita

---

124 theme subject of your verses, i.e. the dead Hermione   **126 shrewdly ebbed** severely
lapsed/wisely receded   **129 one** i.e. Hermione   **131 tongue** praise   **133 professors else**
those dedicated to other religions   **proselytes** converts   **134 who** whoever   **143 prince**
i.e. the dead Mamillius   **145 full a** a full   **151 Unfurnish** deprive

Your mother was most true to wedlock, prince,   *To Florizel*
For she did print your royal father off,
Conceiving you. Were I but twenty-one,
155 Your father's image is so hit in you,
His very air, that I should call you brother,
As I did him, and speak of something wildly
By us performed before. Most dearly welcome!
And your fair princess — goddess! — O, alas!
160 I lost a couple, that 'twixt heaven and earth
Might thus have stood begetting wonder as
You, gracious couple, do. And then I lost —
All mine own folly — the society,
Amity too, of your brave father, whom,
165 Though bearing misery, I desire my life
Once more to look on him.

FLORIZEL   By his command
Have I here touched Sicilia and from him
Give you all greetings that a king, at friend,
170 Can send his brother, and but infirmity,
Which waits upon worn times hath something seized
His wished ability, he had himself
The lands and waters 'twixt your throne and his
Measured to look upon you, whom he loves —
175 He bade me say so — more than all the sceptres
And those that bear them living.

LEONTES   O, my brother —
Good gentleman! — the wrongs I have done thee stir
Afresh within me, and these thy offices,
180 So rarely kind, are as interpreters
Of my behind-hand slackness. Welcome hither,

---

153 print . . . off made an exact copy of Polixenes   155 hit exact   161 begetting producing
163 society company   164 Amity friendship   165 Though . . . him I desire to go on living,
however miserably, in order to see him once more   168 touched arrived in Sicilia/moved
Leontes   169 at friend in friendship   170 but were it not that   171 waits . . . times
accompanies old age   something . . . ability affected the strength he wishes he had
174 Measured traveled   175 sceptres . . . living i.e. living kings   179 offices kindnesses
180 rarely exceptionally   as . . . slackness reveal to me how remiss I have been

As is the spring to th'earth. And hath he too
Exposed this paragon to th'fearful usage,
At least ungentle, of the dreadful Neptune,
185   To greet a man not worth her pains, much less
Th'adventure of her person?

FLORIZEL   Good my lord,
She came from Libya.

LEONTES   Where the warlike Smalus,
190   That noble honoured lord, is feared and loved?

FLORIZEL   Most royal sir, from thence, from him whose
        daughter
His tears proclaimed his, parting with her: thence,
A prosperous south-wind friendly, we have crossed,
To execute the charge my father gave me
195   For visiting your highness. My best train
I have from your Sicilian shores dismissed,
Who for Bohemia bend, to signify
Not only my success in Libya, sir,
But my arrival and my wife's in safety
200   Here where we are.

LEONTES   The blessèd gods
Purge all infection from our air whilst you
Do climate here! You have a holy father,
A graceful gentleman, against whose person,
205   So sacred as it is, I have done sin,
For which the heavens, taking angry note,
Have left me issueless. And your father's blest,
As he from heaven merits it, with you,
Worthy his goodness. What might I have been,
210   Might I a son and daughter now have looked on,
Such goodly things as you.

---

183 paragon i.e. Perdita   **fearful usage** frightening treatment   **184 ungentle** rough
Neptune Roman god of the sea   **185 pains** trouble   **186 Th'adventure . . . person** risking of
her personal safety   **189 Smalus** no definitive source has been found for Smalus   **192 tears
proclaimed** grief at her departure demonstrated her to be   **194 execute** carry out   **charge**
duty/command   **197 bend** direct their course   **203 climate** spend time   **204 graceful** full of
divine grace   **207 issueless** childless   **209 his** of his

Enter a Lord

LORD   Most noble sir,
That which I shall report will bear no credit,
Were not the proof so nigh. Please you, great sir,
215   Bohemia greets you from himself by me.
Desires you to attach his son, who has —
His dignity and duty both cast off —
Fled from his father, from his hopes, and with
A shepherd's daughter.

220 LEONTES   Where's Bohemia? Speak.

LORD   Here in your city. I now came from him.
I speak amazedly, and it becomes
My marvel and my message. To your court
Whiles he was hast'ning, in the chase, it seems,
225   Of this fair couple, meets he on the way
The father of this seeming lady and
Her brother, having both their country quitted
With this young prince.

FLORIZEL   Camillo has betrayed me,
230   Whose honour and whose honesty till now
Endured all weathers.

LORD   Lay't so to his charge:
He's with the king your father.

LEONTES   Who? Camillo?

235 LORD   Camillo, sir. I spake with him, who now
Has these poor men in question. Never saw I
Wretches so quake. They kneel, they kiss the earth,
Forswear themselves as often as they speak.
Bohemia stops his ears, and threatens them
240   With divers deaths in death.

PERDITA   O, my poor father!

---

213 **bear no credit** seem unbelievable   214 **nigh** nearby   216 **attach** arrest   217 **dignity and duty** royal status and his duty to his father   222 **amazedly** in a state of amazement/confusedly, distractedly   **becomes My marvel** befits my astonishment   226 **seeming** apparent   232 **Lay't . . . charge** accuse him directly   236 **Has . . . question** is questioning these miserable/humble men (the Shepherd and the Clown)   238 **Forswear themselves** renounce what they have said   239 **stops** blocks   240 **divers** several

The heaven sets spies upon us, will not have
Our contract celebrated.

LEONTES   You are married?

245 FLORIZEL   We are not, sir, nor are we like to be.
The stars, I see, will kiss the valleys first:
The odds for high and low's alike.

LEONTES   My lord,
Is this the daughter of a king?

250 FLORIZEL   She is,
When once she is my wife.

LEONTES   That 'once' I see by your good father's speed
Will come on very slowly. I am sorry,
Most sorry, you have broken from his liking
255 Where you were tied in duty, and as sorry
Your choice is not so rich in worth as beauty,
That you might well enjoy her.

FLORIZEL   Dear, look up.   *To Perdita*
Though Fortune, visible an enemy,
260 Should chase us with my father, power no jot
Hath she to change our loves. Beseech you, sir,
Remember since you owed no more to time
Than I do now. With thought of such affections,
Step forth mine advocate. At your request
265 My father will grant precious things as trifles.

LEONTES   Would he do so, I'd beg your precious mistress,
Which he counts but a trifle.

PAULINA   Sir, my liege,
Your eye hath too much youth in't. Not a month
270 'Fore your queen died, she was more worth such gazes
Than what you look on now.

LEONTES   I thought of her,

---

243 **contract** betrothal   246 **kiss . . . first** i.e. fall to earth   247 **The . . . alike** random events
of fortune affect those of high and low birth regardless/it is as likely that the high and the low
should be united in marriage as it is that the stars will descend to earth   256 **worth** rank
258 **look up** i.e. keep your spirits up   262 **since . . . now** when you were no older than I am
now   264 **Step . . . advocate** come forward as my supporter   267 **trifle** toy/sexual whim of
yours

Even in these looks I made.— But your petition   *To Florizel*
Is yet unanswered. I will to your father.
275   Your honour not o'erthrown by your desires,
I am friend to them and you, upon which errand
I now go toward him: therefore follow me
And mark what way I make. Come, good my lord.   *Exeunt*

Act 5 Scene 2

Enter Autolycus and a Gentleman

AUTOLYCUS   Beseech you, sir, were you present at this relation?

FIRST GENTLEMAN   I was by at the opening of the fardel, heard the old shepherd deliver the manner how he found it: whereupon, after a little amazedness, we were all
5   commanded out of the chamber. Only this, methought I heard the shepherd say, he found the child.

AUTOLYCUS   I would most gladly know the issue of it.

FIRST GENTLEMAN   I make a broken delivery of the business; but the changes I perceived in the king and Camillo were very
10   notes of admiration. They seemed almost, with staring on one another, to tear the cases of their eyes. There was speech in their dumbness, language in their very gesture. They looked as they had heard of a world ransomed, or one destroyed. A notable passion of wonder appeared in them,
15   but the wisest beholder that knew no more but seeing, could not say if th'importance were joy or sorrow, but in the extremity of the one, it must needs be.

Enter another Gentleman

Here comes a gentleman that happily knows more. The news, Rogero?

---

273 **petition** request   275 **Your . . . desires** provided you have not let lust corrupt your honor (i.e. had sex)/provided your wishes are not incompatible with your status   278 **what . . . make** how far I succeed   **5.2   1 relation** account, narrative   **2 by** nearby   **5 chamber** room/royal presence   **7 issue** outcome (plays on the sense of "child")   **8 broken delivery** incomplete/confused report   10 **notes of admiration** marks of wonder   11 **cases . . . eyes** their eyelids (i.e. by staring in amazement)   **13 as** as if   16 **importance** meaning, import   17 **one** one or the other   18 **happily** perhaps

20   SECOND GENTLEMAN   Nothing but bonfires. The oracle is fulfilled. The king's daughter is found. Such a deal of wonder is broken out within this hour that ballad-makers cannot be able to express it.

Enter another Gentleman

Here comes the lady Paulina's steward. He can deliver you
25   more. How goes it now, sir? This news, which is called true, is so like an old tale that the verity of it is in strong suspicion. Has the king found his heir?

THIRD GENTLEMAN   Most true, if ever truth were pregnant by circumstance. That which you hear you'll swear you see,
30   there is such unity in the proofs. The mantle of Queen Hermione's, her jewel about the neck of it, the letters of Antigonus found with it which they know to be his character, the majesty of the creature in resemblance of the mother, the affection of nobleness which nature shows
35   above her breeding, and many other evidences proclaim her with all certainty to be the king's daughter. Did you see the meeting of the two kings?

SECOND GENTLEMAN   No.

THIRD GENTLEMAN   Then have you lost a sight which was to be
40   seen, cannot be spoken of. There might you have beheld one joy crown another, so and in such manner that it seemed sorrow wept to take leave of them, for their joy waded in tears. There was casting up of eyes, holding up of hands, with countenance of such distraction that they were to be
45   known by garment, not by favour. Our king, being ready to leap out of himself for joy of his found daughter, as if that joy were now become a loss, cries 'O, thy mother, thy mother!' Then asks Bohemia forgiveness, then embraces his son-in-law, then again worries he his daughter with
50   clipping her. Now he thanks the old shepherd, which stands

---

20 bonfires i.e. celebrations   **22 ballad-makers** ballads often provided accounts of contemporary scandals and events   **26 verity** truth   **28 pregnant by circumstance** proven by evidence   **30 mantle** loose sleeveless cloak   **33 character** handwriting   **34 affection of** instinct toward, disposition of   **44 countenance** facial expressions/behavior   **distraction** frenzy   **45 favour** face/appearance   **49 worries he** he harasses   **50 clipping** embracing by like a weather-bitten conduit of many kings' reigns. I never heard of such another encounter, which lames report to follow it and undoes description to do it.

SECOND GENTLEMAN   What, pray you, became of Antigonus, that
55   carried hence the child?

THIRD GENTLEMAN   Like an old tale still, which will have matter to rehearse, though credit be asleep and not an ear open: he was torn to pieces with a bear. This avouches the shepherd's son, who has not only his innocence, which seems much, to
60   justify him, but a handkerchief and rings of his that Paulina knows.

FIRST GENTLEMAN   What became of his bark and his followers?

THIRD GENTLEMAN   Wrecked the same instant of their master's death and in the view of the shepherd, so that all the
65   instruments which aided to expose the child were even then lost when it was found. But, O, the noble combat that 'twixt joy and sorrow was fought in Paulina! She had one eye declined for the loss of her husband, another elevated that the oracle was fulfilled. She lifted the princess from the earth,
70   and so locks her in embracing, as if she would pin her to her heart that she might no more be in danger of losing.

FIRST GENTLEMAN   The dignity of this act was worth the audience of kings and princes, for by such was it acted.

THIRD GENTLEMAN   One of the prettiest touches of all and that
75   which angled for mine eyes, caught the water though not the fish, was when, at the relation of the queen's death, with the manner how she came to't bravely confessed and lamented by the king, how attentiveness wounded his daughter, till, from one sign of dolour to another, she did,
80   with an 'Alas', I would fain say, bleed tears, for I am sure my

---

51 like . . . reigns (weeping) like a fountain that has endured the reigns of many kings
52 lames . . . it makes any account of it seem deficient   53 undoes defies   do express
57 rehearse recount   credit belief   58 with by   avouches vows   59 innocence simple-
mindedness, freedom from cunning   62 bark small ship   67 one . . . elevated
i.e. experienced a mixture of happiness and grief   71 losing being lost   74 prettiest
touches most ingenious/charming aspects   75 caught the water i.e. provoked tears
78 attentiveness intent listening   79 dolour grief   80 fain be compelled to

heart wept blood. Who was most marble there changed colour, some swooned, all sorrowed. If all the world could have seen't, the woe had been universal.

FIRST GENTLEMAN   Are they returned to the court?

85 THIRD GENTLEMAN   No. The princess hearing of her mother's statue, which is in the keeping of Paulina — a piece many years in doing and now newly performed by that rare Italian master, Julio Romano, who, had he himself eternity and could put breath into his work, would beguile nature of her

90 custom, so perfectly he is her ape. He so near to Hermione hath done Hermione that they say one would speak to her and stand in hope of answer. Thither with all greediness of affection are they gone, and there they intend to sup.

SECOND GENTLEMAN   I thought she had some great matter there

95 in hand, for she hath privately twice or thrice a day, ever since the death of Hermione visited that removèd house. Shall we thither and with our company piece the rejoicing?

FIRST GENTLEMAN   Who would be thence that has the benefit of access? Every wink of an eye some new grace will be born.

100 Our absence makes us unthrifty to our knowledge. Let's along.   Exeunt [Gentlemen]

AUTOLYCUS   Now, had I not the dash of my former life in me, would preferment drop on my head. I brought the old man and his son aboard the prince; told him I heard them talk

105 of a fardel and I know not what. But he at that time, overfond of the shepherd's daughter, so he then took her to be, who began to be much sea-sick, and himself little better, extremity of weather continuing, this mystery remained undiscovered. But 'tis all one to me, for had I been the finder

110 out of this secret, it would not have relished among my other discredits.

---

81 marble hard-hearted   87 newly performed recently completed   88 Julio Romano Italian painter who died in 1546, infamous for erotic works   89 beguile cheat   90 custom business ape mimic   91 done created   96 removèd isolated, remote   97 piece add to   98 thence away from there   99 grace wonder   100 unthrifty unprofitable, i.e. we waste an opportunity to add   102 dash trace   103 preferment promotion   104 the i.e. the ship of the 110 relished tasted well   111 discredits misdeeds

Enter Shepherd and Clown

Here come those I have done good to against my will, and
already appearing in the blossoms of their fortune.

SHEPHERD   Come, boy. I am past more children, but thy sons
and daughters will be all gentlemen born.

CLOWN   You are well met, sir. You denied to fight with me
this other day, because I was no gentleman born. See you
these clothes? Say you see them not and think me still no
gentleman born. You were best say these robes are not
gentlemen born. Give me the lie, do, and try whether I am
not now a gentleman born.

AUTOLYCUS   I know you are now, sir, a gentleman born.

CLOWN   Ay, and have been so any time these four hours.

SHEPHERD   And so have I, boy.

CLOWN   So you have, but I was a gentleman born before my
father, for the king's son took me by the hand, and called me
brother, and then the two kings called my father brother, and
then the prince my brother and the princess my sister called
my father father; and so we wept, and there was the first
gentleman-like tears that ever we shed.

SHEPHERD   We may live, son, to shed many more.

CLOWN   Ay, or else 'twere hard luck, being in so preposterous
estate as we are.

AUTOLYCUS   I humbly beseech you, sir, to pardon me all the
faults I have committed to your worship and to give me your
good report to the prince my master.

SHEPHERD   Prithee, son, do, for we must be gentle, now we are
gentlemen.

CLOWN   Thou wilt amend thy life?

AUTOLYCUS   Ay, an it like your good worship.

CLOWN   Give me thy hand. I will swear to the prince thou art
as honest a true fellow as any is in Bohemia.

SHEPHERD   You may say it, but not swear it.

---

113 blossoms full flowering   **117 this** the   **120 Give . . . lie** insult me so that I may challenge
you to a duel   **try** find out   **132 preposterous** utterly absurd; the Clown means to say
"prosperous"   **135 give . . . report** speak well of me   **137 gentle** noble/kind

CLOWN   Not swear it, now I am a gentleman? Let boors and
145   franklins say it, I'll swear it.

SHEPHERD   How if it be false, son?

CLOWN   If it be ne'er so false, a true gentleman may swear it
       in the behalf of his friend, and I'll swear to the prince thou
       art a tall fellow of thy hands and that thou wilt not be drunk.
150   But I know thou art no tall fellow of thy hands and that thou
       wilt be drunk. But I'll swear it, and I would thou wouldst be
       a tall fellow of thy hands.

AUTOLYCUS   I will prove so, sir, to my power.

CLOWN   Ay, by any means prove a tall fellow. If I do not
155   wonder how thou dar'st venture to be drunk, not being a tall
       fellow, trust me not. Hark, the kings and the princes, our
       kindred, are going to see the queen's picture. Come, follow
       us. We'll be thy good masters.   *Exeunt*

Act 5 Scene 3   *running scene 14*

*Enter Leontes, Polixenes, Florizel, Perdita, Camillo, Paulina, Lords and
Attendants*

LEONTES   O grave and good Paulina, the great comfort
       That I have had of thee!

PAULINA   What, sovereign sir,
       I did not well I meant well. All my services
5   You have paid home. But that you have vouchsafed,
       With your crowned brother and these your contracted
       Heirs of your kingdoms, my poor house to visit,
       It is a surplus of your grace, which never
       My life may last to answer.

---

144 boors peasants   **145 franklins** landowners ranking below the gentry   **147 ne'er so false**
completely false   **148 in** on   **149 tall . . . hands** brave/fine man   **151 would** wish   **153 to**
my power as far as I can (perhaps implying his skill at using his **hands** for picking pockets)
157 picture likeness, statue   **5.3   1 grave** wise   **3 What** whatever   **5 paid home** rewarded
fully   **vouchsafed** agreed, granted kindly   **6 contracted** betrothed   **8 which . . . answer**
which for all my life I shall not be able to repay

10 **LEONTES**   O Paulina,
We honour you with trouble. But we came
To see the statue of our queen. Your gallery
Have we passed through, not without much content
In many singularities, but we saw not
15 That which my daughter came to look upon,
The statue of her mother.

PAULINA   As she lived peerless,
So her dead likeness, I do well believe,
Excels whatever yet you looked upon
20 Or hand of man hath done: therefore I keep it
Lonely, apart. But here it is. Prepare
To see the life as lively mocked as ever
Still sleep mocked death. Behold, and say   *Paulina draws a curtain*
    'tis well.   *and reveals*
I like your silence, it the more shows off   *Hermione standing*
25 Your wonder. But yet speak. First, you, my liege,   *like a statue*
Comes it not something near?

LEONTES   Her natural posture!
Chide me, dear stone, that I may say indeed
Thou art Hermione; or rather, thou art she
30 In thy not chiding, for she was as tender
As infancy and grace. But yet, Paulina,
Hermione was not so much wrinkled, nothing
So agèd as this seems.

POLIXENES   O, not by much.

35 **PAULINA**   So much the more our carver's excellence.
Which lets go by some sixteen years and makes her
As she lived now.

LEONTES   As now she might have done,

---

11 **trouble** i.e. demands on your hospitality   12 **gallery** long, large room   13 **content**
pleasure   14 **singularities** objects of note   21 **Lonely** separate (Folio's "Louely" is conceivably
correct, but a printer's error much more likely)   22 **lively mocked** realistically imitated
23 **Still** motionless   **well** well done   26 **something near** somewhat close to resembling her
37 **As** as if

So much to my good comfort, as it is
40   Now piercing to my soul. O, thus she stood,
Even with such life of majesty, warm life,
As now it coldly stands, when first I wooed her!
I am ashamed. Does not the stone rebuke me
For being more stone than it? O royal piece,
45   There's magic in thy majesty, which has
My evils conjured to remembrance and
From thy admiring daughter took the spirits,
Standing like stone with thee.

PERDITA   And give me leave,
50   And do not say 'tis superstition, that
I kneel and then implore her blessing.— Lady,   *Kneels before the*
Dear queen, that ended when I but began,   *statue*
Give me that hand of yours to kiss.

PAULINA   O, patience!   *Prevents Perdita from touching*
55   The statue is but newly fixed; the colour's   *Perdita stands?*
    not dry.

CAMILLO   My lord, your sorrow was too sore laid on,
Which sixteen winters cannot blow away,
So many summers dry. Scarce any joy
Did ever so long live; no sorrow
60   But killed itself much sooner.

POLIXENES   Dear my brother,
Let him that was the cause of this have power
To take off so much grief from you as he
Will piece up in himself.

65   PAULINA   Indeed, my lord,
If I had thought the sight of my poor image
Would thus have wrought you — for the stone is mine —
I'd not have showed it.

LEONTES   Do not draw the curtain.

---

44 stone hard-hearted/dead (from grief)   **47 admiring** full of wonder   **spirits** vital energies
50 superstition idolatry   **55 fixed** painted   **56 sore** painfully/severely   **58 So . . . dry** and
an equal number of summers cannot dry up   **62 cause** i.e. himself   **64 piece up in** add to
67 wrought moved, affected

70 PAULINA   No longer shall you gaze on't, lest your fancy
          May think anon it moves.

    LEONTES   Let be, let be.
          Would I were dead, but that methinks already —
          What was he that did make it?— See, my lord,
75   Would you not deem it breathed? And that those veins
          Did verily bear blood?

    POLIXENES   Masterly done.
          The very life seems warm upon her lip.

    LEONTES   The fixture of her eye has motion in't,
80   As we are mocked with art.

    PAULINA   I'll draw the curtain.
          My lord's almost so far transported that
          He'll think anon it lives.

    LEONTES   O, sweet Paulina,
85   Make me to think so twenty years together!
          No settled senses of the world can match
          The pleasure of that madness. Let't alone.

    PAULINA   I am sorry, sir, I have thus far stirred you, but
          I could afflict you farther.

90 LEONTES   Do, Paulina,
          For this affliction has a taste as sweet
          As any cordial comfort. Still, methinks
          There is an air comes from her. What fine chisel
          Could ever yet cut breath? Let no man mock me,
95   For I will kiss her.

    PAULINA   Good my lord, forbear:
          The ruddiness upon her lip is wet.
          You'll mar it if you kiss it, stain your own
          With oily painting. Shall I draw the curtain?

100 LEONTES   No, not these twenty years.

    PERDITA   So long could I
          Stand by, a looker-on.

---

70 **fancy** imagination   76 **verily** truly   79 **fixture** fixed setting   **motion** movement, life
82 **transported** entranced   86 **settled senses** calm state of mind in   87 **Let't** leave it
92 **cordial** restorative, beneficial to the heart   93 **air . . . her** she seems to breathe
97 **ruddiness** rosy color   98 **mar** spoil

PAULINA   Either forbear,
Quit presently the chapel, or resolve you
105 For more amazement. If you can behold it,
I'll make the statue move indeed, descend
And take you by the hand. But then you'll think —
Which I protest against — I am assisted
By wicked powers.
110 LEONTES   What you can make her do,
I am content to look on. What to speak,
I am content to hear, for 'tis as easy
To make her speak as move.
PAULINA   It is required
115 You do awake your faith. Then all stand still.
On: those that think it is unlawful business
I am about, let them depart.
LEONTES   Proceed:
No foot shall stir.
120 PAULINA   Music; awake her: strike!   *Music*
'Tis time: descend: be stone no more: approach: *To Hermione*
Strike all that look upon with marvel. Come,
I'll fill your grave up. Stir. Nay, come away.
Bequeath to death your numbness, for from him
125 Dear life redeems you.— You perceive she stirs.
Start not. Her actions shall be holy as   *Hermione comes down*
You hear my spell is lawful. Do not shun her
Until you see her die again, for then
You kill her double. Nay, present your hand:
130 When she was young you wooed her, now in age
Is she become the suitor?
LEONTES   O, she's warm!   *Touches her*
If this be magic, let it be an art
Lawful as eating.

---

103 forbear restrain yourself, withdraw   **104 presently** immediately   **chapel** room set aside
for worship   **resolve you** prepare yourself   **109 wicked powers** witchcraft   **116 On** onward
120 strike strike up (sense then shifts to "affect")   **123 fill . . . up** i.e. bring you back to life
124 him i.e. death   **128 for . . . double** by shunning her in this new life, you would kill her
again   **131 Is . . . suitor?** i.e. Must she take your hand?

135   POLIXENES   She embraces him.

      CAMILLO   She hangs about his neck.
      If she pertain to life let her speak too.

      POLIXENES   Ay, and make it manifest where she has lived,
      Or how stol'n from the dead.

140   PAULINA   That she is living,
      Were it but told you, should be hooted at
      Like an old tale. But it appears she lives,
      Though yet she speak not. Mark a little while.—
      Please you to interpose, fair madam. Kneel   *To Perdita*

145   And pray your mother's blessing.— Turn,   *To Hermione*
        good lady,
      Our Perdita is found.

      HERMIONE   You gods, look down
      And from your sacred vials pour your graces
      Upon my daughter's head!— Tell me, mine own.

150   Where hast thou been preserved? Where lived? How found
      Thy father's court? For thou shalt hear that I,
      Knowing by Paulina that the oracle
      Gave hope thou wast in being, have preserved
      Myself to see the issue.

155   PAULINA   There's time enough for that,
      Lest they desire upon this push to trouble
      Your joys with like relation. Go together,
      You precious winners all. Your exultation
      Partake to every one. I, an old turtle,

160   Will wing me to some withered bough and there
      My mate, that's never to be found again,
      Lament till I am lost.

      LEONTES   O, peace, Paulina!
      Thou shouldst a husband take by my consent,

165   As I by thine a wife. This is a match,

---

137 pertain to life is truly alive   **138 make it manifest** explain   **141 hooted** jeered
150 preserved kept alive, protected   **153 in being** alive   **154 issue** outcome/child
156 they . . . relation at this crucial moment others trouble your happiness by relating their
own stories   **159 Partake** extend   **turtle** turtledove, thought to mate for life   **161 mate**
i.e. Antigonus   **162 lost** dead   **165 match** contract

And made between's by vows. Thou hast found mine —
But how, is to be questioned, for I saw her,
As I thought, dead, and have in vain said many
A prayer upon her grave. I'll not seek far —
170   For him, I partly know his mind — to find thee
An honourable husband.— Come, Camillo,
And take her by the hand, whose worth and honesty
Is richly noted and here justified
By us, a pair of kings.— Let's from this place.—
175   What? Look upon my brother.— Both your   *To Hermione,*
     pardons,   *then also Polixenes*
That e'er I put between your holy looks
My ill suspicion. This your son-in-law,
And son unto the king, whom, heavens directing,
Is troth-plight to your daughter.— Good Paulina,
180   Lead us from hence, where we may leisurely
Each one demand, and answer to his part
Performed in this wide gap of time since first
We were dissevered. Hastily, lead away.   *Exeunt*

---

166 between's between us   **170 For** as for   **173 justified** confirmed, acknowledged
179 troth-plight betrothed   **181 demand** question   **183 dissevered** divided

TEXTUAL NOTES

F = First Folio text of 1623, the only authority for the play
F2 = a correction introduced in the Second Folio text of 1632
Ed = a correction introduced by a later editor
SH = speech heading (i.e. speaker's name)

F includes list of parts ("The Names of the Actors") at end of text

1.2.3 burden *spelled* Burthen *in* F **126 And** = F2. F = A **188 do** = Ed. F =
  do's **241 they say** = F2. F = say **318 hobby-horse** = Ed. F = Holy-Horse
2.1.6 SH FIRST LADY = Ed. F = *Lady*
2.3.45 What = F2. F = Who
3.2.10 Silence = Ed. F *prints as a stage direction*
3.3.71 bairn *spelled* barne *in* F **114 made** = Ed. F = mad
4.3.1 SH AUTOLYCUS = Ed. *Not in* F **35 counters** *spelled* Compters *in* F
  53 offends = F2. F = offend
4.4.13 Digest it = F2. F = Digest **14 swoon** = Ed. F = sworne **113 your** =
  F2. F = you **184 out** = Ed. F = on't **241 SH AUTOLYCUS** = Ed. *Not in*
  F **264 kiln** *spelled* kill *in* F **358 square** *spelled* squire *in* F **459 acknowledged** = F2. F = acknowledge **463 who** = F2. F = whom **469 shalt
  see** = Ed. F = shalt neuer see **480 hoop** = Ed. F = hope **550 whom** =
  F2. F = who **710 flayed** *spelled* fled *in* F **806 or** = F2. F = at
5.1.93 SH PAULINA = Ed. *Assigned to Cleomenes in* F
5.3.21 Lonely = Ed. F = Louely

1. This engraving, the frontispiece to Francis Kirkman's *The Wits* (1672–73), depicts a number of famous dramatic characters, with Sir John Falstaff and the Hostess in the foreground, but it is most interesting for showing what a curtained "discovery space" at the back of the stage may have looked like: Hermione posed as the statue would have been revealed when Paulina drew the curtain. The space would also have been used when Prospero "discovers" Miranda and Ferdinand playing chess at the climax of *The Tempest*.

SCENE-BY-SCENE ANALYSIS

ACT 1 SCENE 1

Archidamus and Camillo discuss the relationship between Bohemia and Sicilia. Archidamus comments on the "great difference" between the kingdoms. The deliberate placing of Sicilia and Bohemia at "the ends of opposed winds" leads the way for other "opposites" in the play, such as court versus country and comedy versus tragedy.

ACT 1 SCENE 2

Lines 1–131: Polixenes intends to return home after a nine-month visit to Sicilia. Leontes begs him to stay. Their exchange is courtly, emphasizing the public nature of their roles and the setting, although their references to each other as "brother" suggest a deep personal friendship. Leontes draws his pregnant wife, Hermione, into the conversation and she adds her own pleas that Polixenes will stay. Her language is playful and affectionate toward both men as she reminds them of their childhood friendship. Polixenes' response is lighthearted as he describes himself and Leontes as "twinned lambs that did frisk i'th'sun," an image of innocence (and perhaps a harbinger of its loss). Although Hermione joins in with his banter, Leontes' responses are markedly brief. Polixenes agrees to stay and Leontes says that his wife has only spoken "once" "To better purpose," which was when she agreed to be his "for ever" by marrying him. Polixenes and Hermione walk apart and Leontes watches them.

Lines 132–244: Leontes' aside reveals the intense emotions that have been concealed by his courtly manner. He shows his suspicion and jealousy of Polixenes and Hermione, observing that their relationship is "Too hot, too hot!" (one of many motifs linked to heat and coldness). Although there seems little evidence, he has convinced himself that they are having an affair, and his anger is evident in his disjointed speech and base sexual imagery. He turns to his son, Mamillius, and asks if he is indeed his "calf." The boy responds art-lessly, emphasizing his childhood innocence in comparison to the jealousies of the adult world. Leontes finds some reassurance in the boy's similarity to himself. Polixenes and Hermione notice that he is "unsettled," but he denies it, commenting on Mamillius' similarity to himself as a child, and inquiring after Polixenes' own son. He says that he will walk with Mamillius and asks Hermione to entertain Polixenes, commenting aside that he is "angling now," introducing the motif of entrapment. He watches them, jealously interpreting their smallest actions as signs of love. Camillo arrives and Leontes sends Mamillius away.

Lines 245–403: Leontes informs Camillo that Polixenes "will yet stay longer." Camillo innocently comments that it was Hermione who made him change his mind. Leontes' aside shows that he assumes that the whole court is "whisp'ring" about him. He con-fuses Camillo with questions about Polixenes and court rumors, before telling him his suspicions. Leontes insists that Camillo must have heard talk about his "slippery" wife, but Camillo is shocked and refuses to hear his "sovereign mistress clouded so." He urges Leontes to be "cured / Of this diseased opinion," raising a recurring motif of sickness. Leontes asks Camillo to poison his friend. Camillo refuses, reiterating his belief in Hermione's innocence, but Leontes flies into a rage and Camillo agrees, but only on condition that Leontes return afterward to a normal relationship with Hermione. Camillo urges Leontes to show "a countenance as clear / As friendship wears at feasts," raising the motif of deceptive appearances.

Lines 404–532: Alone, Camillo considers his dilemma: he must either kill Polixenes (thus committing regicide) or be disloyal to his king. As he muses that either option means "a break-neck" for him, Polixenes arrives. He is confused, as Leontes has just walked away without speaking to him. He questions Camillo, whose ambiguous reply of "I dare not know" rouses his suspicions. Polixenes demands that Camillo tell him the truth and Camillo confesses that he has been appointed to murder Polixenes by Leontes, who believes that he has "touched his queen / Forbiddenly." He believes Polixenes when he protests his innocence, but points out that it would be easier to stop the tides than convince Leontes. Camillo suggests that Polixenes leave quickly, and that he will help him depart in secret if Polixenes will take him into his service. Polixenes agrees.

ACT 2 SCENE 1

Lines 1–42: Hermione's attendants tease Mamillius. Hermione asks Mamillius to tell her a "merry" story, but he says that "A sad tale's best for winter," drawing attention to the play's title, and the opposing genres of comedy and tragedy. As he begins to whisper the story in his mother's ear (a visual reminder of the imagined rumors in the previous scene), Leontes arrives.

Lines 43–147: Leontes takes Polixenes' and Camillo's departure as proof of his suspicions. His paranoia seems to be escalating as he claims that not only did they conceal the supposed affair, but that there is "a plot" against his "life" and his "crown." He tells an attendant to take Mamillius away before accusing Hermione of being pregnant with Polixenes' child. Astonished, Hermione denies it, but Leontes makes a public declaration of her adultery and treachery. He orders that she be taken "to prison." Hermione reiterates her innocence. Remaining dignified and calm, she asks the assembled lords to judge her with "thoughts so qualified as your charities" and requests that her ladies may attend her in prison as she is so heavily pregnant.

Lines 148–232: Antigonus warns Leontes that his whole family will "suffer" if he is wrong. The Lords state their belief in Hermione's innocence and Antigonus suggests that "some putter-on" has deceived Leontes. Leontes will not listen and tells them that he has sent Cleomenes and Dion to the oracle of Apollo's temple in "sacred Delphos." He claims that the oracle's "spiritual counsel" will reveal the truth.

ACT 2 SCENE 2

Antigonus' wife, Paulina, arrives at the prison. Her outspoken character is evident as she criticizes the rules that prevent her from seeing the queen. She asks to speak to one of Hermione's attendants and the jailer goes to fetch Emilia, who brings news that Hermione has given birth to a daughter. Emilia reports that Hermione says that she is as innocent as her newborn child, reinforcing the oppositions of innocence/guilt and childhood/adulthood that were established earlier. Paulina curses the "unsafe lunes" of the king and decides that she will tell him of his daughter's birth. She tells Emilia to ask Hermione if she may take the baby to Leontes, suggesting that "he may soften at the sight o'th'child." Emilia says that Hermione has had the same idea, and goes to ask.

ACT 2 SCENE 3

Lines 1–45: Leontes reveals that he has not rested "Nor night nor day" and his fragmented speech and violent imagery show his disordered mind. He regrets that Polixenes "the harlot king" is safe "beyond" his reach, but comments that Hermione is not: he can "hook" her to him and have his revenge. A servant brings news of Mamillius, who is unwell. Leontes blames Mamillius' sickness on his mother's "dishonour" and sends the servant back to his son. As his thoughts return to paranoia and revenge, Paulina enters, carrying the baby. The Lords try to keep her away, saying that Leontes has not slept and does not wish to be disturbed. She points out that their indulgence of Leontes' whims will just "Nourish the cause of his awaking." Insisting that she will speak to him "with words as medicinal as true," she addresses Leontes.

Lines 46–157: Leontes blames Antigonus for Paulina's intrusion, asking if he cannot "rule" his wife, raising issues of power and patriarchy and his own desire for control over Hermione. Paulina reports that the "good queen" has given birth to a daughter, and lays the baby before Leontes. Furious, Leontes commands Antigonus to pick up the "bastard" and give it to Paulina, but Paulina forbids her husband to touch the "princess." When Antigonus obeys his wife, Leontes mocks him and calls everyone "a nest of traitors." He orders that both Paulina and the baby should be burned. Paulina draws the Lords' attention to the fact that the baby is "a copy" of Leontes, emotively describing the fragile perfection of the child as she does so. Leontes orders Antigonus to remove his wife from the chamber, but Paulina remains in control, insisting that she will go of her own accord.

Lines 158–242: Leontes accuses Antigonus of treachery and orders him to take the baby away and burn it within the hour, or he himself will "dash out" its "bastard brains." The Lords beg Leontes to spare the baby. Leontes asks Antigonus what he will do to save the baby's life, and Antigonus bravely replies "Anything," declaring that he would die "To save the innocent." Leontes makes him swear an oath and orders him to take the baby to "some remote and desert place" and abandon it there. Antigonus, bound by his oath, leaves with the child. A servant brings the news that Cleomenes and Dion have returned from the oracle. Leontes orders a public trial for Hermione.

ACT 3 SCENE 1

Cleomenes and Dion discuss the beauty and calmness of Delphos, a contrast to the tension and conflict in the Sicilian court. They hope that the sealed proclamation from Apollo will prove "successful to the queen."

ACT 3 SCENE 2

Lines 1–128: Leontes admits that the trial of Hermione "pushes" against his heart. He expresses his desire that a public trial will clear him of "being tyrannous." Hermione is brought in, accompanied by her attendants and Paulina. The indictment against her is read: she is accused of treason "in committing adultery with Polixenes," of "conspiring with Camillo" to kill Leontes, and of helping Camillo and Polixenes to escape. Hermione responds by pointing out that, as her integrity is already "counted falsehood," her plea of "Not guilty" will not be believed. She insists that the "powers divine" know her innocence. Leontes accuses her of bearing "a bastard by Polixenes" and informs her that the baby has been "cast out." He tells her to "Look for no less than death." Hermione claims that she does not fear dying, as it cannot be any worse than her current suffering, and calls upon the judgment of Apollo. The oracle's proclamation is sent for.

Lines 129–163: Cleomenes and Dion bring in the proclamation, which declares that "Hermione is chaste, Polixenes blameless, Camillo a true subject" and that Leontes is "a jealous tyrant." Everyone is relieved, but Leontes declares the proclamation to be a "falsehood" and insists that the trial continue. As he does so, a servant brings the news that Mamillius is dead. Suddenly, Leontes sees that he has been wrong and unjust: Mamillius' death is Apollo's judgment upon him. Hermione faints and is carried out as Leontes declares that he has "too much believed [his] own suspicion."

Lines 164–260: As Leontes realizes the full extent of his wrongs, Paulina launches an attack on the "tyranny" and "jealousies" that have led Leontes to betray Polixenes and poison "Camillo's honour." She reminds him that he has cast "forth to the crows" his baby daughter and that his son is dead, before revealing that Hermione has also died. She tells Leontes to "despair," as no amount of prayer will "move the gods" to look favorably upon him. Leontes accepts Paulina's criticism, but a Lord tells her to "Say no more." Paulina relents when she sees that Leontes "is touched / To th'noble heart" and asks him to forgive her. She promises never to speak again of Hermione or the children, or of Antigonus, whom she says is "lost too." Leontes replies that he prefers her to speak the truth than to show him pity. He declares that Hermione and Mamillius are to be buried together and that he will mourn them daily.

ACT 3 SCENE 3

This scene is pivotal, marking a shift in action from Sicilia to Bohemia, court to country, and tragedy to comedy.

Lines 1–61: Antigonus, carrying the baby, arrives on the shores of Bohemia. The mariner who has brought him returns to the ship, warning Antigonus that there is a storm brewing and that the coastline is "famous" for predatory animals. Antigonus addresses the baby gently, telling her that he had a dream in which Hermione's ghost appeared to him. The ghost told him that the baby was to be called Perdita, and that he was to leave her in Bohemia. For his role in "this ungentle business" he is destined never to see Paulina again. He believes Hermione must have died and that Perdita must be the "issue" of Polixenes after all. Although his "heart bleeds," he bids Perdita farewell. The storm increases and Antigonus hears a roar. He exits, pursued by a bear.

Lines 62–128: A Shepherd enters, and a change is immediately apparent through his gently humorous ramblings in prose that contrast with Antigonus' tragic blank verse. He is considering the problems of adolescence, such as "getting wenches with child," when he finds Perdita. He assumes that she is the result of an affair, "some behind-door-work," an ironic echo of Leontes' earlier suspicions. He picks up the baby and waits for his son, the Clown. The Clown arrives and gives a muddled account of the shipwreck and Antigonus being killed by the bear, rendering these tragic events comic through his confusion. The Shepherd comments that while his son "met'st with things dying," he himself met "with things newborn," emphasizing the play's shift away from tragedy and death to comedy and regeneration. They find clothes that suggest the baby's high status, and also gold, which they believe has been left by the fairies with the "changeling" child. They decide to keep the baby and the gold, and to bury the remains of Antigonus.

ACT 4 SCENE 1

The meta-theatrical figure of "Time" acts as Chorus, moving the events of the play on by sixteen years.

ACT 4 SCENE 2

Camillo wishes to return to Sicilia, but Polixenes asks him not to, a conversation that evokes that of Polixenes and Leontes at the beginning of the play, one of several such echoes. Polixenes cannot bear to hear Sicilia mentioned as it reminds him of the past's tragic events.

Their conversation turns to Prince Florizel, who has recently been neglecting his "princely exercises." They have heard that he spends his time at the home of a Shepherd "who hath a daughter of most rare note." Polixenes observes that she must be the "angle" (hook) that "plucks" Florizel to the cottage. He decides that they will go in disguise to question the Shepherd.

ACT 4 SCENE 3

Autolycus' song of the spring contrasts with the sad "winter's tale" told by Mamillius in Act 2 Scene 1. It reinforces the rural setting of Bohemia, as well as the theme of regeneration. The sexual innuendo generates comedy and illustrates Autolycus' robust character. Autolycus tells us that he used to be in service of Florizel, but that he now makes his living as a petty thief and con man. He sees the Clown approaching and decides to set a "springe" (trap) for him. The Clown is distracted, trying to remember what he has been sent to buy for the "sheep-shearing feast." Autolycus lies on the ground, groaning and asking for help. He tells the Clown that he has been robbed and that his attackers left him in the "detestable" rags that he is wearing. Concerned, the Clown helps Autolycus up and, as he does so, Autolycus picks his pocket. Ironically, the Clown offers Autolycus money, which he refuses. The Clown asks who attacked him, and with further comic irony, Autolycus describes himself. After the Clown has left, he vows to attend the sheep-shearing and leaves, singing once more.

ACT 4 SCENE 4

Lines 1–62: Florizel, dressed as a shepherd and calling himself "Doricles," compliments Perdita on her costume for the festival. She comments on their reversed roles, raising the issue of status: he has "obscured" his status with "a swain's wearing," and she, a "lowly maid" is "Most goddess-like pranked up," creating dramatic irony as we are aware of her true status. This change in costume establishes the use of disguises throughout the scene, generating comedy and reinforcing the motif of false appearance. Florizel reassures Perdita that his intentions toward her are honorable: his "lusts" do not "Burn hotter" than his "faith." They are interrupted by the arrival of the guests, including Polixenes and Camillo in disguise.

Lines 63–240: Urged by the Shepherd, Perdita welcomes the guests to the sheep-shearing. She distributes flowers to everyone, including the "winter" flowers of "rosemary and rue" to Polixenes and Camillo. She discusses cross-pollinating flowers and the marrying of "A gentler scion to the wildest stock" with Polixenes, reflecting the apparent circumstances in her relationship with Florizel. Perdita and Florizel move aside. Polixenes comments on Perdita's beauty to Camillo and observes that she seems to be "Too noble for this place." The Clown, Mopsa, and Dorcas begin the dance and, as they watch, Polixenes questions the Shepherd about the "fair swain" who is courting his daughter. The Shepherd informs him that Doricles owns rich grazing land. A servant brings news that there is a "pedlar at the door" and Autolycus is shown in, disguised.

Lines 241–344: Autolycus sings an enticing song about his wares, and a comic, bawdy exchange ensues among Mopsa, Dorcas, Autolycus, and the Clown, who fails to recognize Autolycus as the man who "cozened" him. Mopsa and Dorcas join Autolycus in song and the Clown leads them away, offering to buy gifts for both girls.

Lines 345–506: Further entertainment arrives and, as they watch, Polixenes tells Camillo that it is "time to part" Florizel and Perdita. He speaks to Florizel, pretending not to recognize him. Florizel, not recognizing his father, takes Perdita's hand and asks Polixenes to be "witness" to what he is about to say. He makes a public declaration of his love for Perdita. The Shepherd declares that he gives his daughter to Florizel and will "make / Her portion equal to his." As Florizel urges the Shepherd to make their betrothal formal, Polixenes interrupts, asking if Florizel's father knows and suggests that Florizel is wrong not to inform him. Polixenes reveals his true identity, furious with Florizel for attempting to contract a marriage with "a sheephook." He accuses the Shepherd of treachery, the punishment for which is execution, and threatens to have Perdita's beauty "scratched with briers." He forbids Florizel to have any more to do with Perdita, under threat of disinheritance. Polixenes leaves. The Shepherd also vents his anger at the couple before storming out.

Lines 507–667: Florizel guesses Camillo's true identity. Camillo advises him to avoid Polixenes until he has calmed down. Florizel reassures Perdita and declares that he will marry her, even if it means giving up the succession to the throne. He announces his intention to leave Bohemia. Camillo suggests that they go to Sicilia where Florizel can introduce Perdita as his princess and pretend that he has come in reconciliation from Polixenes. Florizel agrees, and Camillo promises to provide him with clothes and attendants. As they draw aside to discuss matters, Autolycus returns.

Lines 668–744: Autolycus is congratulating himself on the number of purses that he has stolen at the shearing. Camillo, Perdita, and Florizel see him and ask him to exchange clothes with Florizel, which he does. Camillo advises Perdita to "disliken / The truth of your own seeming," reminding us that, ironically, her true identity has already been concealed once. Camillo's aside reveals that he intends to tell Polixenes of the lovers' destination, forcing the king to sail to Sicilia, taking Camillo with him. He leaves, as Florizel and Perdita head for the coast.

Lines 745–906: As Autolycus contemplates what he has just witnessed, the Shepherd and the Clown approach. Autolycus stands aside to listen. The Clown urges his father to tell the king that Perdita is "a changeling," not of his "flesh and blood," and that therefore he should not be punished for her actions. As they leave for the palace they are stopped by Autolycus, whom they mistake for a "courtier." Autolycus tells them that Polixenes has boarded a ship and offers to direct them to it. The Shepherd gives him gold in return and they set out, Autolycus revealing aside his intention to do good by his old master, Florizel—and to win some gold for himself by doing so.

ACT 5 SCENE 1

Lines 1–151: In Sicilia, Cleomenes assures Leontes that he has grieved long enough. Leontes will not forgive himself. He is supported by Paulina who, outspoken as ever, reminds him that he "killed" a woman of "unparalleled" goodness. Throughout the scene she continues to remind him of his wife and children. The Lords urge Leontes to marry again, concerned that Sicilia should have an heir, but Paulina reminds them that Apollo has decreed that "King Leontes shall not have an heir / Till his lost child be found." She urges Leontes not to marry again, and he agrees not to without Paulina's "free leave." A servant brings the news that Florizel and his princess have asked to see Leontes. Aware of the absence of state formality surrounding the visit, Leontes wonders whether Florizel has come there out of "need and accident." He sends Cleomenes to fetch them.

Lines 152–278: Leontes greets Florizel, commenting on his likeness to Polixenes. He praises Perdita's beauty and reflects sadly on his own lost children. Florizel presents greetings from Polixenes, pretending that "infirmity" prevents his father from coming in person. As Leontes expresses his pleasure at seeing them, a Lord interrupts with a message from Polixenes, revealing the truth about the couple's flight from Bohemia and demanding that Leontes arrest Florizel. The Lord reports that Polixenes is in Sicilia, accompanied by the Shepherd and the Clown, whom he is questioning. Camillo is also with them, and Florizel realizes that he has been betrayed. Perdita reveals that they are not yet married and they admit that Perdita is not a princess. Leontes expresses sympathy and agrees to try to help them win over Polixenes.

ACT 5 SCENE 2

We learn about the revelation of Perdita's true identity and the reunion of Leontes and Polixenes and Camillo through the conversation of Autolycus and some Gentlemen, a device that suggests that, though these are wonderful events, there is a greater dénouement still to be witnessed onstage. A Third Gentleman reports that the entire party has gone to Paulina's, at Perdita's request, to see a statue of Hermione, and they leave Autolycus to join the party assembling there. Autolycus meets the Shepherd and the Clown who revel in their elevation in rank, bestowed upon them for their kindness in raising Perdita. Autolycus apologizes for his past misdemeanors and they promise to tell the prince that he is "as honest a true fellow as is any in Bohemia."

ACT 5 SCENE 3

Paulina reveals the statue of Hermione and Leontes is overcome by its likeness to his wife. He comments that the statue shows Hermione as older than she was, and Paulina explains that the "carver's excellence" has portrayed her as she would be now. Leontes wistfully compares the cold statue to the "warm life" of Hermione. Perdita kneels and reaches out to touch the statue, but Paulina stops her. Camillo, Polixenes, and even Paulina try to comfort Leontes, who is overcome, but he will not allow Paulina to cover Hermione again. As everyone comments on how lifelike the statue is, Paulina claims that she can make it move and speak. Leontes commands her to do so and Paulina pronounces a "spell" to music. In a visual affirmation of the regeneration that characterizes the latter half of the play, Hermione steps down from the plinth, although whether this is an act of magic or the revelation that she has been alive all this time is not certain. Leontes and Hermione embrace, and Perdita kneels again before her mother. Hermione blesses her daughter. Leontes declares that Paulina and Camillo will marry and, despite the tragic deaths of Antigonus and Mamillius, the play ends in unity and celebration.

THE WINTER'S TALE IN PERFORMANCE: THE RSC AND BEYOND

The best way to understand a Shakespeare play is to see it or ideally to participate in it. By examining a range of productions, we may gain a sense of the extraordinary variety of approaches and interpretations that are possible—a variety that gives Shakespeare his unique capacity to be reinvented and made "our contemporary" four centuries after his death.

We begin with a brief overview of the play's theatrical and cinematic life, offering historical perspectives on how it has been performed. We then analyze in more detail a series of productions staged over the last half-century by the Royal Shakespeare Company. The sense of dialogue between productions that can only occur when a company is dedicated to the revival and investigation of the Shakespeare canon over a long period, together with the uniquely comprehensive archival resource of promptbooks, program notes, reviews, and interviews held on behalf of the RSC at the Shakespeare Birthplace Trust in Stratford-upon-Avon, allows an "RSC stage history" to become a crucible in which the chemistry of the play can be explored.

Finally, we go to the horse's mouth. Modern theater is dominated by the figure of the director, who must hold together the whole play, whereas the actor must concentrate on his or her part. The director's viewpoint is therefore especially valuable. Shakespeare's plasticity is wonderfully revealed when we hear directors of highly successful productions answering the same questions in very different ways.

FOUR CENTURIES OF *THE WINTER'S TALE:* AN OVERVIEW

The Winter's Tale was one of four plays described by Simon Forman, Elizabethan quack doctor and astrologer, in his commonplace book. Forman saw it at the Globe on Wednesday, May 15, 1611, and wrote a rough outline of the plot, although he failed to mention either the bear or Hermione's statue coming back to life. He was especially impressed by Autolycus, drawing the moral, "Beware of trusting feigned beggars or fawning fellows."[1] Richard Burbage, leading tragedian with the King's Men, probably played Leontes, and Robert Armin, the company's scholarly comedian, renowned for his wit and his singing, would have been Autolycus. The play must have been popular since there are recorded performances at court on November 5, 1611, another in spring 1613 as part of the wedding celebrations of Princess Elizabeth and Frederick V, the Elector Palatine, one in 1618, and another on January 18, 1624, before the Duchess of Richmond. The Revels Accounts also record that "The Winter's Tale was acted on Thursday night at Court, the 16 Janua[ry] 1633, by the K[ing's] players and liked."[2]

The play was not, however, much liked by Restoration audiences when the theaters reopened in 1660. The change of tone and location between the two halves of the play, the sixteen-year time gap, and the geographical solecism of a sea coast in landlocked Bohemia all offended prevailing neoclassical tastes. The same issues have worried some subsequent critics and directors.

In 1754 Macnamara Morgan's popular adaptation, *The Sheep-Shearing: or, Florizel and Perdita,* solved the problem by eliminating Leontes and Hermione entirely. It focused on the pastoral scenes, with Spranger Barry as Florizel and Isabel Nossiter as Perdita. The action was set in Bithynia, an ancient province of Asia Minor, rather than Bohemia (a change based on a suggestion in Thomas Hanmer's edition of the play). The Old Shepherd is finally revealed as a disguised Antigonus! Two years later David Garrick produced his version, *Florizel and Perdita, A Dramatic Pastoral.* The setting was returned to Bohemia; this version also featured the pastoral scenes but now included the restoration in the final act. Garrick explained his intentions in the prologue:

> The five long acts from which our three are taken
> Stretch'd out to sixteen years, lay by, forsaken.
> Lest then this precious liquor run to waste,
> 'Tis now confin'd and bottled for your taste.
> 'Tis my chief wish, my joy, my only plan
> To lose no drop of that immortal man![3]

Garrick's version had the benefit of a star-studded cast, with Garrick himself as Leontes, his leading lady Hannah Pritchard as Hermione, and the rising star Susannah Cibber as Perdita. It was a great success and was frequently revived until the end of the century, often in a double bill with *Catherine and Petruchio*, a similarly abridged version of *The Taming of the Shrew*. The Prince of Wales (and future King George IV) fell in love with the young actress Mary Robinson when she took over the part of Perdita in the early 1780s. He sent her love letters signed "Florizel" and she became known as "Perdita," then she left the stage and became a famous society beauty and fashion icon. The affair with the prince ended in a public scandal, but Perdita, despite being partially paralyzed as a result of rheumatic fever, remade herself as a novelist, feminist pamphleteer, and poet, highly regarded by leading intellectuals such as William Godwin and Samuel Taylor Coleridge.[4]

It was John Philip Kemble who restored Shakespeare's play to the stage in 1802 at Drury Lane and later Covent Garden. While restoring the first three acts, with minor alterations, Kemble still omitted the figure of Time, a practice continued by several subsequent producers. The reviewer in *The Gentleman's Magazine* details with disapproval the eclectic mix of props and costumes used by Kemble, describing them as "The usual perloinings [*sic*] from the fashions of James I, Charles I, and Oliver's courts, and the common country garb of our own time." He goes on to comment that "It remains for our classical managers to inform us, how this association of scenes, dresses, and decorations, of different ages, times, and places, could, with any degree of propriety, probability, or consistency, be brought together in one point of view; leaving it to them to fix their own data, architecture, customs, or manners."[5] Most critics, however, were impressed. The theater historian Dennis Bartholomeusz argues in his study of the play in performance that, in combining Gothic and Grecian settings, Kemble was responding, "whether consciously or not, to the different levels of time in the play."[6] Kemble's Leontes was generally admired, while his sister Sarah Siddons' Hermione was regarded as one of her greatest roles: "*Kemble*, in Leontes, evinced a perfect knowledge of his author, and displayed a judgment and feeling which justly place it among his most successful parts. The agonies of extreme jealousy with which his mind is tortured, were admirably depicted . . . The Hermione of Mrs. Siddons towers above all praise."[7]

Actor-manager William Charles Macready also produced the play and played Leontes at Drury Lane and Covent Garden. Critics were still carping about the play's form and structure. They compared Macready unfavorably to Kemble. His most distinguished Hermione was Helen Faucit, who wrote a detailed account of her experience:

My first appearance as Hermione is indelibly imprinted on my memory by the acting of Mr Macready as I have described it in the statue scene. Mrs Warner [formerly the actress Mary Amelia Huddart, widely admired for her own performance as Hermione] had rather jokingly told me, at one of the rehearsals, to be *prepared* for something extraordinary in his manner, when Hermione returned to life. But prepared I was not, and could not be, for such a display of uncontrollable rapture . . . It was the finest burst of passionate speechless emotion I ever saw, or could have conceived. My feelings being already severely strained, I naturally lost something of my self-command, I looked as the gifted Sarah Adams afterwards told me, "like Niobe, all tears" [*Hamlet*, 1.2.149]. Of course, I behaved better on the repetition of the play, as I knew what I had to expect and was somewhat prepared for it; but the intensity of Mr Macready's passion was so real, that I never could help being moved by it, and feeling much exhausted afterwards.[8]

Samuel Phelps' production at Sadler's Wells achieved critical and popular success with an interpretation of Leontes based on Coleridge's assessment of the character as a tormented man prone to jealousy. An innovation was the setting of the play in ancient Greece:

> Mr Phelps, though occasionally given to over-vehemence in his renderings of emotion, plays with genuine feeling always. The torments of his jealousy as Leontes are unmistakeable, his pathos strikes home . . . The scenery is entirely new, for the most part consisting of felicitous representations of classical interiors, decorated in the polychromatic style. The famous scene of the statue is so managed as to produce a most beautiful stage effect. The light is so thrown, and the drapery is so arranged, that the illusion is all but perfect, the stately figure of Mrs Warner, who looks the statue admirably, contributing in no small degree to the beauty of the picture. The moment the curtain was removed, and Hermione was discovered, the applause of the audience broke with immense force.[9]

By far the most spectacular production, however, was at the Princess' Theatre in 1856, when, as the London *Times* review put it, "Mr. Charles Kean's principle of making the stage a vehicle for historical illustration was never carried out so far as in his revival of the *Winter's Tale*."[10] Archaeological research supplied details for the Sicilian setting which opened with a view of the Temple of Minerva at Syracuse, followed by a Greek banquet in Act 1, enlivened by the introduction of dances including the "warlike Pyrrhic dance" with "[t]hree dozen ladies of the *corps de ballet*, attired in glittering armour as youthful warriors." Hermione's trial in Act 3 took place in the theater at Syracuse. The previously banished figure of Time now reappeared as

> an episodical allegory, consisting of three distinct tableaux— first, by that contrivance which allows stage goddesses and spirits to fly without visible ropes . . . we have Luna in her car, personified, accompanied by stars, who are personified like-

wise. These disappear to make way for Time—not the old gentleman, with sithe [sic] and hour-glass, but Chronos, father of Zeus—who delivers his speech sitting on this mundane globe, as its ruler. He is succeeded by Phoebus in his car, copied from Flaxman's shield of Achilles, and an antique vase. This group, while it has all the effect of an exquisite piece of sculpture, is lighted in a manner that almost dazzles the eye, and it is impossible to conceive the solar glory more vividly personified.[11]

Meanwhile, Bohemia reverted to Bithynia so as to allow maximum contrast with the barbaric tribes of Asia Minor for the pastoral scenes when "the sheep-shearing holyday is heightened into a Dionysiac orgie [sic], in which something like 200 dancers are employed."[12] Florizel was played as a breeches part (a male part played by a female actor) by a Miss Heath and Ellen Terry made her first stage appearance as Mamillius.[13] Kean's production provided not only "gorgeous spectacle, but good and sufficient acting,"[14] and the play's enthusiastic reception seems to have been enhanced by the presence of Queen Victoria on the opening night. The satirical magazine *Punch* was less impressed, claiming:

> Mr Punch has it upon authority to state that the Bear at present running in Oxford Street in the *Winter's Tale* is an archaeological copy from the original bear of Noah's Ark. Anything more modern would have been at variance with the ancient traditions reproduced in the drama. Further, by one of those curious coincidences that too rarely repay the industry of genius, we hear that among the engagements of scene-shifters newly made at the Princess', there are three individuals named HAM, SHEM, and JAPHET.[15]

The chief innovation in the 1887 production was American actor Mary Anderson's doubling of the roles of Hermione and Perdita. The show opened in Nottingham before transferring to the Lyceum and going on to a triumphant tour of the United States. Critical views were divided, most feeling that Anderson was more successful as

Perdita and criticizing the cutting of the text as well as Anderson's verse-speaking. The London *Times* was blunt:

> There is small advantage in having the Bohemia of Shakespeare's fancy restored and the crazy archaeology of Charles Kean discarded if such tampering as this with a Shakespearian subject is to be allowed. Nor does the evil stop here. To the grotesque effect of the doubling of the parts in the statue scene, must be added a certain confusion of identity between mother and daughter which detracts from the spectator's enjoyment of the play as a whole.[16]

In 1906 Herbert Beerbohm Tree produced another spectacular three-act version with a text cut by nearly half to allow for change of the elaborate sets, which included a running brook, several trees, and a donkey. The performances of the distinguished cast—Ellen Terry as Hermione, Charles Warner as Leontes, and Maud Tree as Paulina—were overwhelmed by sets and orchestra.

Harley Granville-Barker's 1912 production at the Savoy Theatre revolutionized the staging of Shakespeare's plays forever and his influence on modern production practices is still evident.[17] Critics were quick to recognize its significance:

> Mr. Barker's production of "The Winter's Tale" on Saturday last is probably the first performance in England of a play by Shakespeare that the author would himself have recognised for his own since Burbage—or, at any rate, Davenant—retired from active management.[18]

> Yes, there is no other word for it save the word that in popular usage denotes a special kind of artistic assault on conventionalism; it is Post-Impressionist Shakespeare.[19]

Granville-Barker was influenced by the work of William Poel's Elizabethan Stage Society, which attempted to re-create original performance conditions in his production of *Hamlet* in 1881. In New York

2. The clean lines of modernity: Time introduces the audience to Perdita, the Old Shepherd, and Florizel in Harley Granville-Barker's 1912 production at the Savoy Theatre.

Northrop Ames directed a production of *The Winter's Tale* in similar conditions at the New Theatre in 1910. But it was Granville-Barker's *Winter's Tale* that crystallized the new production style. His most telling resource was a simple thrust stage:

> For the management of the action Mr. Barker has revived the Elizabethan plan with a difference. The stage has three planes, or steps, with two side-doors in the foreground, through which courtiers and messengers make their entrances and exits. There is only one interval, after the third act, to mark off the two periods of the story, and the act-drop occasionally descends upon the actors when they are speaking (this, by the way, is taken from the theatre of the Restoration), so that they begin a speech in mid-stage and finish it before the curtain. Set speeches they deliver at the very edge of the stage (there are no footlights, but search-lamps converging on the stage from the

dress-circle), addressing them directly to the audience, the proper method, of course, of the old "platform." The rustics dance and sing to pipe and tabor; there is no orchestra.[20]

Those critics who liked the production admired the performances. John Palmer called Henry Ainley's Leontes "the finest piece of Shakespearian acting I have yet seen" and was equally enthusiastic about Lillah McCarthy's Hermione.[21] Not everyone was convinced, however, and the production closed after six weeks: "Mr Granville Barker, in a distressful striving after the artistic, has achieved that mingling of discordant, ill-related elements, that impossible jangling of different keys, which can never be far removed from vulgarity."[22]

Peter Brook's 1951 production at the Phoenix Theatre achieved popular and critical success, despite continued misgivings about the play itself:

But for all its structural shortcomings *The Winter's Tale* has eminence, charm, of an indefinably old-fashioned kind, and Mr Peter Brook's production discovers in it a certain strength as well. Most of this stems from Mr Gielgud's very fine performance as Leontes, whose jealousy is so unquestionably real and terrible that we are not worried by the fact that its causes are flimsy and its consequences far-fetched. He is well partnered by Miss Diana Wynyard's handsome and long-suffering Hermione and Miss Flora Robson's staunch Paulina (though I am not sure that Shakespeare did not see this officious lady as a slightly more comic character than Miss Robson makes her).[23]

Brook was clearly influenced by Barker's ideas, but theater historian Dennis Bartholomeusz concludes that while "Barker was very much in play" in terms of the simple set and fluid performance style, "Barker's other important principle of intimacy, dictated by the thrust-stage, was not a part of Brook's design. The production was not as radical in its sweep as Granville-Barker's, nor quite as original."[24]

In recent years the play has regained some of its early popularity, and those issues that rendered it problematic for theater audiences attuned to a realist mode of representation seem less daunting to those willing to suspend their disbelief and, as required by Paulina, to awake their poetic and theatrical faith. Most recent productions have nevertheless been performed under the aegis of the subsidized theaters such as the Royal Shakespeare Company and the Royal National Theatre. RSC productions are discussed in detail below, while the most significant production at the National has been Nicholas Hytner's modern dress version in 2001 with Alex Jennings as Leontes, Claire Skinner as Hermione, and Deborah Findlay as Paulina. A play as ever of two halves, it had critics mixed in their views as to which worked better. Most were impressed by Hytner's inventive updating: "His contrasting versions of contemporary life suggest Establishment and drop-out, old order and New Age, Windsor and Spencer."[25] Sicilia became a "sleek monochrome box . . . peopled by sycophants in grey suits," while "Bohemia is an explosion of colour: Glastonbury-cum-Woodstock, with no morris-dance romping or unfunny clowns, no yokels and no wenches."[26] All were agreed that "Findlay, always subtle and always substantial, gives the outstanding performance of the production: she's never a shrew or simply a visionary."[27] The part of Paulina has again and again proved to be one of the most rewarding female roles in Shakespeare.

Perhaps the most admired production of modern times was that of Annabel Arden for Simon McBurney's Complicite company, who specialize in vivid storytelling through highly physical theater. The production opened in January 1992 at the Seymour Theatre Centre, Sydney, then was played in Hong Kong and toured the UK before a run at London's Lyric Hammersmith. *Daily Telegraph* critic Charles Spencer caught its dazzling quality in a suitably effervescent review:

> Complicite's use of movement and body language brilliantly illuminates the text, and almost every scene has a vitality that forces you to consider the play afresh.
>
> The play begins with disco music, popping champagne corks and manic games of blind-man's-buff, yet it quickly becomes clear that the party spirit is not shared by Leontes.

Simon McBurney brings a fidgety, sweaty intensity to the role of the troubled king, and in one superb scene he is discovered standing on top of a wardrobe, gazing miserably down on the happy innocents beneath him as his heart is gnawed by destructive jealousy.

Annabel Arden's production captures harrowingly the full trauma of the first half of the play, as Leontes creates a winter world of death and despair. The physical and emotional violence McBurney brings to the tormented king as he rages among the toys in his young son's nursery has the sickening impact of a kick in the solar plexus.

In the second half Complicite let their hair down in their own inimitable way. The scenes in Bohemia have an infectious, anarchic energy, with a vintage comic performance from Marcello Magni as that normally tedious rogue Autolycus. Jettisoning Shakespeare, and talking in a ludicrous mixture of Italian and heavily accented English, he comes on as a hilarious parody of a libidinous Latin, pinching handbags from the audience, flogging dodgy cassette tapes and offering healing laughter after all the grief of the earlier acts.

In a haunting, slow-motion procession with the nine-strong cast changing into costumes of mourning as they march, the production takes us back to Leontes's tragic court. There is a stillness in these final scenes which forms a fine contrast with the earlier manic activity, a real sense of wonder as the dead come to life and the divided family are miraculously reunited. The moment when Leontes embraces the "statue" of his wife Hermione and cries "She's warm" achieves an astonishing depth of emotion.

The cast double and treble their roles (even McBurney plays the clown as well as Leontes), and all make memorable contributions. There must be a special praise, however, for Kathryn Hunter, who is not so much an actress as a human chameleon. In the course of the show she plays a young child (Mamillius), a passionate middle-aged woman (Paulina) and a comic old man (the shepherd) with a verisimilitude that beggars belief.[28]

The Winter's Tale has not proved itself a play with wide international appeal, but there have been a number of ambitious modern productions in the United States and elsewhere. Ingmar Bergman took his Royal Dramatic Theatre of Sweden's production to the Brooklyn Academy of Music in 1995. It was set in the early nineteenth century in a Swedish manor house and played as a play-within-a-play put on by the guests at a young woman's birthday party. It contained:

> not one but two bears, one brown, the other white . . . The brown bear is a comic interpolation. The white bear is the beast that figures in Shakespeare's best-known stage direction: "Exit pursued by a bear." This bear, being polar, also more or less locates Mr. Bergman's vision of Shakespeare's settings of Sicily and Bohemia. They're now far closer to the chill of the Arctic Circle than to the reviving warmth of the Mediterranean sun. This may be why the play's dark first half . . . now has such emotional impact that the light-hearted conclusion seems more of a dream than Shakespeare possibly intended.[29]

Brian Kulick directed a version for New York's Public Theater in 2000 to mixed reviews. Most critics concluded that the production was "most successful at the breezy comic business that fills much of the latter half of the play."[30] Barry Edelstein's Off-Broadway production attempted to update the play but, as one critic pointed out, "The kind of topsy-turvy worlds these plays evoke is not easy to reconcile with business suits and modern technology," but concluding: "The damage here comes not from Edelstein's often handsome stage images, which are underscored with elegance by Michael Torke's superb jazz-tinged piano score and the subtle lighting of Jane Cox, but from the drab delivery of some of Shakespeare's most challenging verse, which drains too much of the color from this exceedingly colorful play."[31]

Barbara Gaines' production for her Chicago Shakespeare Theater is discussed in "The Director's Cut," below.

There have been a number of films of *The Winter's Tale*, including a 1910 silent version. Several stage productions have been filmed, including Frank Dunlop's with Laurence Harvey as Leontes in 1968 and Gregory Doran's 1997–98 RSC production with Antony Sher, Alexandra Gilbreath, and Estelle Kohler. Jane Howell directed the play for BBC television in 1981 with Jeremy Kemp as Leontes. This was one of the more successful productions in the BBC series, as film historian Michael Brooke suggests:

> One of the most daringly stylised productions of the entire project, its stripped-down approach to design and staging working particularly well on television . . . Production designer Don Homfray (who had already moved towards a minimalist approach with Rodney Bennett's production of *Hamlet* the previous year) reduced the sets to a couple of cones, a tree (which Howell said was a deliberate homage to Samuel Beckett's similarly spartan *Waiting for Godot*) and a plain wedge-shaped background with a passage cut through the centre, and the changing seasons were conveyed by shifts in the colour of the sets and lighting (stark white for winter, green and fertile for spring).[32]

The style proved an imaginative transposition of the world of the play to the medium of the small screen. At the time of writing, there is yet to be a modern big screen adaptation, though one directed by Waris Hussein, with Dougray Scott as Leontes, is due for release in 2009.

AT THE RSC

The Winter's Tale — a "Problem Play"?

Writing in 1958, two years before the launch of the RSC, Nevill Coghill still felt it necessary to defend six continuing areas of concern regarding the play, among them the suddenness of Leontes' jealousy, the bear, Time, and the statue scene.[33] To these could be added the "broken-backed" nature of the play, split between two very different worlds and eras, which features so regularly in criticism and reviews. To today's reviewers and audiences, these concerns are no longer seen as dramaturgical failings. Nevertheless, how each director decides to address these challenges, together with their choice of period and place, and the balance between public and personal, continues to a great extent to define each production.

Popular as the play now is in its own right, *The Winter's Tale* is often performed as part of a themed season. In 1960 it gained status as the last in the chronological sequence of six Shakespearean comedies that launched the RSC. Later productions, however, continue to occur in the context of Shakespeare's late plays (1969, 2002, 2006); the 1984 community tour coupled it more interestingly with Arthur Miller's *The Crucible*, with which it has strong thematic and dramaturgical parallels.

Venues

The twentieth-century productions of *The Winter's Tale* at Stratford were all on the main stage: the scale and intensity of the emotions, the extrovert energy of the sheep-shearing festival, and the very size of the cast enabled the play to fill the large Royal Shakespeare Theatre (RST) space comfortably, while the non-naturalism of the various "problematic" sequences makes a clear separation between audience and action attractive. However, in 1984 the RSC toured a small-scale production to non-theater venues; this very successfully explored the possibilities inherent in a staging that was intimate, as well as involving a promenading audience surrounding and taking part in the action. These principles were reapplied in both the twenty-first-century productions: Matthew Warchus' Roundhouse production made significant use of onstage promenaders to contribute to the visual picture, even though these had to be cut when the production transferred to the RST; Dominic Cooke's production for the intimate neo-Elizabethan Swan Theatre in 2006 went further, converting the whole of the stalls to a playing and promenading space, and although designer and director were unable to resist incorporating a mini proscenium arch acting space into the design, the key scenes were made public and played among the audience.

Period and Place

Although the appeal to the oracle at Delphos suggests the classical world, no RSC director has opted for this setting, standard throughout the late nineteenth and early twentieth centuries, perhaps because the era contains less resonance for our generation and the costumes can be alienating.

More surprisingly, the possible Renaissance setting has not proved popular either. Peter Wood's predominantly medieval 1960 production came closest: "both costumes and décor evoked a mythical Renaissance, a world in which anything could happen and anything did."[34] In 1976, the RST was converted into a hexagonal, galleried "Elizabethan-style" thrust stage for the season; even so, John Barton ignored this context, choosing to set his *Winter's Tale* in Lapland, establishing a primitive, ritualistic setting.

Both the 1980s mainhouse productions (Ronald Eyre, 1981; Terry Hands, 1986) were described as Regency. Those in the 1990s were both early twentieth century: Gregory Doran (1999) opted for a "Ruritanian" setting, allowing echoes of tsarist autocracy within a recognizably modern world; Adrian Noble (1992) chose an English equivalent, with his 1930s Bohemia repeatedly compared to the painter Stanley Spencer's Cookham, a kind of idealized English village.

Trevor Nunn (1969), Noble (1984), Warchus (2002), and Cooke (2006) all opted for the mid-twentieth century. In Nunn's case, he was choosing a totally contemporary setting, the only director to do so. Noble's setting was postwar Sicily, combining the tiaras, medals, and ball gowns of an "ambassadorial reception"[35] with Mafia connotations. Warchus, too, drew out Mafia implications, but set his production in America, combining Hollywood film noir effects in Sicilia with an Appalachian setting for Bohemia.

Visual Setting and Emotional Color

Within these periods, overall visual choices for these productions were remarkably similar, dictated by the cyclical and seasonal nature of the play and the theme of death and rebirth. Design choices thus almost inevitably start the play in a wintry world, with white or monochrome dominating both costumes and set (1969, 1981, 1986, 2002, 2006); others have opted instead for deep autumnal colors or the regal spectrum of purples and cold lilacs. The set here is usually minimalist and symbolic, while costume choices are stylish and sophisticated.

In strong contrast, Bohemia moves us through spring to the high summer of the sheep-shearing. Here designers always provide an explosion of color, a high level of rustic naturalism, and a stage crowded with scenery, colorful costumes, and visual detail. Warm colors and bright lights predominate.

The final movement returns us to the petrified winter of Sicilia; these scenes, by reverting to the previous sparse setting and cold and limited color spectrum, and by using lighting that frequently constricts the playing area, show us a world frozen and often dark, until the advent of Perdita and Florizel brings with it light and indications of return to life.

Music

The musical underscoring of the action follows a similar trajectory. Minimalist solo instruments (e.g. sitar in 1976, piano in 1986) and sounds of "haunting . . . remote melancholy"[36] are typical in Sicilia, while in Bohemia a live band not only appears regularly onstage as part of the sheep-shearing festivities, but also often provides full-blooded offstage accompaniment to scene changes and even Autolycus' solo songs: these often have a music hall or vaudeville tone regardless of the period setting. The Appalachian bluegrass band of Warchus' Bohemia also played throughout the interval, getting the audience into the mood for the second half.

1960: On the Brink of a New Era

Peter Wood's production in the first year of the RSC faced both forward and backward, showing us *The Winter's Tale* at a clear turning point. Reviewers were still hampered by their negative preconceptions of the play, but were willing to have these overturned, as the *Financial Times* reviewer indicated: "triumphing over the bristling incredibilities and complex snags of this melodramatic fairytale . . . [the] company have achieved a small theatrical near-miracle."[37] The production was generally highly regarded. The *Daily Telegraph* reviewer noted how

Mr Wood gave it a sombre setting of rusts and dark blues and employed some sheer magic with his lighting so that as

Leontes soliloquises in corrosive error, his words wing out from the darkening stage as from his soul straight into our hearts. Under this treatment the bear that makes his dinner of Antigonus and the imagined sea coast of Bohemia fall into place as part of Shakespeare's bodying force [sic] of the strangest imaginings.[38]

Jacques Noel's set design was economical and flexible, using "the vast empty spaces of the Stratford stage to conjure up medieval palaces, great plains and mighty seas."[39] Yet its "modernism" clearly looked back fifty years to Granville-Barker and Gordon Craig, and elements of the resplendent barbarism that characterized the previous Stratford production in 1948 still lingered on. The New Statesman critic described the trial scene as displaying "barbaric magnificence . . . swirling cloaks of crimson velvet, grotesquely armed soldiery, savagely grinning masks, all the grim pomp and tawdry splendour of Medievalism gone mad."[40] The costumes throughout were regal and imposing, in rich colors, with deep ruffs, cloaks, and flowing sleeves, while Mamillius was dressed as "a miniature copy of his father."[41] The production focused as much on the public roles as the private experience—imposing crowns were worn throughout, though Wood broke with tradition in excluding the court from the final scene. A further controversial innovation was to transform the usual "genteel trippings" of the sheep-shearing into "a full-bodied fertility rite."[42]

Eric Porter's Leontes was universally lauded, "meet[ing] the play's initial difficulty by 'striking twelve' at once, thrusting the action forward with burning force and ferocity . . . [yet] still a man and not a monster . . . The hysterical tyrant of the play's opening and the benign penitent of its close are credibly one and the same."[43] Elizabeth Sellers' "serene . . . long-suffering" Hermione was virtually ignored by the critics, but Peggy Ashcroft revolutionized perceptions of Paulina, repositioning her from the expected "querulous character part"[44] as a "female Polonius"[45] or a "terrible scold and barking harridan"[46] to establish her as a leading role, a woman "endowed . . . with profound common sense and practical humanity . . . epitomis[ing] the generosity and sadness of age."[47]

3. Paulina, a force for good: Peggy Ashcroft presenting the baby to Leontes (Eric Porter) in Peter Wood's 1960 production.

Thus, while in many ways Wood's production belonged to the pre-RSC tradition, it clearly also provided a transition that allowed a serious reevaluation of the play and its potential, enabling the interpretations to come.

1969: Cubism and Carnaby Street

By contrast, Trevor Nunn's innovative and highly controversial production brought *The Winter's Tale* sharply up to date, both in setting and approach. Dressed all in white on a bare white set, the Sicilian characters wore "contemporary neck-buttoned jackets and bell-bottomed trousers"[48] with Polixenes "a splash of scarlet,"[49] while the Bohemian sheep-shearing festival featured "a bunch of hippies on a musical picnic."[50] References to Carnaby Street and the scandalous nude musical *Hair* abounded. In keeping with the mood of the 1960s, Nunn was interested in "a representative individual . . . [not] a crowned king."[51] The crowns were accordingly absent, and the

4. "Hippies on a musical picnic": Judi Dench as Perdita takes a tumble with her Florizel (David Bailie) in Trevor Nunn's 1969 production.

play opened in Mamillius' nursery, rather than in the context of a royal banquet.

Despite this human emphasis, the production was heavily stylized. As the lights went down, the audience heard "a deep voice speak[ing] out of the air, hushing the theatre in mystery."[52] Meanwhile, strobe lighting illuminated a rotating glass cube in which an agonized Leontes was imprisoned, his arms and legs outstretched like Leonardo's *Renaissance Man*. A spotlight then picked out "another glass box, a tiny one this time, with a tiny mannikin revolving in it."[53] The lights finally came up on a nursery filled with further symbolic toys, including a giant rocking horse on which Leontes and Mamillius rode together and a "school-boy's top" (2.1.123) which "fill[ed] the theatre with a gently evocative humming which recur[red] at the end of the play."[54] The cube, too, recurred at the end, providing the setting in which Hermione's statue was displayed.

The problem of Leontes' jealousy was also given a stylized solution. "Mr. Nunn simply makes it a condition of the story and establishes it by a stunning change of lighting in which we see Hermione and Polixenes as they appear in his fevered dream."[55] Thus the audience was able both to believe in Hermione's purity and to experience Leontes' imaginings themselves, seeing them through his eyes, as Barber's startled reaction indicates: "[Hermione] actually appeared to fawn upon Polixenes."[56] Similar stylization was used in the trial scene, in which Hermione fainted in slow motion. Finally, a single actress, Judi Dench, was cast in the roles of both Perdita and Hermione, in order to underline "the allegorical meaning of the end of the play . . . [in which Leontes] finds his daughter returned to him in the form of his wife."[57]

Dench proved immensely successful in both parts. J. C. Trewin's comments in the *Birmingham Post* may seem hyperbolic, but are typical in both tone and content of the general critical response:

> As Hermione the actress affected me like the pure clear beauty of a starlight night. We have not had in our time a performance of more simply expressed emotion . . . As Perdita, she is enchantingly the queen of the sheep-shearing, dancing like a wave of the sea and speaking . . . neither with a brittle gentility nor with a country accent too forced . . . Miss Dench's response to the verse is unerringly exact.[58]

Despite this effusive praise for Dench herself, the concept of the doubling proved less successful. The roles had last been combined by Mary Anderson in 1887, when Perdita's lines in the final scene had been cut, and the character played there by a stand-in who kept her back to the audience. Nunn's solution was more tricksy than this: a stand-in for Hermione in the first half of the scene enabled Dench to deliver Perdita's lines; a rapid swap then introduced a stand-in Perdita, allowing Dench to take over as Hermione. Even though this sleight of hand worked effectively, the audience was inevitably distracted, focusing on the theatrical tour de force rather than surrendering totally to the emotion of the final scene.

Nunn's production proved immensely influential. The stylized white decor, the focus on the personal rather than political, the youthful protagonists, the highlighting of Mamillius, his toys and nursery, the doubling of Hermione and Perdita, and the mid-twentieth-century setting have all been reused repeatedly since. Nunn was also responsible for introducing the business in which Paulina hands the baby to Leontes in Act 2 Scene 3, and also the first postwar director to use Hermione herself to speak the words of Antigonus' dream.

1976: Ritual in Lapland

John Barton's 1976 production, co-directed with Trevor Nunn, was heavily cut throughout. It stands apart from the mainstream of RSC productions of *The Winter's Tale*, and has generated comparatively little attention since. The Arctic setting, chosen for the symbolism of Lapland's solstice festivals, failed to capture reviewers' imagination, and the lack of the usual contrast between Sicilia and Bohemia was heavily criticized. The interpretation focused strongly on storytelling and emphasized ritual throughout, notably in the trial scene and in its use of motifs such as the bear.

Hermione and Perdita were linked by exoticism. Critic Richard David stated: "This Hermione was not the simple symbol of nobility and sincerity that is sometimes seen, but a conspicuously foreign princess,"[59] and Roger Warren compared Perdita to a "Byzantine icon."[60] Reviewer Harold Hobson praised Marilyn Taylerson's Hermione for her "unexpectedly sharp tongue . . . there is not a scrap of flirtatiousness in her";[61] Ian McKellen gave a "bristling performance" as Leontes "in a part ideally suited to his temperament and verse-speaking abilities."[62]

The one influential innovation was the repositioning of Hermione's statue, traditionally placed upstage center with both court and audience looking up at her. Barton positioned her by the proscenium left, facing out, with the court looking diagonally down at her from upstage, thus enabling the audience to see everyone's reactions. This restaging won universal praise for enhancing the emotional power of the play's resolution.

1981: A Smiling Villain?

Ronald Eyre's production was notable for the unusual and highly praised performance of Patrick Stewart as a Leontes who covered his jealousy with "gaiety" and "dangerous geniality," although in retrospect clearly "jealous from the start."[63] In keeping with this, the opening exchanges between the central trio were informal, characterized by friendly, youthful horseplay and jokes. However, both Hermione and Leontes wore crowns for the final scene, emphasizing a public as well as a private dimension to their reconciliation.

Sheila Hancock's Paulina also won praise: "equally original . . . a compassionate friend rather than tart scold."[64] However, the overall Brechtian style of the production was less popular: "four coldly clinical lamps"[65] shone down onto the acting area; the white costumes appeared sterile rather than stylish; the set was high and blank-walled.

As in 1976, the production's "dominant visual motif" was "that of the theatre, of performing a story."[66] Here a masque introduced the action, foreshadowing what was to come: as director, Leontes

> darted anxiously about the stage, wearing a clown's red bulbous nose, blowing a toy trumpet and carrying a jester's bladder . . . Autolycus . . . led in an enormous black bear. A polonaise signalled the entrance of Hermione [dressed as Flora and carrying a sheaf of wheat], partnered by Polixenes . . . A gigantic figure of Time [entered and] . . . at the stroke of twelve . . . Mamillius emerged from beneath Time's cloak.[67]

1984: *The Winter's Tale* on Tour

In 1984 a small-scale tour visited "non-velvet" venues, from cathedrals and sports halls to an agricultural showground. *The Winter's Tale* was performed in promenade, the set consisting of a pair of movable rostra, "audience and acting area joined on a shared floor covered with countless Oriental carpets."[68]

The audience were not just bystanders but were "invited to create the billowing shore of Bohemia with a white sheet [and] . . . sit at

5. Autolycus leads in a bear in Ronald Eyre's 1981 production.

tables with the cast to munch bread and quaff Ribena."[69]
"Hermione's [trial] was breathtakingly staged, with innocent queen
and jealous king facing each other across half a mile of carpet cor-
doned off by officious ushers like a royal procession."[70] At the end,
the rostra were pushed together to provide a raised acting area for
"the beauty and gravity of those final scenes, with the statue coming
to life amid flickering candles."[71]

Alun Armstrong and Lynn Farleigh were praised for "human-
scale" performances, "real warm people under their high tragedy of
royal treachery,"[72] while Julian Curry's "dignified, mystified Polix-

enes," Janet Dale's "outstandingly notable Paulina, elegant and beautifully spoken," and Jennifer Landor's "pulsatingly attractive Perdita" were all repeatedly singled out for appreciation.[73]

1986: Boy Eternal

Terry Hands' 1986 production showed a clear reaction against former minimalism. The mosaic floor was "covered by a vast polar bear skin, whose huge head stare[d] out at the audience, the play's softness and savagery personified."[74] The backdrop was an enormous fragmented mirror, angled to reflect and duplicate the action. "Regency costumes [were] white—tailcoats, boots and all."[75] Jeremy Irons' youthful Leontes was accompanied by numerous equally youthful attendants in an informal court.

The action opened with a slow-motion snowball fight acted out behind a white gauze and remained informal as the protagonists removed their outerwear and accepted warming drinks. A highly flirtatious Polixenes and Hermione gave ample cause for jealousy, to an extent that undermined the later scenes, yet for once this was a Leontes that hardly needed justification, interpreted as petulant obsessive child unable to control his temper or stop until he had destroyed all around him. The trial appeared to be held in the royal nursery with Irons dragging furniture around to set the scene himself.

A continuing focus on clothing and moments of disguise, underlining the tension between appearance and reality, unified the play, as did repeated use of the bear motif and the doubling of Perdita and Hermione (Penny Downie), though this time at the expense of Perdita's final lines, with a silent stand-in throughout the final scene.

1992: Balloons and a Gauze Box

Adrian Noble's main house production, "[crammed] with imaginative detail,"[76] was praised as "a real ensemble show, full of pain, wild comedy and hard-won joy"[77] and "the best Stratford *Winter's Tale* in two decades."[78]

A deceptively simple set from Anthony Ward offered a Sicilia characterized by a versatile gauze box filled with gilt ballroom chairs

and a "Bohemian sheep-shearing that [was] no self-conscious pastoral but a joyous small-town fair with bunting and a brass band."[79]
Balloons dominated everything, floating from the chairs for Mamillius' party in Act 1 Scene 1 or providing bawdy humor at the feast in
Act 4 Scene 4; Autolycus even made his first appearance descending
from above on a tree of green balloons which provided the central
focus for Bohemia.

Noble's stage pictures were visually and emotionally powerful,
adding depth and narrative; the sweeping circular choreography of
the mass entrances and exits unified the production. The play
opened with Mamillius alone downstage center, shaking a toy snow-
storm to conjure up a birthday party within the gauze box; it ended
with Hermione's statue in the same position, looking up at a court
staring down at her from the box. Her trial took place "i'th'open
air" (3.2.109), backed by solemn attendants bearing umbrellas;
"Leontes' defiance called forth Apollo's wrath in a huge storm full
of howling wind, scurrying courtiers, lightening and shattered
umbrellas skidding madly across the stage."[80]

Samantha Bond's queen was "radiantly comfortable in her
advanced pregnancy . . . confident in her husband's love and sensuous in a way that was plainly innocent but capable of being misun-
derstood," showing pity rather than anger at her trial, while John
Nettles "was not a Leontes who brought his doubts onstage with
him; one saw the aberration descend."[81]

1999: Ibsenesque Jealousy

Greg Doran's production began in darkness to the escalating sound of
mocking whispers, as the backlit figure of Leontes in ermine and full
regalia processed downstage. Similar soundtracks accompanied later
scene changes. Robert Jones' set reflected the sense of claustrophobia:
"King Leontes' palace in Sicilia [was] a haunted and haunting place.
The walls of the great chamber narrow[ed] towards the back in
thrilling perspective . . . White sheets billow[ed] above like gleaming
clouds big with rain, suggesting both the plenitude and the dangers of
nature."[82] At the end of the trial, the stage sky literally fell.

Both costuming and interpretation gave this late Victorian/early
Edwardian production a strong Ibsenesque flavor. Antony Sher, as

6. An allusion to Our Lady, the Virgin Mary: Hermione's statue (Alexandra Gilbreath) in Gregory Doran's 1999 production.

Leontes, based his performance on detailed medical research into psychotic jealousy: he wept and embraced Hermione even as he accused her. Alexandra Gilbreath's Hermione had an unusually distant relationship with the wheelchair-bound Mamillius, but was obviously a loving and devoted wife; her goodness was an active rather than passive force. Like Bond, she offered pity and love rather than anger. London *Times* reviewer Benedict Nightingale wrote of her trial: "[Hermione] has clearly spent weeks on bread and water in some cramped dungeon. This frail sweaty figure speaks with simple humility and utterly unaffected dignity. She has been bitterly wronged—and she is more queen than ever she was."[83]

Bohemia was characterized by piles of wool bales on an industrial scale; Perdita (here doubled with Mamillius by Emily Bruni) was controversially more the shepherd girl than a princess-in-waiting.

The final scene offered a full reconciliation. A torchlit procession entered to find Hermione revealed, downstage left, in the same position as at her trial, and in a similar enclosure, but now head bowed, amid banks of candles, like a statue of the Virgin Mary. "The ending [was] all wonder, humour, forgiveness and joy born out of sadness, . . . a salvation . . . both earned and divinely bestowed."[84]

2002: An American Tale

Matthew Warchus' Roundhouse production was set in mid-twentieth-century America. It generated praise for the "awesome menace" of Douglas Hodge's shaven-headed Mafia gangster Leontes,[85] but the generally bad-tempered reviews were clearly influenced by the critics' dislike of being dragged out of central London to this new venue, as well as by the lengthy technical delays at the start and a cast still uncomfortable with their accents. In a mainly seated auditorium, Warchus had made a brave effort at a promenade element, but this added to the first-night confusion.

The Sicilian sections were dominated by increasing film noir shadows and a sinister soundtrack by Gary Yerson. The proceedings began in a nightclub, all tuxedos, evening gowns, and white tablecloths, with Mamillius as MC providing a symbolic "Lady Vanishes" conjuring trick. The opening dialogue was recast for Leontes and Polixenes and delivered at the microphone before the scene became more private. Anastasia Hille's "trophy wife" Hermione, "a Midwestern beauty-contest winner of recent and earnest gentility,"[86] flirted happily but chastely with Polixenes, and Leontes was obviously controlling anger (and drink) from the start. Act 1 Scene 2 was played in the deserted nightclub, a now pajama-wearing Mamillius running away from Hermione to hide under the table.

From then on, a bare stage and suggestive lighting set the increasingly darkening scene. Even those familiar with the play experienced "a moment of pure terror when . . . Leontes hurl[ed] the infant Perdita from a high balcony"[87] and were "very frightened"[88] by the bear. Myra Lucretia Taylor was a forceful Paulina, played here as a Southern black housekeeper. The most powerful scene in this production was the trial: Hermione in prison shift was "tethered to the floor" in the center of an empty stage while her accuser circled her in the darkened auditorium; she resembled "a deer . . . being used to warm up the dogs in a game of bear-baiting."[89]

The statue sequence, however, lacked its usual impact, perhaps partly because the emotional peak had been reached during the first half, perhaps partly because of the detail and liveliness of the "Bohemian" scenes, here transferred to Appalachia, but perhaps owing to the lack of any supra-individual context.

However, two interesting new touches occurred in Act 5: in the first, Perdita fainted when Leontes turned against the lovers, a faint that brought back memories of Hermione and triggered both interest and remorse; in the second, after the reconciliation, Leontes noticed Hermione looking toward rather than, as usual, away from Polixenes—his "What? Look upon my brother" became a (possibly mock) reversion to jealousy before he laughed and begged their pardons.

2006: Promenading in the Swan

Dominic Cooke's promenade production in the Swan opened at a New Year's Eve party, cast and audience joining hands together to sing "Auld Lang Syne" below a crazily-angled clock. Time was a dominant motif, interpreted here as both narrator and gardener, visible at his tasks throughout the play, tending both land and tale, and underlining, too, the cyclical, seasonal nature of the story.

Designer Mike Britton's transformation of the Swan looked

impressive and was very effective. The mix of promenaders in the stalls and seated audience elsewhere worked successfully, with acting areas at both stalls and gallery levels integrating and involving the whole theater, and the level of audience participation was carefully judged. Much use was made of two mobile rostra, as in Noble's 1984 tour. This was an intelligent, clear, and uncontroversial production, whose intimate scale and unusual staging provided its main innovations and offer an exciting point of departure for the future.

Exit, Pursued by a Bear

Shakespeare's most famous stage direction has been interpreted both naturalistically and symbolically. In Barton's ritualistic Lapland, an elderly shaman with a bear mask conducted Antigonus out; in 1986 the giant white bearskin covering the stage reared up and engulfed him; in 1999 the silk clouds that had loomed over Leontes' palace took bear form and swallowed him up. Impressive though these theater-high manifestations were, the stylized solutions generated mixed responses, while the naturalistic bears of 1981, 1992, 2002, and 2006 were found both convincing and genuinely frightening. In many cases Antigonus deliberately sacrifices himself to protect the baby; occasionally a ghostly Hermione appears to protect her daughter. Often (most notably in 1976 and 1986) the bear motif is used to unify the play, reappearing in various guises throughout.

Time, That Tries All

Shakespeare's source was subtitled *The Triumph of Time* and directors have repeatedly used the concept to unify the play, emphasizing Time's role as "Shakespeare's ultimate protagonist."[90] Time opened Nunn's production as voice-over, and Eyre's as a stage-high masque character, while Cooke's production started with the chimes of midnight and unfolded beneath a giant carriage clock, as well as featuring Time the gardener as a constant onstage presence. Both Noble (1984) and Doran used a "quietly ticking clock" in the background.[91]

In 1986, Time was a jolly old man with a Warwickshire accent, hovering on large feathered wings; in 1999 he was a numinous figure with the fallen sky draped around his shoulders; in 1976 he was both bear and shaman. Often Leontes has done penance during his speech, or Perdita and Florizel met under his gaze. Just occasionally he has been displaced: in Noble's 1992 production his speech arrived "by balloon-post" to be read out "by a puzzled Camillo, casting bemused looks heavenwards,"[92] while in 2002 Warchus cut the speech altogether—instead, the Shepherd and his son ended their jig of joy holding up the baby between them and a full-grown Perdita danced on, unraveling the "baby" which became her train, only stopping as Florizel launched a (real) hawk across the theater, the lights coming down as their eyes met.

Snapper-up of Unconsidered Trifles

Autolycus has been barely mentioned here, despite the attention-grabbing bravura of his role. Vital though he is to the performance and successful as his various interpreters have been, his key characteristics and even stage business have remained remarkably constant throughout the period, implicit in the script's very strong blueprint here.

Every director has found symbolic ways of unifying the play; often these have been provided by the very aspects that seemed most problematic to early generations, such as the bear and Time. Doubling, costume echoes, reiterated technical effects, recurrent design motifs such as Noble's balloons, repeated blocking such as the 2006 fainting, even the clear progression of the seasons have all made the play a satisfying and coherent whole, moving from the "sad tale" of the opening acts to an ending "full of grace and forgiveness."[93]

THE DIRECTOR'S CUT: INTERVIEWS WITH ADRIAN NOBLE, BARBARA GAINES, AND DOMINIC COOKE

Adrian Noble, born in 1950, arrived at the RSC from the Bristol Old Vic, where he had directed several future stars in productions of classic plays. His *Henry V* on the main stage of the Royal Shakespeare Theatre in Stratford sowed the seed for Kenneth Branagh's film. Among his other major productions during his two decades at the RSC were *Hamlet*, again with Branagh in the title role; *The Plantagenets*, based on the *Henry VI / Richard III* tetralogy, and the two parts of *Henry IV*, with Robert Stephens as Falstaff. Stephens returned in 1993 to play Lear in Noble's second production of the tragedy for the company. Noble's 1994 *Midsummer Night's Dream* was made into a film. He was Artistic Director from 1991 to 2003, since when he has been a freelance director. His production style is characterized by strong use of colors and objects (such as umbrellas and balloons), and fluid scenic structure. He talks here about his 1984 small-scale touring production and, in more detail, his 1992 main stage production of *The Winter's Tale*, with John Nettles as Leontes and Samantha Bond as Hermione.

Barbara Gaines grew up outside New York City. She fell in love with Shakespeare's sonnets as a youngster and gained her first dramatic experience working for her father, a film director, during summer breaks. She graduated from Northwestern University in 1968 and had a successful career as an actress in New York and theater educator in Chicago. In 1986, she founded her Shakespeare Repertory Theater, later renamed the Chicago Shakespeare Theater. From modest beginnings it has grown to become one of the largest producing theaters in Chicago. Gaines has directed many of the plays herself, often having particular successes with less frequently performed works, such as *Antony and Cleopatra* and *Troilus and Cressida*. Here she talks about her 2003 production of *The Winter's Tale*.

Dominic Cooke, born in 1966, was educated at the University of Warwick. As an Associate Director at the RSC he undertook a number of highly successful productions, notably in the genres of comedy and romance. They combined theatrical energy with lucidity of storytelling. He also developed new theater writing for the company and directed an acclaimed production of Arthur Miller's *The Crucible*, shortly after the dramatist's death. In 2007 he became Artistic Director of the Royal Court, the British theater's leading house for contemporary drama. He talks here about his "promenade" production of *The Winter's Tale*, performed in the Swan during the RSC's Complete Works Festival of 2006–07.

How did you and your designer set about creating the distinctive worlds of Sicilia and Bohemia? The contrast between them is very important, isn't it?

Noble: I've done the play twice and didn't create contrasting worlds for either production. The first occasion was for a tour, mostly of cathedrals. It was the first promenade production [in which the audience are standing and become involved in the scenes] ever done by the RSC and its provenance is quite relevant. Back in the eighties I'd been to Lincoln to see John Caird's touring production of *Romeo and Juliet*. I missed the train on the way back so I went to visit Lincoln Cathedral. It struck me smack between the eyes that this was where we should be playing. It was at the center of the community, and so it was both a sacred and a profane space. For the first time I wanted to do the tour! The space was crucial because I could see in it the possibility of doing something that was both sacred—i.e. that told the underlying story of *The Winter's Tale* very clearly—but also profane, in the sense that it could reveal all of the wonderful contradictions of the human flesh in a marvelous way, and all very close up in a promenade production. The sacred aspect is as follows. It strikes me that underpinning the play is a very traditional medieval morality story: of the Fall, of somebody almost unknowingly falling from grace, then repentance and finally redemption. A very simple story, but one of the most important stories one could ever possibly tell about human beings, because we are all seriously flawed. I took that experience forward when I did the play with John Nettles in 1992. Anthony Ward designed it and as I said to him, it's not two worlds. It happens in one world. It's one story. To create totally different scenery for one and the other is just rubbish. We used the same scenery for both. We didn't use much but it was very beautiful. There was a box which created an inner world and an outer world, which seemed to me to be a very useful tool for this play.

Gaines: Creating a sense of place and, yes, contrast, is essential in staging this story. I wanted to feel an icy chill in Sicilia and, by contrast, a warmth within Bohemia. One of my first visual inspirations was a Russian doll box, those brilliantly painted wooden dolls that fit one inside of another. The story of *The Winter's Tale* is multiple stories, one fitting inside another, inside another, compacted by the collapsing of time.

It was winter in that chilly court of jealousy, all in tones of black, white, and grays—and it was snowing. (In Chicago, every dog owner who walks along the lakefront has a visceral knowledge of that crystal clear, midwinter cold!) In Bohemia, I saw a Russian peasant-inspired world, soaked in warmth and unabashed color. I imagined these two polar worlds both set against a black, reflective surface. A simple back wall and floor of reflective black seemed to push the essential emotional elements of Sicilia and Bohemia to their extremes. The reflectivity of a nonliteral, nonspecific set felt right because this play for me is a reflection of life and all its changes and colors and reverberations. Those mirror images reflected upon the set suggested the repetition of time—within the wide borders of this play, and within all of our lives and our stories. Our search for love and the vortex of jealousy are universal: human life on this planet has existed tens of thousands of years—as have love and jealousy. Boxes within boxes within boxes—the ripple of time passing through all of our stories.

The contrast between those two places symbolizes interiorly the antithesis within all of us, our lighter and darker elements. As life goes on, we face that darkness, and search for more light: *that* is the search within this play. Shakespeare understood that years, and lifetimes, are encompassed by it. The play emerges emotionally from the recesses of the dark sides of our souls, where our fears, jealousies, and self-doubts dwell. Like Leontes, we are afraid. We're afraid to till that interior landscape, yet we must: crises force us to. Life, with its wheel of fortune, also gives us Bohemia—a landscape of light, warmth, companionship, community, love, and color. Then in Act 5 we find ourselves in yet another place of human existence—a place of the spirit and of transcendence.

Cooke: We started with two key principles. The first was to do with time periods. It seemed to me to be very important to get the audience to have a direct and emotional response to the sixteen years' passage of time in the play, and the change that symbolizes. We thought about what period in our living memory had seen the most significant change, particularly in terms of the relationship between generations. We came up with the idea that if we started the play in the mid-fifties, with that kind of post–Cold War McCarthyist paranoia and formality, then in Act 4 you would get this extraordinary transformation to the world of the late sixties: Woodstock, hippies, and flower power. The late sixties would resonate with the pastoral imagery in that part of the play and also the feeling of a melting of barriers and boundaries, a move toward a more informal world. It gave Autolycus the feel of roving hippie and crook, a beatnik outsider, and it allowed an atmosphere at the sheep-shearing of a new generation coming through who were freer and more ready to follow their instinct. That connected with another theme of the play, the danger to the state of Florizel, a young person in a position of political power, following his instinct. These two eras just seemed emotionally right. We didn't labor the point or make a massive issue out of the differences between the two periods, it was mainly done with costume; more of a reference to the period rather than a literal setting.

The second principle was to perform the play promenade, which meant that the audience were on their feet and actually physically involved in the scenes. This idea came from noticing that the structure of the play is built around communal events: the trial scene, the

7. The involved, promenading audience: the trial scene in Dominic Cooke's 2006 production in the Swan Theatre.

sheep-shearing, and the unveiling of the statue. These were events that the audience could be directly involved in. We also turned the opening scenes into another communal event, a New Year's Eve party. This again referred to the idea of time passing; the cyclicality of time, the idea that, like the country, the court has its seasonal rituals. As the play progressed we moved from midwinter through spring into summer and ended back in winter. The way we staged the play was that the audience were part of these communal events but there were other scenes that they were watching from outside. You were both implicated as an active witness in the communal events, and then watching the consequences of those events and choices being played out privately in rooms around the palace. We played those two dynamics.

What is your view of what causes Leontes' sudden explosion of suspicion, and did that come about or develop during rehearsal?

Noble: Shakespeare requires us to be almost unprepared for it—it's written that way. We see a tiny crack and then suddenly a fissure a thousand miles deep. It struck me that we had got to start from what is written, rather than easing our way in in a comfortable fashion. In other words, not work out in advance a whole series of neuroses that would eventually lead to that explosion. If there were a series of neuroses they have to be hidden from the audience. You start from the objective, i.e. the way the words are written on the page, so it has to be sudden, it has to be instantaneous, it has to be violent, it has to be Old Testament. Then John Nettles and I worked out a psychological pattern and a series of choreographic patterns on stage that would allow that to be expressed. Exactly what John thought you'd have to ask him; in a way that's not my business, that's his mystery. I did certain things like freezing the action; I used that method from the beginning of the play. There's a feeling about the beginning of the play whereby people are clinging on to joy, clinging on to memories, whether of the nine months they've all been having this marvelous time hanging out in Sicily or of their childhood—they're hanging on to something. I dramatized that by using a lot of freeze-frames, allowing Antigonus and Camillo to walk around and look at beautiful things frozen in

8. Court celebrations (with balloons) suspended in the freeze-frame moment of jealousy, Leontes isolated as Hermione paddles Polixenes' palm: Adrian Noble's 1992 production.

time, which allowed me dramatically to use the same device when Leontes starts to go. We froze on Polixenes and Hermione, so Leontes could get within literally inches and look into her eyes, examine in a scientific way how she positioned her hand, whether it was ambiguous, all of those things. If you look through Shakespeare's canon, I think the most violent emotion he explores is sexual jealousy. It's corrosive, it's lethal, it's obscene. Whether it's Othello, whether it's the father to the daughter in *Romeo and Juliet*, whether it's *The Winter's Tale*, it's an obscene, uncontrollable emotion. It's also completely irrational: the handkerchief?! The handkerchief is as absurd as the palm paddling in *The Winter's Tale*. They're tiny things but they are the matter upon which these catastrophes rest.

Gaines: I came to rehearsal knowing it because I have felt it, been hit by it, as many people have—you turn a corner and see something you don't expect. The suddenness is completely realistic. Yes, Leontes goes further than most people: he goes mad, he is insane with jealousy. I went into rehearsal trusting Shakespeare—and in this play and in this passage in particular, he gives the actor everything he needs in the punctuation alone, forcing us to a place of teetering, breath-knocked-out-of-you imbalance: "Inch-thick, knee-deep, o'er head and ears a forked one!— / Go, play, boy, play. Thy mother plays, and I / Play too." Thoughts spill one into the other, with three mid-stop lines within one verse line. You can hardly take a breath, you can hardly think because this fit comes upon you as if you're struck by lightning. The thoughts are heaped one upon another— Shakespeare's writing at this moment is like a cyclone and it whirls you around. Meeting Leontes in rehearsal is like meeting that part of ourselves that we don't want to remember, that we hope never to meet again, but whom we *do* know. And there was no one in rehearsal who hadn't been there. It was overwhelming working that scene, overwhelming and ultimately thrilling—because it is life itself. There's no mask. When played well, there's no actor performing in it. It is life, it is shocking and cataclysmic, a terrifying journey into the abyss of the soul.

"I have *tremor cordis* on me: my heart dances, / But not for joy, not joy." I don't in any way see this as a fairy-tale moment. Perhaps it happens because he is a king, because he has only himself to answer to. But more important than being a king is being a frightened man. Because there's also terror that lives in jealousy, the terror of being a cuckold, of the shame and the humiliation of it. Something inside Leontes, some dark place that's always been there, is triggered in that moment, [thinking] "When I lose love, there is no world for me to hold on to. If I lose the people I trust, then my life is a sham, my kingdom is a sham, my child must be a bastard." I think that's the key: when he believes himself betrayed by the people closest to him, his first instinct is to destroy. None of us are that far away from being Leontes, at least in our imaginations.

Cooke: I guess I wasn't really interested in the "why" but the "what." It seems to me that the play is not really about why Leontes has become the way he has. It's about irrational behavior and the disastrous consequences of that behavior, especially in powerful people. So, for me, backstory was really only important inasmuch as it supported the actor in playing the present moment action. I'd read a lot in preparation and we had a psychoanalyst come into rehearsal to talk about Leontes' jealousy—both jealousy of Polixenes taking his wife away but also a homoerotic jealousy; that in some ways his wife was taking his potential lover away. These notions are really interesting but I don't know how relevant they are. The cause of Leontes' breakdown is not fully explored by Shakespeare and in some ways, I believe, it is as random as the appearance of the bear in the play. These events have a spiritual logic—they bring about a journey that the characters need to go on. Their cause is almost divine, rather than rooted in a literal world.

How important for you was the pagan, classical setting—the consultation of the oracle, the thunderbolt that seems to come from Jupiter?

Noble: I wouldn't say it was pagan. I would say that was part of the mystery of it. I would absolutely say it is sacred. It's numinous; it's the acceptance that there is mystery in our lives. If you have a faith then there is the possibility of some sort of invisible but ubiquitous force for good. It is interesting that Paulina says at the end, "It is required / You do awake your faith." I've done the play twice and, actually, I've done it all over the world—the tour went all over England and then to Warsaw and Kraków; my other *Winter's Tale* went all over Europe, the Far East, and to New York and Washington—and I've seen this extraordinary thing happen every single night. The audience know that there's a trick to it, but they remain profoundly moved by the transformation of the statue. One could say that Christianity is a metaphor; the fallen man, the crucifixion of Christ, the twelve disciples. But metaphor works on the human imagination in a very particular way. That scene is a metaphor, and we know it's a metaphor, but it touches us in a very mysterious and *very* potent way. It almost never fails to work. Shakespeare has set us up in using means that are in a way purely man-made, but there are visions that are sacred and things that happen beyond the material. They are of the numinous variety. It's not just a pagan play, it's a secular play, and it has another dimension, a holy dimension.

Gaines: There is a deep and abiding spirituality in this play but, no, the pagan, classical setting did not influence our production in any literal sense. These pagan gods certainly have more power than this king because, ultimately, it's in the spirit world that judges him, and Leontes loses sight of that. In rejecting the spirit world, his hubris must be tamed, he must be brought to his knees. His dear son dies, his queen dies, and his life is left in a pile of rubble. Consulting the oracle is a metaphor for making contact with our universal conscience. Spirituality for me exists beyond a single religion. I think these last plays dwell in this other realm. Spiritual guidance and influence run throughout them—here in *The Winter's Tale*, in *Pericles*, certainly in *Cymbeline*, and in *The Tempest*. These stories are elevated beyond the rules or the traditions of any single religion. They embody a reverence for life.

Cooke: It's important in that the play is mythic. It's not a literal world. It's full of psychological and emotional truth but it is conscious of itself, like the other late Shakespeare plays, as a story. It's truthful but not literal. Its connection with the classical world is that the play is concerned with an idea of spiritual laws—that there are certain spiritual laws that, if broken, will be paid for. This seems to be a very Ancient Greek notion. What we did was create a world where a divine presence existed. This, for me, is in the play—when Apollo's judgment is disobeyed, disaster strikes. We accentuated this in the trial scene by using the sound of approaching thunder as Apollo's oracle was read out. So we respected the epic, classical gesture of the play without getting caught up in a kitsch world of men in skirts!

How did you stage the moment when Antigonus exits "pursued by a bear"?

Noble: It seemed to me that it's one of those things you shouldn't duck as a director. I tried to make it as amazing, fabulous, and extraordinary as possible. I had a huge bear and staged it quite vividly. It seemed to be the thing to do. When we were on the road we had this huge sheet that the whole audience held and rippled, so they were literally creating the stage upon which Antigonus was walking. They created this strange link with death. Then literally from among the audience we had the bear coming out. You can't short change things like that. It's like people who say there shouldn't be a good fight at the end of *Hamlet*. It's just a swizz for the audience!

Gaines: The stage was very dimly lit, almost black. You hardly saw anything but what you *thought* you saw was terrifying. A huge, white polar bear, perhaps eight feet tall with a ferocious face and tremendous teeth, ran toward the audience on that deep thrust stage—a slathering, drooling beast coming straight at you as it ran up the center aisle. It was so quick and the sound so overpowering and the scream of Antigonus so terrifying, that all together in this brief moment, it was shocking. Then there was a quick blackout and we saw Antigonus' blood on the white carpet. We cared for him, and so that spot of blood was devastating.

Cooke: We had a very scary, life-size bear and it came through the audience. We tried to make it as real as possible and not send it up. I think that all these late Shakespeare plays work best when you commit to the here and now of what is happening and make that as real and as truthful as you possibly can, not comment or send it up. As Shakespeare's career develops it seems to me he writes more from a place of the unconscious. There is a mythic, poetic, divine, spiritual logic to the late plays. They're not really naturalistic plays. I think it also comes from a lifetime of having worked in the theater and understanding what an audience will accept, and how far they will go imaginatively when a play has an emotional logic. The last scene of *Cymbeline* played truthfully is very powerful, yet on the page you think it's faintly ridiculous! I think that comes from a lifetime of being an actor and writer and understanding that if an event is truthful and real, and by that I don't mean naturalistic, an audience will accept it. It's almost as if the play conjures up a bear at this point and we delivered one that was as real as possible. We also made it clear that Antigonus lured the bear away from the child—almost offering himself as a sacrifice for having exiled and abandoned the child.

One of the distinctive features of the play is the sixteen-year gap between the end of Act 3 and the beginning of Act 4. What consequences did that have for your production?

Noble: The first thing is that you have got to tell the story of what has happened. I think one of the wonderful things about the play and one of the reasons it engages an audience in an almost unique way is that it's partly about getting a second chance. It's a notion that chimes in so many ways with people. Leontes does these terrible, terrible things but he gets a second chance; that's why it's so moving. It must be like running over a child. It's out of your control. You know you shouldn't have done it; you shouldn't have gone out, or you shouldn't have stayed that long in the café or whatever. You can't go back and change it but you can have a second chance, but it requires a huge amount of time.

You have to punctuate the play in a very profound way, not just through the character of Time, the Chorus—which you've just got to do well, in a nice, imaginative way that will entertain. Funnily enough, it is the next scene that helps you do that more than anything—the scene between Polixenes and Camillo. Get two great actors and give them a nice little scene to do and you can tell that story. Then you get this extraordinary setting of Bohemia and these folk who are completely different to anybody we've seen before. Act 4 Scene 4 is one of the most creative and fertile bits of writing or dramaturgy in the whole of the canon. In that scene Shakespeare invented what in the twentieth century we call musical comedy, the form which has dominated the American stage for seventy or eighty years: the form in which there's a book and music or song, there's a story, usually a principal love story, often a clash of the generations, and usually a subplot with a song as well. The songs are there partly to create an atmosphere and a world, and also to advance the narrative; the state of the play is different at the end of the song than it was at the beginning, the story has progressed. It's quintessential Rodgers and Hammerstein. That is the template for modern musical theater. Coming out of the sixteen-year gap for Shakespeare was probably the most creative thing he could have done! He invents a new form, it's absolutely amazing! That's why some people can't really cope. They can't quite get it and want to cut chunks of it. But look at it for what it is and it's *Carousel*. It's an absolutely phenomenal piece of writing.

Gaines: Sicilia was set in 1906, so when we returned sixteen years later to the court, it was 1922. One of the primary reasons for choosing this period was that clothing had so radically changed, helping the audience understand the gulf of time that had passed between one act and another. The corseted bodices and big bustles of the Edwardian period had given way to the natural, unconstricted, and shorter silhouettes of the twenties.

Also in this same period a seismic shift in our worldview occurred. Between 1906 and 1922, the worst war humanity ever perpetrated invaded our consciousness. Man's inhumanity to man was unleashed—on a world scale mirroring Leontes' loss of all restraint on a personal, intimate scale—outrageous, unrestricted rage that can destroy a family or a continent. I wanted that heaviness and that weight to be inside these people. The historical significance of a world war in the intervening years is powerful, reflecting the cataclysmic changes that can happen in the span of just sixteen years. The war became an outward manifestation of the interior and personal war inflicted by Leontes' madness.

Is there a danger of all that jollification at the sheep-shearing feast turning into a sentimental idealization of the pastoral life, in contrast to the machinations of the court?

Cooke: I don't think so. If you really read it closely I think it's very rooted in the reality of rural life. Also, the rural world may have its humor and romance but it's shot through with pain, loss, and darkness. The scene starts with a serious argument between Florizel and Perdita about the doomed future of their relationship; it features a moment where a father disowns a son and another a daughter and Autolycus spends most of the scene ripping people off and mocking the locals. Even Mopsa and Dorcas' song is full of sexual jealousy.

It's the minor notes that need to be served in realizing the scene. Even the dances have their significance in terms of fertility and the cycles of nature. I don't think Shakespeare has any sentimental notions about nature—the country can be a frightening place, as well as a beautiful one. This duality is there in many other of his plays: *As You Like It*, for example.

What was your take on Autolycus: lovable rogue or something more sinister?

Noble: He's out to make a buck, really, I don't think he's any more sinister than that. He tries to manipulate people and he's caught out, and the people whom he would regard as unsophisticated in fact get the better of him in the end—the Clown and the Old Shepherd.

Gaines: I think he's the most charming thief, but he *is* a criminal— he steals things that are precious to people. But it just goes to show that if you can make us laugh, you can get away with just about anything! On the other hand, if he stole a locket that my grandmother gave me, I'd want to strangle him. As far as we know, Autolycus is the worst thing Bohemia has going, and when you juxtapose his crimes to Sicilia's, they're obviously not in the same ballpark. If you took Autolycus and made him a miserable bastard, you'd be committing an artistic "crime" yourself because he's so full of the joy of life. He's one of the cleverest petty villains in Shakespeare. So does he belong in jail? Yes, but just keep letting him out long enough to keep us laughing.

Cooke: I really learned a lot about him through doing that production. If ever I do it again I'll start from a different place. He's not really a lovable rogue. He's funny, but I think he's a damaged outsider who wants to get his revenge on the world for having rejected him. He's a watchful, cunning wolf. The more I learned about him the more I understood that actually there is an amazingly amoral self-interest at work in that character. Sure, there's humor, but like Perdita, Hermione, and, to an extent, Florizel, he's displaced.

How did you stage the moment where the "statue" of Hermione is revived?

Noble: When I did the promenade production it was done right smack in the middle of the audience, with seven hundred people standing up, crowding around it. They were literally within two feet of it, so could see it from all angles. That meant we were the witnesses. We were the people who were required to awaken our faith. We were put on the spot by Paulina. When you do it inside a proscenium arch it seems to me that the people watching should be the focus, not the statue. I did a clever thing where I got the statue on stage without anybody knowing it was on; suddenly she was there but with her back to us. She was right downstage on the lip of the stage and in a semicircle around her were the witnesses who were watching her. So the light was on their faces watching her. Therefore we got the energy through *them*, through their faces, their belief. It was interesting because it worked either way.

Gaines: A thrust stage is a lot less forgiving in staging a scene like this one. I wanted the moment to be thrilling and I wanted it to be heartbreaking: someone we have loved and lost forever comes back to life. What is more miraculous than that?—but there's such heartache between them. In that moment, I wanted us to remember the sorrow and feel the joy.

On our deep thrust stage, the simple, three-step pedestal was positioned downstage of the proscenium arch, and so the statue was within a few feet of many. Paulina moved aside a curtain to reveal her statue. The skin color was the same tone as the "stone" of Hermione's simple, classically draped dress—a pale, off-white color—and skin and dress all looked like one piece. The lighting washed the entire statue in a cool, blue light, and as Hermione came to life, the figure was transformed to a soft, warm amber. As you watched the rose color return to her cheeks, you actually felt life being breathed into this statue. I remember so often people leaning forward in their seats as the statue would begin to move. The moment was accompanied by the music of a single oboe. It was a moment of grace and of forgiveness. It begs the question: how much are we willing to forgive a great harm and injustice?

Cooke: Following our logic of communal events it became like the end of a party, so that the audience were involved in it. That made it in a way cyclical, because our production began with a New Year's Eve party. We tried as much as possible to play off the reactions of the court rather than the statue. I have to say that I was a bit inspired in that by Adrian Noble's production. I knew that production quite well because it was on at the RSC when I was an Assistant Director there. I didn't work on it but I loved it and saw it lots of times and I thought it was a stroke of genius the way he staged that scene, because of course it's not about what she's feeling, it's about what everyone else is feeling in relation to her. It's their rebirth, especially Leontes', that we're witnessing, as much as hers. We had to fly in Kate [Fleetwood], who was playing Hermione, onto this platform, hidden behind a canopy. When she was revealed the audience were watching her back and observing the reactions of Leontes and the royal family, as well as all of the courtiers who'd been there at the first scene. It was very moving to see them all sixteen years older. It was very difficult to achieve and took quite a few previews before we could get it right. She was in a very iridescent, pearl-gray dress that caught the light. So we played it off a lot of the reactions of the courtiers, and Leontes.

It may well be that the boy actor who played Mamillius in Shakespeare's original production doubled as Perdita, giving an extra layer of meaning to the idea of the lost child being found. But can the finding of Perdita ever really compensate for the loss of Mamillius?

Noble: That isn't a question about drama, it's a question about the nature of grief and loss. Inside the play I think he gives us a pretty accurate and insightful portrait of grief. Parents should not bury their children. It should not happen. It's an abomination, and the grief will never ever go away. I don't think Shakespeare says it ever does go away. But he does give you a miracle. There's no question at all that the saving of Perdita is a miracle. Her life is saved through divine intervention. That bear should eat that baby. On both occasions I've done it I've made that very clear. I've had the bear sniffing around the baby, pawing the baby, looking at the baby and not killing the baby. Someone is looking after her. So the weight of emotion you get when Perdita is reunited with her father and then her mother is overwhelming. I think Shakespeare gives you that, but you can't take grief away. It's not a set of scales that balance out.

Gaines: In no sense can Mamillius be replaced by Perdita. No child is replaced by another. Also, I wanted to cast the boy younger, eight or nine years old—much younger than Perdita at age sixteen. The younger he is, the more innocent he is, the more moving his lines, and the more horrific his death. He's an extraordinary child— a storyteller—and the world is less rich without him.

Cooke: No. I've seen it done like that and it can really work. If you have male actors or, as they would have been, boy actors, I think it works because there is always a fascinating duality when a young man is playing a woman. But I think a woman in her early twenties playing a little boy is potentially a very painful thing. I can't abide adults playing children; it always seems fake and theatrical in a cod way, so we didn't go down that path.

I don't think the finding of Perdita can compensate for the loss of Mamillius. There's a strong sense of loss as well as joy at the end of the play, which is one of the reasons why it's the greatest ending of any play, ever. It's shot through with melancholy. There's a strong sense, when Leontes sees the statue before it comes to life, that his grief for Hermione is still alive and that there's a part of him that will never recover. You feel that when the play is done honestly. Although there's this redemptive ending, a rebirth, or at the very least, a second chance, there's also a strong sense that damage has been done that cannot be compensated for. It's a very bittersweet ending.

What about the moment at the end when Camillo is married off to Paulina? It often gets a laugh in the theater, but maybe there's a rightness about it, since they are both such good people?

Noble: I think you'd have to have a very dull production for it *not* to get a laugh. If you don't get a laugh on that you're in real trouble! Because you like them both so much and so it's fabulous. It's one of those lovely things that happen. If the audience don't laugh at that it's because they weren't moved by the reconciliation before; it's partly relief, so you've got to get a laugh there otherwise you're in real trouble. It's like a tap.

Gaines: I wouldn't deny that laugh for anything in the world. It leaves us happy. "O, peace, Paulina!" That's why they laugh—Leontes tells her to shut up! Of course you can play it many ways, but we need to laugh. Frankly, we *deserve* to laugh. What's better than a good belly laugh as two old friends get married? The theatricality of these last moments is brilliant. It's yet another kind of rebirth, and in this, too, we see the threads connecting this play to his other late plays, which end in reunion, forgiveness, and rebirth. But, personally, if I were Paulina, I'd be annoyed to death . . .

Cooke: They're both highly skilled political animals as well, so there's a good match in that respect. One of the things I discovered about Camillo through doing the play is what a consummate politician he is. I think Paulina is as well, in her own way. Not that she is politic in a Machiavellian, sly way; she's very impassioned and direct, but nonetheless she's a skilled rhetorician. I think Shakespeare is often conservative in his view of youth: it's often the older characters that he really values the most. In *All's Well That Ends Well* it's characters like Lafew and the Countess that make the soundest judgment and the young ones, Bertram and Helen, that are impulsive and narcissistic. Young people follow their hearts, and following your heart is not always the best way to respond to the world, especially if you're in a powerful family. There's a kind of harmony in Camillo's betrothal to Paulina, and an audience enjoys the tying up of ends at the close of a play. In this respect, Shakespeare plays, especially in these late works, with convention. He plays with the conventional happy ending in a very knowing way. Again, *Cymbeline* is a really interesting point of comparison, where everything is resolved to a ridiculous degree as in a fairy tale; he's playing with an audience's hopes and expectations and acknowledging that in some ways every story is generic, but at the same time he's committing to the emotional reality of the play. There's huge pleasure for an audience in that.

9. Autolycus the con man: Richard Katz in Dominic Cooke's 2006 production.

SHAKESPEARE'S CAREER
IN THE THEATER

BEGINNINGS

William Shakespeare was an extraordinarily intelligent man who was born and died in an ordinary market town in the English Midlands. He lived an uneventful life in an eventful age. Born in April 1564, he was the eldest son of John Shakespeare, a glove maker who was prominent on the town council until he fell into financial difficulties. Young William was educated at the local grammar in Stratford-upon-Avon, Warwickshire, where he gained a thorough grounding in the Latin language, the art of rhetoric, and classical poetry. He married Ann Hathaway and had three children (Susanna, then the twins Hamnet and Judith) before his twenty-first birthday: an exceptionally young age for the period. We do not know how he supported his family in the mid-1580s.

Like many clever country boys, he moved to the city in order to make his way in the world. Like many creative people, he found a career in the entertainment business. Public playhouses and professional full-time acting companies reliant on the market for their income were born in Shakespeare's childhood. When he arrived in London as a man, sometime in the late 1580s, a new phenomenon was in the making: the actor who is so successful that he becomes a "star." The word did not exist in its modern sense, but the pattern is recognizable: audiences went to the theater not so much to see a particular show as to witness the comedian Richard Tarlton or the dramatic actor Edward Alleyn.

Shakespeare was an actor before he was a writer. It appears not to have been long before he realized that he was never going to grow into a great comedian like Tarlton or a great tragedian like Alleyn. Instead, he found a role within his company as the man who patched up old plays, breathing new life, new dramatic twists, into tired repertory pieces. He paid close attention to the work of the university-educated dramatists who were writing history plays and tragedies for the public stage in a style more ambitious, sweeping, and poetically grand than anything that had been seen before. But he may also have noted that what his friend and rival Ben Jonson would call "Marlowe's mighty line" sometimes faltered in the mode of comedy. Going to university, as Christopher Marlowe did, was all well and good for honing the arts of rhetorical elaboration and classical allusion, but it could lead to a loss of the common touch. To stay close to a large segment of the potential audience for public theater, it was necessary to write for clowns as well as kings and to intersperse the flights of poetry with the humor of the tavern, the privy, and the brothel: Shakespeare was the first to establish himself early in his career as an equal master of tragedy, comedy, and history. He realized that theater could be the medium to make the national past available to a wider audience than the elite who could afford to read large history books: his signature early works include not only the classical tragedy *Titus Andronicus* but also the sequence of English historical plays on the Wars of the Roses.

He also invented a new role for himself, that of in-house company dramatist. Where his peers and predecessors had to sell their plays to the theater managers on a poorly paid piecework basis, Shakespeare took a percentage of the box-office income. The Lord Chamberlain's Men constituted themselves in 1594 as a joint stock company, with the profits being distributed among the core actors who had invested as sharers. Shakespeare acted himself—he appears in the cast lists of some of Ben Jonson's plays as well as the list of actors' names at the beginning of his own collected works—but his principal duty was to write two or three plays a year for the company. By holding shares, he was effectively earning himself a royalty on his work, something no author had ever done before in England. When the Lord Chamberlain's Men collected their fee for performance at court in the Christmas season of 1594, three of them went along to the Treasurer of the Chamber: not just Richard Burbage the tragedian and Will Kempe the clown, but also Shakespeare the scriptwriter. That was something new.

The next four years were the golden period in Shakespeare's

career, though overshadowed by the death of his only son, Hamnet, aged eleven, in 1596. In his early thirties and in full command of both his poetic and his theatrical medium, he perfected his art of comedy, while also developing his tragic and historical writing in new ways. In 1598, Francis Meres, a Cambridge University graduate with his finger on the pulse of the London literary world, praised Shakespeare for his excellence across the genres:

> As Plautus and Seneca are accounted the best for comedy and tragedy among the Latins, so Shakespeare among the English is the most excellent in both kinds for the stage; for comedy, witness his *Gentlemen of Verona*, his *Errors*, his *Love Labours Lost*, his *Love Labours Won*, his *Midsummer Night Dream* and his *Merchant of Venice:* for tragedy his *Richard the 2*, *Richard the 3*, *Henry the 4*, *King John*, *Titus Andronicus* and his *Romeo and Juliet*.

For Meres, as for the many writers who praised the "honey-flowing vein" of *Venus and Adonis* and *Lucrece*, narrative poems written when the theaters were closed due to plague in 1593–94, Shakespeare was marked above all by his linguistic skill, by the gift of turning elegant poetic phrases.

PLAYHOUSES

Elizabethan playhouses were "thrust" or "one-room" theaters. To understand Shakespeare's original theatrical life, we have to forget about the indoor theater of later times, with its proscenium arch and curtain that would be opened at the beginning and closed at the end of each act. In the proscenium arch theater, stage and auditorium are effectively two separate rooms: the audience looks from one world into another as if through the imaginary "fourth wall" framed by the proscenium. The picture-frame stage, together with the elaborate scenic effects and backdrops beyond it, created the illusion of a self-contained world—especially once nineteenth-century developments in the control of artificial lighting meant that the auditorium could be darkened and the spectators made to focus on the lighted stage. Shakespeare, by contrast, wrote for a bare platform stage with a standing audience gathered around it in a courtyard in full daylight. The audience were always conscious of themselves and their fellow spectators, and they shared the same "room" as the actors. A sense of immediate presence and the creation of rapport with the audience were all-important. The actor could not afford to imagine he was in a closed world, with silent witnesses dutifully observing him from the darkness.

Shakespeare's theatrical career began at the Rose Theatre in Southwark. The stage was wide and shallow, trapezoid in shape, like a lozenge. This design had a great deal of potential for the theatrical equivalent of cinematic split-screen effects, whereby one group of characters would enter at the door at one end of the tiring-house wall at the back of the stage and another group through the door at the other end, thus creating two rival tableaux. Many of the battle-heavy and faction-filled plays that premiered at the Rose have scenes of just this sort.

At the rear of the Rose stage, there were three capacious exits, each over ten feet wide. Unfortunately, the very limited excavation of a fragmentary portion of the original Globe site, also in 1989, revealed nothing about the stage. The first Globe was built in 1599 with similar proportions to those of another theater, the Fortune, albeit that the former was polygonal and looked circular, whereas the latter was rectangular. The building contract for the Fortune survives and allows us to infer that the stage of the Globe was probably substantially wider than it was deep (perhaps forty-three feet wide and twenty-seven feet deep). It may well have been tapered at the front, like that of the Rose.

The capacity of the Globe was said to have been enormous, perhaps in excess of three thousand. It has been conjectured that about eight hundred people may have stood in the yard, with two thousand or more in the three layers of covered galleries. The other "public" playhouses were also of large capacity, whereas the indoor Blackfriars theater that Shakespeare's company began using in 1608—the former refectory of a monastery—had overall internal dimensions of a mere forty-six by sixty feet. It would have made for a much more intimate theatrical experience and had a much smaller capacity, probably of about six hundred people. Since they paid at least six-pence a head, the Blackfriars attracted a more select or "private" audience. The atmosphere would have been closer to that of an indoor performance before the court in the Whitehall Palace or at Richmond. That Shakespeare always wrote for indoor production at court as well as outdoor performance in the public theater should make us cautious about inferring, as some scholars have, that the opportunity provided by the intimacy of the Blackfriars led to a sig-nificant change toward a "chamber" style in his last plays—which, besides, were performed at both the Globe and the Blackfriars. After the occupation of the Blackfriars a five-act structure seems to have become more important to Shakespeare. That was because of artifi-cial lighting: there were musical interludes between the acts, while the candles were trimmed and replaced. Again, though, something similar must have been necessary for indoor court performances throughout his career.

Front of house there were the "gatherers" who collected the money from audience members: a penny to stand in the open-air yard, another penny for a place in the covered galleries, sixpence for the prominent "lord's rooms" to the side of the stage. In the indoor "private" theaters, gallants from the audience who fancied making themselves part of the spectacle sat on stools on the edge of the stage itself. Scholars debate as to how widespread this practice was in the public theaters such as the Globe. Once the audience were in place and the money counted, the gatherers were available to be extras on stage. That is one reason why battles and crowd scenes often come later rather than early in Shakespeare's plays. There was no formal prohibition upon performance by women, and there certainly were women among the gatherers, so it is not beyond the bounds of possi-bility that female crowd members were played by females.

The play began at two o'clock in the afternoon and the theater had to be cleared by five. After the main show, there would be a jig—which consisted not only of dancing, but also of knockabout comedy (it is the origin of the farcical "afterpiece" in the eighteenth-century theater). So the time available for a Shakespeare play was about two and a half hours, somewhere between the "two hours' traffic" men-tioned in the prologue to *Romeo and Juliet* and the "three hours' spectacle" referred to in the preface to the 1647 Folio of Beaumont and Fletcher's plays. The prologue to a play by Thomas Middleton refers to a thousand lines as "one hour's words," so the likelihood is that about two and a half thousand, or a maximum of three thousand, lines made up the performed text. This is indeed the length of most of Shakespeare's comedies, whereas many of his tragedies and histories are much longer, raising the possibility that he wrote full scripts, possibly with eventual publication in mind, in the full knowledge that the stage version would be heavily cut. The short Quarto texts published in his lifetime—they used to be called "Bad" Quartos—provide fascinating evidence as to the kind of cutting that probably took place. So, for instance, the First Quarto of *Hamlet* neatly merges two occasions when Hamlet is overheard, the "Fishmonger" and the "nunnery" scenes.

The social composition of the audience was mixed. The poet Sir John Davies wrote of "A thousand townsmen, gentlemen and whores, / Porters and servingmen" who would "together throng" at the public playhouses. Though moralists associated female playgoing with adultery and the sex trade, many perfectly respectable citizens' wives were regular attendees. Some, no doubt, resembled the modern groupie: a story attested in two different sources has one citizen's wife making a post-show assignation with Richard Burbage and ending up in bed with Shakespeare—supposedly eliciting from the latter the quip that William the Conqueror was before Richard III. Defenders of theater liked to say that by witnessing the comeuppance of villains on the stage, audience members would repent of their own wrongdoings, but the reality is that most people went to the theater then, as they do now, for entertainment more than moral edification. Besides, it would be foolish to suppose that audiences behaved in a homogeneous way: a pamphlet of the 1630s tells of how two men went to see *Pericles* and one of them laughed while the other wept. Bishop John Hall complained that people went to church for the same reasons that they went to the theater: "for company, for custom, for recreation . . . to feed his eyes or his ears . . . or perhaps for sleep."

Men-about-town and clever young lawyers went to be seen as much as to see. In the modern popular imagination, shaped not least by *Shakespeare in Love* and the opening sequence of Laurence Olivier's *Henry V* film, the penny-paying groundlings stand in the yard hurling abuse or encouragement and hazelnuts or orange peel at the actors, while the sophisticates in the covered galleries appreciate Shakespeare's soaring poetry. The reality was probably the other way round. A "groundling" was a kind of fish, so the nickname suggests the penny audience standing below the level of the stage and gazing in silent openmouthed wonder at the spectacle unfolding above them. The more difficult audience members, who kept up a running commentary of clever remarks on the performance and who occasionally got into quarrels with players, were the gallants. Like Hollywood movies in modern times, Elizabethan and Jacobean plays exercised a powerful influence on the fashion and behavior of the young. John Marston mocks the lawyers who would open their lips, perhaps to court a girl, and out would "flow / Naught but pure Juliet and Romeo."

THE ENSEMBLE AT WORK

In the absence of typewriters and photocopying machines, reading aloud would have been the means by which the company got to know a new play. The tradition of the playwright reading his complete script to the assembled company endured for generations. A copy would then have been taken to the Master of the Revels for licensing. The theater book-holder or prompter would then have copied the parts for distribution to the actors. A partbook consisted of the character's lines, with each speech preceded by the last three or four words of the speech before, the so-called cue. These would have been taken away and studied or "conned." During this period of learning the parts, an actor might have had some one-to-one instruction, perhaps from the dramatist, perhaps from a senior actor who had played the same part before, and, in the case of an apprentice, from his master. A high percentage of Desdemona's lines occur in dialogue with Othello, of Lady Macbeth's with Macbeth, Cleopatra's with Antony, and Volumnia's with Coriolanus. The roles would almost certainly have been taken by the apprentice of the lead actor, usually Burbage, who delivers the majority of the cues. Given that

10. Hypothetical reconstruction of the interior of an Elizabethan playhouse during a performance.

apprentices lodged with their masters, there would have been ample opportunity for personal instruction, which may be what made it possible for young men to play such demanding parts.

After the parts were learned, there may have been no more than a single rehearsal before the first performance. With six different plays to be put on every week, there was no time for more. Actors, then, would go into a show with a very limited sense of the whole. The notion of a collective rehearsal process that is itself a process of discovery for the actors is wholly modern and would have been incomprehensible to Shakespeare and his original ensemble. Given the number of parts an actor had to hold in his memory, the forgetting of lines was probably more frequent than in the modern theater. The book-holder was on hand to prompt.

Backstage personnel included the property man, the tire-man who oversaw the costumes, call boys, attendants, and the musicians, who might play at various times from the main stage, the rooms above and within the tiring-house. Scriptwriters sometimes made a nuisance of themselves backstage. There was often tension between the acting companies and the freelance playwrights from whom they purchased scripts: it was a smart move on the part of Shakespeare and the Lord Chamberlain's Men to bring the writing process in-house.

Scenery was limited, though sometimes set pieces were brought on (a bank of flowers, a bed, the mouth of hell). The trapdoor from below, the gallery stage above, and the curtained discovery space at the back allowed for an array of special effects: the rising of ghosts and apparitions, the descent of gods, dialogue between a character at a window and another at ground level, the revelation of a statue or a pair of lovers playing at chess. Ingenious use could be made of props, as with the ass's head in *A Midsummer Night's Dream*. In a theater that does not clutter the stage with the material paraphernalia of everyday life, those objects that are deployed may take on powerful symbolic weight, as when Shylock bears his weighing scales in one hand and knife in the other, thus becoming a parody of the figure of Justice who traditionally bears a sword and a balance. Among the more significant items in the property cupboard of Shakespeare's company, there would have been a throne (the "chair of state"), joint stools, books, bottles, coins, purses, letters (which are brought on stage, read, or referred to on about eighty occasions in the complete works), maps, gloves, a set of stocks (in which Kent is put in *King Lear*), rings, rapiers, daggers, broadswords, staves, pistols, masks and vizards, heads and skulls, torches and tapers and lanterns which served to signal night scenes on the daylit stage, a buck's head, an ass's head, animal costumes. Live animals also put in appearances, most notably the dog Crab in *The Two Gentlemen of Verona* and possibly a young polar bear in *The Winter's Tale*.

The costumes were the most important visual dimension of the play. Playwrights were paid between £2 and £6 per script, whereas Alleyn was not averse to paying £20 for "a black velvet cloak with sleeves embroidered all with silver and gold." No matter the period of the play, actors always wore contemporary costume. The excitement for the audience came not from any impression of historical accuracy, but from the richness of the attire and perhaps the transgressive thrill of the knowledge that here were commoners like themselves strutting in the costumes of courtiers in effective defiance of the strict sumptuary laws whereby in real life people had to wear the clothes that befitted their social station.

To an even greater degree than props, costumes could carry symbolic importance. Racial characteristics could be suggested: a breastplate and helmet for a Roman soldier, a turban for a Turk, long robes for exotic characters such as Moors, a gabardine for a Jew. The figure of Time, as in *The Winter's Tale*, would be equipped with hourglass, scythe, and wings; Rumour, who speaks the prologue of *2 Henry IV*, wore a costume adorned with a thousand tongues. The wardrobe in the tiring-house of the Globe would have contained much of the same stock as that of rival manager Philip Henslowe at the Rose: green gowns for outlaws and foresters, black for melancholy men such as Jaques and people in mourning such as the Countess in *All's Well That Ends Well* (at the beginning of *Hamlet*, the prince is still in mourning black when everyone else is in festive garb for the wedding of the new king), a gown and hood for a friar (or a feigned friar like the duke in *Measure for Measure*), blue coats and tawny to distinguish the followers of rival factions, a leather apron and ruler for a carpenter (as in the opening scene of *Julius Caesar*—and in *A Midsummer Night's Dream*, where this is the only sign that Peter Quince is a carpenter), a cockle hat with staff and a pair of sandals for a pilgrim or palmer (the disguise assumed by Helen in *All's Well*), bodices and kirtles with farthingales beneath for the boys who are to be dressed as girls. A gender switch such as that of Rosalind or Jessica seems to have taken between fifty and eighty lines of dialogue—Viola does not resume her "maiden weeds," but remains in her boy's costume to the end of *Twelfth Night* because a change would have slowed down the action at just the moment it was speeding to a climax. Henslowe's inventory also included "a robe for to go invisible": Oberon, Puck, and Ariel must have had something similar.

As the costumes appealed to the eyes, so there was music for the ears. Comedies included many songs. Desdemona's willow song, perhaps a late addition to the text, is a rare and thus exceptionally poignant example from tragedy. Trumpets and tuckets sounded for ceremonial entrances, drums denoted an army on the march. Background music could create atmosphere, as at the beginning of

Twelfth Night, during the lovers' dialogue near the end of *The Merchant of Venice*, when the statue seemingly comes to life in *The Winter's Tale*, and for the revival of Pericles and of Lear (in the Quarto text, but not the Folio). The haunting sound of the hautboy suggested a realm beyond the human, as when the god Hercules is imagined deserting Mark Antony. Dances symbolized the harmony of the end of a comedy—though in Shakespeare's world of mingled joy and sorrow, someone is usually left out of the circle.

The most important resource was, of course, the actors themselves. They needed many skills: in the words of one contemporary commentator, "dancing, activity, music, song, elocution, ability of body, memory, skill of weapon, pregnancy of wit." Their bodies were as significant as their voices. Hamlet tells the player to "suit the action to the word, the word to the action": moments of strong emotion, known as "passions," relied on a repertoire of dramatic gestures as well as a modulation of the voice. When Titus Andronicus has had his hand chopped off, he asks "How can I grace my talk, / Wanting a hand to give it action?" A pen portrait of "The Character of an Excellent Actor" by the dramatist John Webster is almost certainly based on his impression of Shakespeare's leading man, Richard Burbage: "By a full and significant action of body, he charms our attention: sit in a full theatre, and you will think you see so many lines drawn from the circumference of so many ears, whiles the actor is the centre . . ."

Though Burbage was admired above all others, praise was also heaped upon the apprentice players whose alto voices fitted them for the parts of women. A spectator at Oxford in 1610 records how the audience was reduced to tears by the pathos of Desdemona's death. The puritans who fumed about the biblical prohibition upon cross-dressing and the encouragement to sodomy constituted by the sight of an adult male kissing a teenage boy on stage were a small minority. Little is known, however, about the characteristics of the leading apprentices in Shakespeare's company. It may perhaps be inferred that one was a lot taller than the other, since Shakespeare often wrote for a pair of female friends, one tall and fair, the other short and dark (Helena and Hermia, Rosalind and Celia, Beatrice and Hero).

We know little about Shakespeare's own acting roles—an early allusion indicates that he often took royal parts, and a venerable tradition gives him old Adam in *As You Like It* and the ghost of old King Hamlet. Save for Burbage's lead roles and the generic part of the clown, all such castings are mere speculation. We do not even know for sure whether the original Falstaff was Will Kempe or another actor who specialized in comic roles, Thomas Pope.

Kempe left the company in early 1599. Tradition has it that he fell out with Shakespeare over the matter of excessive improvisation. He was replaced by Robert Armin, who was less of a clown and more of a cerebral wit: this explains the difference between such parts as Lancelet Gobbo and Dogberry, which were written for Kempe, and the more verbally sophisticated Feste and Lear's Fool, which were written for Armin.

One thing that is clear from surviving "plots" or storyboards of plays from the period is that a degree of doubling was necessary. *2 Henry VI* has over sixty speaking parts, but more than half of the characters only appear in a single scene and most scenes have only six to eight speakers. At a stretch, the play could be performed by thirteen actors. When Thomas Platter saw *Julius Caesar* at the Globe in 1599, he noted that there were about fifteen. Why doesn't Paris go to the Capulet ball in *Romeo and Juliet*? Perhaps because he was doubled with Mercutio, who does. In *The Winter's Tale*, Mamillius might have come back as Perdita and Antigonus been doubled by Camillo, making the partnership with Paulina at the end a very neat touch. Titania and Oberon are often played by the same pair as Hippolyta and Theseus, suggesting a symbolic matching of the rulers of the worlds of night and day, but it is questionable whether there would have been time for the necessary costume changes. As so often, one is left in a realm of tantalizing speculation.

THE KING'S MAN

The new king, James I, who had held the Scottish throne as James VI since he had been an infant, immediately took the Lord Chamberlain's Men under his direct patronage. Henceforth they would be the King's Men, and for the rest of Shakespeare's career they were favored with far more court performances than any of their rivals.

There even seem to have been rumors early in the reign that Shakespeare and Burbage were being considered for knighthoods, an unprecedented honor for mere actors—and one that in the event was not accorded to a member of the profession for nearly three hundred years, when the title was bestowed upon Henry Irving, the leading Shakespearean actor of Queen Victoria's reign.

Shakespeare's productivity rate slowed in the Jacobean years, not because of age or some personal trauma, but because there were frequent outbreaks of plague, causing the theaters to be closed for long periods. The King's Men were forced to spend many months on the road. Between November 1603 and 1608, they were to be found at various towns in the south and Midlands, though Shakespeare probably did not tour with them by this time. He had bought a large house back home in Stratford and was accumulating other property. He may indeed have stopped acting soon after the new king took the throne. With the London theaters closed so much of the time and a large repertoire on the stocks, Shakespeare seems to have focused his energies on writing a few long and complex tragedies that could have been played on demand at court: *Othello*, *King Lear*, *Antony and Cleopatra*, *Coriolanus*, and *Cymbeline* are among his longest and poetically grandest plays. *Macbeth* only survives in a shorter text, which shows signs of adaptation after Shakespeare's death. The bitterly satirical *Timon of Athens*, apparently a collaboration with Thomas Middleton that may have failed on the stage, also belongs to this period. In comedy, too, he wrote longer and morally darker works than in the Elizabethan period, pushing at the very bounds of the form in *Measure for Measure* and *All's Well That Ends Well*.

From 1608 onward, when the King's Men began occupying the indoor Blackfriars playhouse (as a winter house, meaning that they only used the outdoor Globe in summer?), Shakespeare turned to a more romantic style. His company had a great success with a revived and altered version of an old pastoral play called *Mucedorus*. It even featured a bear. The younger dramatist John Fletcher, meanwhile, sometimes working in collaboration with Francis Beaumont, was pioneering a new style of tragicomedy, a mix of romance and royalism laced with intrigue and pastoral excursions. Shakespeare experimented with this idiom in *Cymbeline* and it was presumably with his blessing that Fletcher eventually took over as the King's Men's company dramatist. The two writers apparently collaborated on three plays in the years 1612–14: a lost romance called *Cardenio* (based on the love-madness of a character in Cervantes' *Don Quixote*), *Henry VIII* (originally staged with the title "All Is True"), and *The Two Noble Kinsmen*, a dramatization of Chaucer's "Knight's Tale." These were written after Shakespeare's two final solo-authored plays, *The Winter's Tale*, a self-consciously old-fashioned work dramatizing the pastoral romance of his old enemy Robert Greene, and *The Tempest*, which at one and the same time drew together multiple theatrical traditions, diverse reading, and contemporary interest in the fate of a ship that had been wrecked on the way to the New World.

The collaborations with Fletcher suggest that Shakespeare's career ended with a slow fade rather than the sudden retirement supposed by the nineteenth-century Romantic critics who read Prospero's epilogue to *The Tempest* as Shakespeare's personal farewell to his art. In the last few years of his life Shakespeare certainly spent more of his time in Stratford-upon-Avon, where he became further involved in property dealing and litigation. But his London life also continued. In 1613 he made his first major London property purchase: a freehold house in the Blackfriars district, close to his company's indoor theater. *The Two Noble Kinsmen* may have been written as late as 1614, and Shakespeare was in London on business a little over a year before he died of an unknown cause at home in Stratford-upon-Avon in 1616, probably on his fifty-second birthday.

About half the sum of his works were published in his lifetime, in texts of variable quality. A few years after his death, his fellow actors began putting together an authorized edition of his complete *Comedies, Histories and Tragedies*. It appeared in 1623, in large "Folio" format. This collection of thirty-six plays gave Shakespeare his immortality. In the words of his fellow dramatist Ben Jonson, who contributed two poems of praise at the start of the Folio, the body of his work made him "a monument without a tomb":

And art alive still while thy book doth live
And we have wits to read and praise to give . . .
He was not of an age, but for all time!

SHAKESPEARE'S WORKS: A CHRONOLOGY

1589–91	*? Arden of Faversham* (possible part authorship)
1589–92	*The Taming of the Shrew*
1589–92	*? Edward the Third* (possible part authorship)
1591	*The Second Part of Henry the Sixth*, originally called *The First Part of the Contention Betwixt the Two Famous Houses of York and Lancaster* (element of co-authorship possible)
1591	*The Third Part of Henry the Sixth*, originally called *The True Tragedy of Richard Duke of York* (element of co-authorship probable)
1591–92	*The Two Gentlemen of Verona*
1591–92 perhaps revised 1594	*The Lamentable Tragedy of Titus Andronicus* (probably co-written with, or revising an earlier version by, George Peele)
1592	*The First Part of Henry the Sixth*, probably with Thomas Nashe and others
1592/94	*King Richard the Third*
1593	*Venus and Adonis* (poem)
1593–94	*The Rape of Lucrece* (poem)
1593–1608	*Sonnets* (154 poems, published 1609 with *A Lover's Complaint*, a poem of disputed authorship)
1592–94/ 1600–03	*Sir Thomas More* (a single scene for a play originally by Anthony Munday, with other revisions by Henry Chettle, Thomas Dekker, and Thomas Heywood)
1594	*The Comedy of Errors*
1595	*Love's Labour's Lost*

1595–97	*Love's Labour's Won* (a lost play, unless the original title for another comedy)
1595–96	*A Midsummer Night's Dream*
1595–96	*The Tragedy of Romeo and Juliet*
1595–96	*King Richard the Second*
1595–97	*The Life and Death of King John* (possibly earlier)
1596–97	*The Merchant of Venice*
1596–97	*The First Part of Henry the Fourth*
1597–98	*The Second Part of Henry the Fourth*
1598	*Much Ado About Nothing*
1598–99	*The Passionate Pilgrim* (20 poems, some not by Shakespeare)
1599	*The Life of Henry the Fifth*
1599	"To the Queen" (epilogue for a court performance)
1599	*As You Like It*
1599	*The Tragedy of Julius Caesar*
1600–01	*The Tragedy of Hamlet, Prince of Denmark* (perhaps revising an earlier version)
1600–01	*The Merry Wives of Windsor* (perhaps revising version of 1597–99)
1601	"Let the Bird of Loudest Lay" (poem, known since 1807 as "The Phoenix and Turtle" [turtledove])
1601	*Twelfth Night, or What You Will*
1601–02	*The Tragedy of Troilus and Cressida*
1604	*The Tragedy of Othello, the Moor of Venice*
1604	*Measure for Measure*
1605	*All's Well That Ends Well*
1605	*The Life of Timon of Athens*, with Thomas Middleton
1605–06	*The Tragedy of King Lear*
1605–08	? contribution to *The Four Plays in One* (lost, except for *A Yorkshire Tragedy*, mostly by Thomas Middleton)

1606	*The Tragedy of Macbeth* (surviving text has additional scenes by Thomas Middleton)
1606–07	*The Tragedy of Antony and Cleopatra*
1608	*The Tragedy of Coriolanus*
1608	*Pericles, Prince of Tyre*, with George Wilkins
1610	*The Tragedy of Cymbeline*
1611	*The Winter's Tale*
1611	*The Tempest*
1612–13	*Cardenio*, with John Fletcher (survives only in later adaptation called *Double Falsehood* by Lewis Theobald)
1613	*Henry VIII (All Is True)*, with John Fletcher
1613–14	*The Two Noble Kinsmen*, with John Fletcher

FURTHER READING AND VIEWING

CRITICAL APPROACHES

Adelman, Janet, "Masculine Authority and the Maternal Body: The Return to Origins in the Romances," in her *Suffocating Mothers: Fantasies of Maternal Origin in Shakespeare's Plays, Hamlet to The Tempest* (1992), pp. 193–238. Strong psychoanalytic reading.

Barton, Anne, "Leontes and the Spider: Language and Speaker in Shakespeare's Last Plays," in *Shakespeare's Styles*, ed. Philip Edwards, Inga-Stina Ewbank, and G. K. Hunter (1980), pp. 131–50. Astute on language.

Cavell, Stanley, *Disowning Knowledge in Seven Plays of Shakespeare* (2003). Skeptical philosophical interrogation.

Coghill, Nevill, "Six Points of Stage-Craft in *The Winter's Tale*," *Shakespeare Survey* 11 (1958), pp. 31–42. Influential essay on some problems in the play.

Colie, Rosalie L., "Perspectives on Pastoral: Romance, Comic and Tragic," in *Shakespeare's Living Art* (1974), pp. 243–83. Deeply thoughtful, with excellent sense of genre.

Egan, Robert, *Drama Within Drama: Shakespeare's Sense of His Art in King Lear, The Winter's Tale, and The Tempest* (1972). Good attention to self-conscious artfulness.

Felperin, Howard, *Shakespearean Romance* (1972). Sophisticated generic reading.

Frey, Charles H., *Shakespeare's Vast Romance: A Study of "The Winter's Tale"* (1980). Detailed critical reading.

Frye, Northrop, *A Natural Perspective: The Development of Shakespearean Comedy and Romance* (1965). Concise, beautifully written, goes to the mythic core.

Lyne, Raphael, *Shakespeare's Late Work* (2007). Excellent introduction to the play in comparison to the other "late romances."

Sanders, Wilbur, *The Winter's Tale*, Critical Introductions to Shakespeare (1987). Strong close reading.

THE PLAY IN PERFORMANCE

Bartholomeusz, Dennis, *"The Winter's Tale" in Performance in England and America 1611–1976* (1982). Exemplary stage history.

Brooke, Michael, "*The Winter's Tale* on Screen," www.screenonline .org.uk/tv/id/564832/index.html. Overview of film and television versions.

Draper, R. P., *The Winter's Tale, Text and Performance* (1985). Interpretation via staging.

Gilbreath, Alexandra, "Hermione in *The Winter's Tale*," in *Players of Shakespeare 5*, ed. Robert Smallwood (2003), pp. 74–90. Another actor's perspective.

Jones, Gemma, "Hermione in *The Winter's Tale*," in *Players of Shakespeare 1*, ed. Philip Brockbank (1989), pp. 153–66. On playing the lead female role.

McCabe, Richard, "Autolycus in *The Winter's Tale*," in *Players of Shakespeare 4*, ed. Robert Smallwood (1998), pp. 60–70. Insight into the Clown.

Royal Shakespeare Company, "Exploring Shakespeare: *The Winter's Tale*," www.rsc.org.uk/explore/winterstale/2336_2341 .htm. Website with good range of materials on performance.

Sher, Antony, "Leontes in *The Winter's Tale*," in *Players of Shakespeare 5*, ed. Robert Smallwood (2003), pp. 91–112. On playing the part.

Tatspaugh, Patricia, *The Winter's Tale*, Shakespeare at Stratford (2001). Valuable survey of RSC productions.

Williams, George Walton, "Exit Pursued by a Quaint Device: The Bear in *The Winter's Tale*," *The Upstart Crow*, 14 (1994), pp. 105–9. On a particularly famous stage direction.

For a more detailed Shakespeare bibliography and selections from a wide range of critical accounts of the play, with linking commentary, visit the edition website, www.rscshakespeare.co.uk.

AVAILABLE ON DVD

The Winter's Tale, directed by Jane Howell (BBC Television Shakespeare, 1981, DVD 2005). Stylized and effective.

The Winter's Tale, directed by Robin Lough for television, from Gregory Doran's RSC stage production (transmitted 1999, DVD 2005), with Antony Sher and Alexandra Gilbreath as Leontes and Hermione.

REFERENCES

1. *Eyewitnesses of Shakespeare: First Hand Accounts of Performances 1590–1890*, ed. Gamini Salgado (1975), p. 33. The authenticity of this document has been questioned in the past but is now generally accepted.
2. *The Winter's Tale: A Casebook*, ed. Kenneth Muir (1969), p. 24.
3. Quoted in Muir, *Winter's Tale*, p. 28.
4. See further, Paula Byrne, *Perdita: The Life of Mary Robinson* (2004).
5. "Of the Impropriety of Theatrical Representations, as Far as They Relate to the Scenes, Dresses, and Decorations, Etc.," in *The Gentleman's Magazine and Historical Chronicle*, 72 (March 1802), pp. 231–2.
6. Dennis Bartholomeusz, "John Philip Kemble—*The Winter's Tale* in a Picture Frame," in his *The Winter's Tale in Performance in England and America 1611–1976* (1982), pp. 42–63.
7. London *Times* review of *The Winter's Tale*, 26 March 1802.
8. Helen Faucit, Lady Martin, in a letter to Lord Tennyson on 1 November 1890, quoted in *Blackwood's Edinburgh Magazine*, January 1891, pp. 1–37, and partly reprinted in *Shakespeare in the Theatre: An Anthology of Criticism*, ed. Stanley Wells (2000), pp. 67–72.
9. London *Times* review, 28 November 1845.
10. London *Times* review, 1 May 1856.
11. London *Times* review, 1 May 1856.
12. London *Times* review, 29 April 1856.
13. The production and her experiences are discussed in detail in *Ellen Terry's Memoirs* (1932, repr. 1969).
14. Review in *The Athenaeum*, 3 May 1856, p. 561.
15. Review in *Punch; or the London Charivari*, 10 May 1856, p. 90.
16. London *Times* review, 12 September 1887.
17. Detailed discussion of the production can be found in Dennis Kennedy, "Shakespeare Alive," in his *Granville Barker and the Dream of Theatre* (1985), pp. 123–47.
18. John Palmer, *The Saturday Review*, 28 September 1912.
19. A. B. Walkley, in a review (originally unsigned) in the London *Times*, 23 September 1912.
20. Walkley, London *Times* review, 23 September 1912.

21. John Palmer, *Saturday Review*, 28 September 1912.

22. *The Athenaeum*, 28 September 1912, p. 351.

23. Peter Fleming, review in *The Spectator*, 6 July 1951.

24. Dennis Bartholomeusz, "Boston, New York, London; Connecticut, Ontario, Oregon—1912–1975," in his *Winter's Tale in Performance in England and America*, pp. 165–96.

25. Susannah Clapp, *Observer* review, 27 May 2001.

26. Clapp, *Observer* review, 27 May 2001.

27. Clapp, *Observer* review, 27 May 2001.

28. Charles Spencer, *Daily Telegraph*, 2 April 1992, quoted with permission of the author.

29. Vincent Canby, *New York Times* review, 2 June 1995.

30. Charles Isherwood, review in *Variety*, 10 July 2000, p. 31.

31. Charles Isherwood, review, "Off Broadway, *The Winter's Tale*," *Variety*, 3 February 2003, p. 43.

32. Michael Brooke, "The Winter's Tale," www.screenonline.org.uk/tv/id/527466/index.html.

33. Nevill Coghill, "Six Points of Stage-craft in *The Winter's Tale*," *Shakespeare Survey*, 11 (1958), pp. 31–41.

34. Robert Speaight, "The 1960 Season at Stratford-upon-Avon," *Shakespeare Quarterly*, 11 (1960).

35. Patricia Tatspaugh, *The Winter's Tale*, Shakespeare at Stratford (2001), p. 47.

36. Herbert Kretzmer, *Daily Express*, 1 June 1976.

37. Richard Findlater, *Financial Times*, 31 August 1960.

38. Kenneth Young, *Daily Telegraph*, 31 August 1960.

39. Julian Holland, *Evening Mail*, 31 August 1960.

40. Jeremy Brooks, *New Statesman*, 10 September 1960.

41. Bernard Levin, *Daily Express*, 31 August 1960.

42. *Sunday Times* (uncredited), 4 September 1960.

43. Findlater, *Financial Times*, 31 August 1960.

44. *Evening Standard*, 31 August 1960.

45. Levin, *Daily Express*, 31 August 1960.

46. Michael Billington, *Peggy Ashcroft* (1988), p. 187.

47. Billington, *Peggy Ashcroft*, p. 187.

48. Don Chapman, *Oxford Mail*, 16 May 1969.

49. John Armour, *Glasgow Herald*, 17 May 1969.

50. Chapman, *Oxford Mail*, 16 May 1969.

51. Trevor Nunn, in conversation with Peter Ansorge, *Plays and Players*, September 1970.

52. Peter Lewis, *Daily Mail*, 16 May 1969.

53. B. A. Young, *Financial Times*, 16 May 1969.

54. Young, *Financial Times*, 16 May 1969.

55. Irving Wardle, London *Times*, 16 May 1969.

56. John Barber, *Daily Telegraph*, 16 May 1969.

57. Trevor Nunn in conversation, *Plays and Players*, September 1970.

58. J. C. Trewin, *Birmingham Post*, 17 May 1969.

59. Richard David, *Shakespeare in the Theatre* (1978), p. 62.

60. Roger Warren, "Theory and Practice: Stratford 1976," *Shakespeare Survey*, 30 (1977), pp. 169–79.

61. Harold Hobson, London *Sunday Times*, 6 June 1976.

62. Michael Coveney, *Plays and Players*, August 1976.

63. Roger Warren, "Interpretations of Shakespearian Comedy, 1981," *Shakespeare Survey*, 35 (1982), p. 148.

64. Warren, "Interpretations of Shakespearian Comedy," p. 148.

65. Tatspaugh, *Winter's Tale*, p. 41.

66. Tatspaugh, *Winter's Tale*, p. 42.

67. Tatspaugh, *Winter's Tale*, p. 43.

68. Michael Coveney, *Financial Times*, 22 October 1984.

69. Coveney, *Financial Times*, 22 October 1984.

70. Anthony Masters, London *Times*, 27 October 1984.

71. Coveney, *Financial Times*, 22 October 1984.

72. Robin Thornber, *Guardian*, 31 August 1984.

73. Coveney, *Financial Times*, 22 October 1984.

74. Martin Hoyle, *Financial Times*, 1 May 1986.

75. Hoyle, *Financial Times*, 1 May 1986.

76. Kirsty Milne, *Sunday Telegraph*, 5 July 1992.

77. Charles Spencer, *Daily Telegraph*, 3 July 1992.

78. Michael Billington, *Guardian*, 3 July 1992.

79. Milne, *Sunday Telegraph*, 5 July 1992.

80. Robert Smallwood, "Shakespeare Performed: Shakespeare at Stratford-upon-Avon, 1992," *Shakespeare Quarterly*, 44 (1993), p. 349.

81. Smallwood, "Shakespeare Performed," p. 349.

82. John Peter, London *Sunday Times*, 10 January 1999.

83. Benedict Nightingale, London *Times*, 8 January 1999.

84. Peter, London *Sunday Times*, 10 January 1999.

85. Charles Spencer, *Daily Telegraph*, 15 April 2002.

86. Rhoda Koenig, *Independent*, 17 April 2002.

87. Michael Billington, *Guardian*, 15 April 2002.

88. Koenig, *Independent*, 17 April 2002.

89. Koenig, *Independent*, 17 April 2002.
90. Michael Billington, *Guardian*, 9 January 1999.
91. Billington, *Guardian*, 9 January 1999.
92. Paul Taylor, *Independent*, 3 July 1992.
93. Spencer, *Daily Telegraph*, 3 July 1992.

ACKNOWLEDGMENTS AND PICTURE CREDITS

Preparation of "*The Winter's Tale* in Performance" was assisted by a generous grant from the CAPITAL Centre (Creativity and Performance in Teaching and Learning) of the University of Warwick for research in the RSC archive at the Shakespeare Birthplace Trust. The Arts and Humanities Research Council (AHRC) funded a term's research leave that enabled Jonathan Bate to work on "The Director's Cut."

Picture research by Michelle Morton. Grateful acknowledgment is made to the Shakespeare Birthplace Trust for assistance with reproduction fees and picture research (special thanks to Helen Hargest).

Images of RSC productions are supplied by the Shakespeare Centre Library and Archive, Stratford-upon-Avon. This library, maintained by the Shakespeare Birthplace Trust, holds the most important collection of Shakespeare material in the UK, including the Royal Shakespeare Company's official archives. It is open to the public free of charge.

For more information see www.shakespeare.org.uk.

1. "The Wits" in private collection © Bardbiz Limited
2. London Savoy Theatre, directed by Harley Granville-Barker (1912). Reproduced by permission of the Shakespeare Birthplace Trust
3. Directed by Peter Wood (1960) Angus McBean © Royal Shakespeare Company
4. Directed by Trevor Nunn (1969) Joe Cocks Studio Collection © Shakespeare Birthplace Trust
5. Directed by Ronald Eyre (1981) Reg Wilson © Royal Shakespeare Company

The Modern Library presents paperback editions of individual Shakespeare plays from

The Royal Shakespeare Company

Antony and
Cleopatra

King Lear

Macbeth

The Sonnets and
Other Poems

The Winter's Tale

With new commentary, as well as definitive text and cutting-edge notes from the RSC's *William Shakespeare: Complete Works,* the first authoritative, modernized edition of Shakespeare's First Folio in more than 300 years.

Hamlet

Love's Labour's Lost

A Midsummer Night's Dream

Richard III

The Tempest

Also available in hardcover
William Shakespeare: Complete Works

"Timely, original, and beautifully conceived . . . a remarkable edition."
—James Shapiro, professor, Columbia University, bestselling author of *A Year in the Life of Shakespeare: 1599*

MODERN LIBRARY IS ONLINE AT
WWW.MODERNLIBRARY.COM

MODERN LIBRARY ONLINE IS YOUR GUIDE
TO CLASSIC LITERATURE ON THE WEB

THE MODERN LIBRARY E-NEWSLETTER

Our free e-mail newsletter is sent to subscribers, and features sample chapters, interviews with and essays by our authors, upcoming books, special promotions, announcements, and news. To subscribe to the Modern Library e-newsletter, visit **www.modernlibrary.com**

THE MODERN LIBRARY WEBSITE

Check out the Modern Library website at
www.modernlibrary.com for:

- The Modern Library e-newsletter
- A list of our current and upcoming titles and series
- Reading Group Guides and exclusive author spotlights
- Special features with information on the classics and other paperback series
- Excerpts from new releases and other titles
- A list of our e-books and information on where to buy them
- The Modern Library Editorial Board's 100 Best Novels and 100 Best Nonfiction Books of the Twentieth Century written in the English language
- News and announcements

Questions? E-mail us at **modernlibrary@randomhouse.com**.
For questions about examination or desk copies, please visit
the Random House Academic Resources site at
www.randomhouse.com/academic